PHILIP R. WHITE, Ph.D. Johns Hopkins University, is Senior Staff Scientist at the Roscoe B. Jackson Memorial Laboratory, in Bar Harbor, Maine. Dr. White previously taught at the University of Missouri, Yale University, the Sorbonne, and Pennsylvania State University and held research fellowships at the Boyce Thompson Institute and the University of Berlin. After leaving the Rockefeller Institute at Princeton, he became head of the Division of General Physiology of the Institute for Cancer Research in Philadelphia. Dr. White is the recipient of the Annual Prize of the American Association for the Advancement of Science, the Stephen Hales Award of the American Society of Plant Physiology, the Centenary Medal of the Botanical Society of France, and the Medal of Honor of the University of Liége and is a Past President of the Tissue Culture Association.

THE CULTIVATION OF
ANIMAL AND PLANT CELLS

By

PHILIP R. WHITE

The Roscoe B. Jackson Memorial Laboratory
Bar Harbor, Maine

SECOND EDITION

THE RONALD PRESS COMPANY , NEW YORK

DEDICATION

To ALL THOSE RESTLESS SPIRITS who, wandering
beyond the narrow boundaries of established pastures,
keep the paths between fields open and in the process
occasionally find here and there a tussock which is in
truth greener, more nourishing and worthy to be used
for the seeding of new fields, I dedicate this volume.

"Entia non sunt multiplicanda praeter
necessitatem"
"Things are not to be made more complicated
than necessary."
—WILLIAM OF OCCAM, 1270–1349

PREFACE

THE SAME three objectives sought in the preparation of the First Edition of this book still apply: to present the major techniques of cell culture for both plant and animal materials in a sufficiently extended and detailed fashion so that they can be used by all those who may choose to enter the field professionally; to present a group of simple techniques by which anyone without previous experience beyond that of a good biology course may be able to make interesting and effective, if less professional, cultures and may perhaps be led gradually into the greater refinements of the field; and to emphasize as adequately as is conveniently possible the essential importance of the cell itself, as the basic physiological entity out of which all (or at least almost all) those societies called "organisms" are constituted. This book still remains the only one combining the botanical and zoological aspects of what should be looked upon as one field.

The general plan of the First Edition has been retained. In the process of completely revising the book, the chapter on nutrients is largely new, and a number of new methods have been introduced. Of particular importance are those for handling peripheral blood in studies of cytogenetics and human constitutional disease. A new chapter on "cloning" and new material on cultivation of plant cells should prove especially useful.

I have tried to keep the presentation as simple and concise as seems compatible with completeness and lucidity, and have wherever possible used photographs and drawings in place of long descriptions. I have not attempted an inclusive survey of the field in all its past and present ramifications. In fact, I have sedulously avoided such a survey. I have concentrated rather on those matters which may suggest to the reader new fields of conquest and provide him with the basic information and the technique necessary for an intelligent approach to those fields.

Books are always to some extent cooperative projects. I should like to acknowledge specifically the new photographs provided for this volume by H. Derman (Fig. 2B), H. B. Tukey (Fig. 2C). George O. Gey (Fig. 6), E. Leitz & Co. (Fig. 31), Clifford Grobstein (Fig. 60), Edith Peterson (Fig. 61), Leroy Stevens (Fig. 62), Etienne V. Lasfargues (Fig. 64), Rita Levi-Montalcini (Fig. 66), Murray B. Bornstein (Fig. 67), and C. E. Ford and the editors of *Nature* (Fig. 68). I should like to acknowledge permission of Bellco Glass Co. (Fig. 23), Charity Waymouth (Fig. 52), and Morgan Harris (Fig. 53) to use line drawings from their work, and of T. D. C. Grace and Paul S. Moorhead for allowing me to paraphrase material from their publications. Photographs republished from the earlier edition were acknowledged there. Those taken from other publications are cited individually in the text. The drawings are mostly from the able hand of Mrs. Ruth Soper; I am most grateful, for they add immeasurably to the usefulness of the work.

PHILIP R. WHITE

Bar Harbor, Maine
March 1963

CONTENTS

THE CULTIVATION OF
ANIMAL AND PLANT CELLS

"ONE CAN thus construct the following two hypotheses concerning the origin of organic phenomena such as growth: either this origin is a function of the organism as a whole—or growth does not take place by means of any force residing in the entire organism, but each elementary part possesses an individual force, a separate life.

"We have seen that all organisms consist of essentially like parts, the cells; that these cells are formed and grow according to essentially the same laws; that these processes are thus everywhere the result of the same forces. If, therefore, we find that some of these elementary parts . . . are capable of being separated from the organism and of continuing to grow independently, we can conclude that each of the other elementary parts, each cell, . . . would be capable of developing independently if only there be provided the external conditions under which it exists in the organism. The eggs of animals are in fact such cells, capable of living separated from the organism. Among the lower plants any cell can be separated from the plant and continue to grow. . . . We must therefore ascribe an independent life to the cell as such. That not every cell grows, when separated from the organism, is no more an argument against this theory than is the fact that a bee soon dies when separated from its swarm a valid argument against the individual life of the bee."

THEODORE SCHWANN (1839), pp. 188–190.

❊   ❊   ❊

"THERE has been, so far as I know, up to the present, no planned attempt to cultivate the vegetative cells of higher plants in suitable nutrients. Yet the results of such attempts should cast many interesting sidelights on the peculiarities and capacities which the cell, as an elementary organism, possesses. They should make possible, conclusions as to the interrelations and reciprocal influences to which the cell is subjected within the multicellular organism."

G. HABERLANDT (1902), p. 69.

Chapter 1

THE PROBLEM

Cells and Why We Should Cultivate Them

The development of the living body is one of the most complex and important phenomena with which science must concern itself. What are the steps in this development? How is it directed and controlled? Why does this control sometimes fail? What are health and disease?

Descartes taught us that philosophical problems (and by that he meant all scientific problems) could best be solved by reducing them to their simplest elements. This concept, although less clearly stated, had in fact long before been the basis for the Aristotelian procedure of describing things at ever decreasing levels of complexity. We can apply the same method to the study of the construction, development, and function of organisms.

Aristotle (340 B.C.)[1] and Theophrastus (320 B.C.) described animals and plants as being made up of homogeneous elements: blood and sap, flesh and fiber, nerves and veins, bone and wood. Having no lenses for closer examination, they could make their definitions no more exact than this. With the development of the microscope, however, Malpighi (1675) and Grew (1682) were able to carry the analysis much further and to establish the idea that these elements were literally "woven" (*tissé*) into tissues of still finer elements. Hooke had shown in 1667 that Grew's "tissues," which Theophrastus had called "fiber" and Aristotle "bone," were in fact made up of still smaller units which he called "cells." A half-century later, Brown recognized the ubiquity of "nuclei" in the fleshy as well as the fibrous or bony materials, especially in plants (1833). Dujardin (1835) noted that the semifluid substance which commonly lines the cellular skeleton in the living parts of plants and animals has also a ubiquitous and hence obviously important role. This covering he called the "sarcode," the forerunner of our protoplast. These three concepts: of the ubiquity of the (lifeless) "cell" of Hooke, the "nucleus" of Brown,

---

[1] References are to the bibliography at the end of this volume.

and the "sarcode" of Dujardin were crystallized in 1838 in the "cell theory," jointly formulated by Schleiden (1838), a botanist, and Schwann (1839), a zoologist. Schwann (see the first epigraph of this chapter) clearly stated that living cells are independent individuals, with the same sort of individuality as have the bees in a swarm. The solitary bee can neither long survive nor multiply its race in isolation; the functional unit, the fully competent *organism* is the swarm, not the bee, yet, given proper conditions a bee can be transplanted from one swarm to another or can be maintained as an incomplete unit for some time outside the swarm. It is with this sort of unit that "cell culture" has to deal.

If we are to fully understand the aims and methods of cell culture and their importance in the science of biology, we must remember that the cell theory had two distinct aspects. First, it recognized that the compartmentalization which Hooke had noted in dead materials (cork, pith, etc.) was a universal characteristic of all or nearly all parts of both plants and animals, that the cell was therefore a *structural* unit of all living creatures. This facet of the theory gained quick acceptance and has become an unconscious part of our thinking, in spite of those exceptions, like the protozoa, where it seems not to apply. But second, the theory clearly stated the corollary that these ubiquitous structural units were also distinct and potentially totipotent *physiological* and developmental units.

The idea that an "animal" or "plant" is no more than a "society" of cooperating cells has by no means gained general acceptance. For there is an alternative hypothesis, also resting on a considerable mass of observations, which postulates that somewhere in the developmental history of the individual organism the cells have progressively lost parts of their original competence, that they have become irreversibly segregated for particular functions and cannot be returned to a totipotent state. Until recently no mechanism for such segregation was known, but a possible one has now been described in the variations in chromosome number and pattern in different organs and tissues, reported both in plants (Winkler, 1935; D'Amato, 1952; Tschermak-Woess, 1956; and others) and in animals (Hsu, 1959; Walker, 1958; Fraser and Short, 1958). Actively growing parts such as skin, the intestinal lining, a regenerating liver, or the apical meristem of a plant are generally diploid, while specialized tissues such as the tapetal layer or the endosperm of plants or the adrenal cortex of animals are sometimes found to be just as consistently polyploid. Physiological segregations at the tissue or organ level, whether reversible or not, are certainly just as ubiquitous as are the cells themselves, so that the hypothesis of functional development which emphasizes "the organism as a whole" rather than the cellular constituents has today many adherents. Sharp (1926) has given an excellent presentation of this view. His introductory chapter and the papers of Baker (1952) deserve careful reading.

If all cells of an organism are essentially alike and, within the genetic pattern, totipotent, then the differences in behavior of cells of a given type in different situations in the body must result from the responses of those cells to their environment and especially to other cells in the organism. It should be possible to restore suppressed functions by isolating the cell from those external influences which were responsible for the suppression. If, on the other hand, there has been a true segregation and loss of function, so that the cells in the mature organism are no longer totipotent, then no modification of a given cell line's environment could hope to restore the lost function. It is clear that a decision between these two alternative hypotheses is essential to any valid concept of the origin of form and function. And it is also clear that one of the most promising techniques for arriving at such a decision lies in the segregation of cells, tissues, and organs from the associated members of the body, and their maintenance and study as isolated units under as nearly optimal and as fully controlled conditions as possible. The attempt to reduce an organism to its constituent cells and to study these cells as elementary organisms is thus a project of fundamental importance in the solution of basic biological questions. This is the problem of cell culture.

Schleiden and Schwann (1839), who formulated the concept of cellular totipotency, and Virchow (1858), the medical pathologist who popularized that concept, made no attempt to put it to experimental proof. Nor did Claude Bernard (1878), whose complementary idea of the "internal environment" sought to explain how independent cells might be integrated into a functional society, carry out experiments which might settle the question.

The first consistent effort to do so seems to have been that of Vöchting (1878). First he dissected plants into smaller and smaller fragments while keeping those fragments growing. He found a clear-cut polarity to be characteristic of every fragment, irrespective of size, and, by extrapolation, probably of every cell. Thus the distal portion of a stem always produced leaves and the proximal portion roots, but whether a given cell produced leaves or roots depended on that cell's fortuitous position, whether distal to or proximal to the nearest cut surface or uninjured growing point. If a 3-foot piece of willow was left intact, the distal foot of stem would produce only roots, but if a 6-inch piece was isolated from this same piece, either by removal or merely by severing the bark, the proximal 3 inches would produce leaves instead of roots. The morphogenetic pattern was a function of "the organism as a whole," considering here the autonomous fragment as the organism. Yet the cell appeared to be totipotent, its actual expression being the result of influences coming from outside (Fig. 1). This point of view was developed for animals a generation later by Child (1941), whose "axial gradients" are comparable to Vöchting's concepts of polarity.

Parallel with these dissections Vöchting carried on complementary studies in synthesis, by grafts and transplants (1892, 1894). Here the emphasis was not on the *lability* of a tissue, on the shifting of develop-

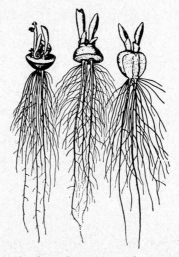

FIGURE 1. Cell lability—the dependence of morphogenetic expression on fortuitous position. Tubers of *Corydalis solida,* cut in two perpendicular planes and allowed to regenerate. The cells at the center of the tuber, which in an intact plant serve only for the storage of food, have produced three distinct kinds of members: leaves (left), roots (center), or merely wound callus (right), depending on their spatial relationships to the plane of the cut. (Goebel, 1908, p. 220, Fig. 111.)

mental pattern with changes in environment, but rather on the *stability* of pattern against different backgrounds. No matter to what host a scion was transplanted it always developed according to a pattern fixed by its species of origin. Not only the morphology but the physiology as well remained unaltered even when dependent on tissues of another species. A segment of Jerusalem artichoke stem (*Helianthus tuberosa*) could be grafted onto a root of the sunflower (*H. annuus*) and a sunflower top then grafted onto the artichoke. All three survived and functioned successfully yet the intercalated artichoke segment stored its carbohydrate as inulin while the sunflower root and top stored theirs as starch. The existence of sectorial and periclinal chimeras, whether of artificial (Figs. 2A and 2B) or of natural origin (Fig. 2C) provides striking examples of this persistence of segregations in contiguous cells and tissues.

Vöchting's dissection experiments had demonstrated the essential totipotency of the cell within its species limitations (Fig. 1). His trans-

FIGURE 2. Cell fixity—the limitations placed on morphogenetic expression by genetic constitution. Chimeras in animals and plants. (A) Graft chimeras in amphibia. Segments of larvae of *Rana palustris,* light in color, and of *R. sylvatica,* with dark pigmentation, have been grafted together in the early embryonic stages. Each retains its own specific characteristics in intimate anatomical and physiological contact with the other. (Harrison, 1904.) (B) Chimeras of *Poinsettia* produced by somatic mutation in the apical meristem such that the fully developed leaf is separated both sectorially and periclinally into segments of different constitution. (Dermen, 1950, p. 324, Fig. 8.) (C) Chimeras in apple fruit, resulting from grafting of two species together. Buds arise at the line of suture which contain cells of both sorts; these buds in turn give rise to flowers and fruits which are made up of segments with distinct specific characteristics. (Photo from H. B. Tukey.)

plantation experiments had demonstrated the restrictions which species places on these potencies (Figs. 2A and 2B). A generation later, Spemann (1936) and his followers carried out similar transplantations in animal bodies, with results of similar import and of the greatest importance for our understanding of morphogenesis.

Roux (1885) carried this analysis a step further by isolating the chick medullary plate and keeping it alive for some days in saline solution. This he did in an effort to determine the factors involved in the closure of the medullary tube. At about the same time, Arnold (1887) was "cultivating" leucocytes and other cells by an ingenious method. He soaked very thin slices of elder pith in aqueous humor of the frog. These were then implanted under the skin or in the peritoneal cavity of frogs where they were soon invaded by leucocytes. He then removed the slices of pith at intervals to dishes of saline solution or of aqueous humor and observed that the leucocytes migrated from the pith into the "nutrient," where they survived for some time. He studied their mitotic divisions, made drawings of many types of cells (Fig. 3), and clearly demonstrated their individuality and partial independence. Ljunggren (1898) maintained bits of skin alive in ascitic fluid. Jolly (1903) likewise kept leucocytes alive in serum. These were, however, with the possible exception of Arnold's work, little more than brief technical tours de force, without intended or implied general biological significance. Somewhat closer to the main stream of cell culture, and very similar to Arnold's studies, was the work of Leo Loeb (1902), who followed the progressive migration of cells into a blood clot or a block of gelatin implanted either in the ear of a rabbit or intraperitoneally. This was essentially an internal and hence rather unmanageable type of "tissue culture."

The ultimate objective of Vöchting's type of dissection would be the cultivation of individual cells, as, indeed, Arnold, Jolly, and Loeb had done. But the idea of cultivating single isolated body cells in vitro as a general biological procedure, seems not to have been explicitly formulated until 1902. In that year Haberlandt, a botanist, set forth the problem frankly and lucidly (see the second epigraph of this chapter). The discipline which he thus outlined is that which, in the half-century since his paper, has crystallized into what we know today as "tissue culture" or, perhaps preferably, "cell culture."

But the imagination needed to formulate the broad outlines of a new technique is not always coupled with the other qualities required to put that technique into actual practice. Where Vöchting and after him Rechinger (1893) had sought to determine the "limits of divisibility" of plant materials, Haberlandt (1902) boldly took his point of departure directly from the cell theory and assumed that there were no limits of divisibility. He therefore chose to work with single cells, an aim which

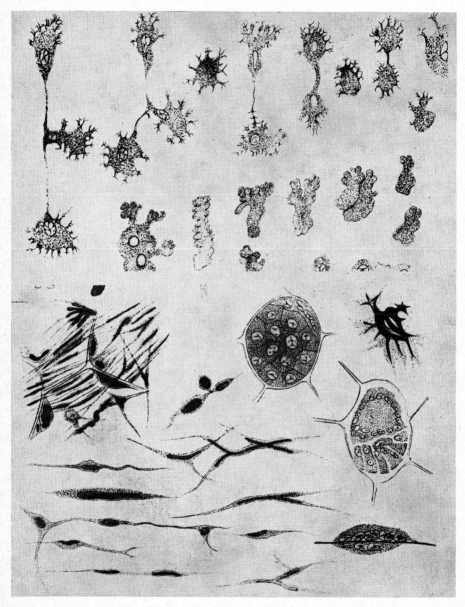

FIGURE 3. Pictures of frog cells, drawn in 1887 by Arnold. Above: leucocytes which have migrated in vitro away from a slice of elder pith, removed to a dish containing aqueous humor after implantation in the peritoneal cavity of a frog. Below, left: fibroblasts as seen in sections of pith. Below, right: macrophages. Note the multinucleate giant cells.

during his lifetime proved to be an elusive ideal. It is only recently that Sanford, Earle, and Likely (1948) and Puck (Puck and Marcus, 1955) with animals and Muir (Muir, Hildebrandt, and Riker, 1954), Torrey (1957), and Jones *et al.* (1960) with plants have succeeded in developing methods for obtaining colonies from single somatic cells (see Chapter 7). These methods have come into current use only since 1957.

Haberlandt fully appreciated the importance of the photosynthetic process for all living material. He consequently assumed that by cultivating green cells he would eliminate the need to provide carbohydrate in the nutrient. In this he apparently lost sight of the fact that green cells are relatively mature and highly differentiated units in which the meristematic function is largely in abeyance. Haberlandt was, moreover, faced with a number of difficulties which are inherent in plant anatomy and morphogenesis. Most cells of plants are not bathed in any free, complete nutrient medium. The xylem sap, although rich in inorganic materials, lacks many of the organic constituents needed to maintain life. The phloem sap, which contains elaborated organic materials, is in direct contact with only a very few specialized cells. Most plant cells must obtain the greater part of their nutriment by diffusion through neighboring cells. Except for the liquid endosperms, which do not exist in most plants, there are no "natural" nutrients which one might extract from plants and use for the cultivation of cells and for subsequent analysis. Even the endosperms, where they exist, are generally present in only minute amounts. The coconut milk recently introduced with some success as a nutrient for plant-cell cultures is an exception. Plant cells, moreover, with rare exceptions, are surrounded by a rigid pellicle of cellulose. This prevents them from seeking and engulfing food, thus greatly restricting the forms of food which they can use. It prevents them from adhering satisfactorily to solid substrata. And, since excision involves rupturing this pellicle and exposing the protoplast naked to the surrounding medium in a way that seldom occurs in nature, there results a considerable and unavoidable shock. Further, "growth" in a plant is normally restricted to a few specialized regions of the body, leaving all other parts in a relatively inert or at least dormant condition as far as capacity for immediate cell division is concerned, thereby greatly restricting the experimenter in his choice of materials.

These inherent difficulties frustrated all of Haberlandt's attempts to cultivate plant cells in vitro. His efforts and those of his immediate successors were, without exception, disappointing. The attempt to attack the problem directly was regretfully abandoned with the remark that "At any rate, the cultivation of isolated cells in nutrient solutions should make possible an experimental approach to many important problems from a new point of view" (Haberlandt, 1902). Haberlandt turned to an indirect approach, that of the study of wound healing, and never personally returned to the original problem.

Animal tissues, fortunately, present none of the above-named difficulties, at least to anything like a comparable degree. Animal cells throughout the body are regularly bathed in one of three characteristic and essentially complete nutrient fluids: the blood, interstitial fluid, or lymph. Two of these, the blood and lymph, can be removed from the body easily and in considerable quantity. They serve as basic "natural" nutrients for animal cells, in which such cells can be immersed without serious shock. These fluids can be analyzed at leisure to determine which of their constituents are truly essential. Further, animal cells are, for the most part, surrounded by a tough but mobile pellicle in place of the semirigid pellicle of the plant cell. They can therefore be removed from the body with a minimum of shock; anyone who has worked with both sorts will appreciate this difference. Animal cells adhere well to a variety of solid substrata. They are capable of autonomous movement and phagocytosis, so they can be fed on relatively complex nutrient materials which they themselves transform into constituents which pass readily into the protoplasts. And finally, "growth" regularly takes place in all parts of the animal body and, in the sense of replacement, occurs throughout the life of the animal. There is thus comparatively little obvious restriction placed on the experimenter in choosing favorable materials for cultivation. These facts have largely affected the development of cell culture in the two kingdoms. As a result, progress passed in the first decade of this century entirely into the hands of the zoologists.

At about the same time that Haberlandt was formulating the concept of cell and tissue culture, a controversy was raging among zoologists as to whether the fibrillae observed in histological preparations, which connect the neurocenters with their end-organs, originate from the nerve cell, from the end-organ, or from the intervening ground substance. A considerable body of opinion supported an origin *de novo* from the ground substance. This view was held by the great German anatomist Hensen. The chief proponents of an origin by outgrowth from the neurone were Ramon y Cajal and His. Classic histology had proved incompetent to settle the question. Harrison had tried transplanting the neural crest to various parts of the body, without arriving at a definite answer. Turning then to the methods suggested by Haberlandt and tested cursorily by Arnold, Roux, Ljunggren, and Jolly, Harrison settled the controversy in two now classic papers (1907, 1910). He cultivated the neuroblast of the frog in clotted lymph and observed the growth of the fibrillae from the central body (Fig. 4A). This was the first successful "tissue culture." Harrison followed the presentation of his experimental results with a brilliant exposé of the possibilities of this method of approach (1912).

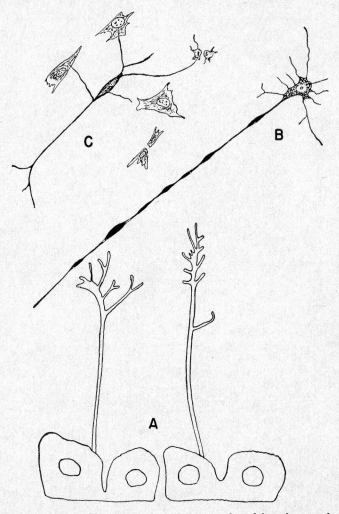

FIGURE 4 (A) Neuroblast of the frog, grown in clotted lymph: two drawings of a single nerve fiber, drawn 50 minutes apart to show the extensive changes in outline which such a growing fiber undergoes. Excepting Arnold's 1887 figure, this is probably the oldest picture of a growing metazoan cell in culture. (Harrison, 1908, Fig. 22.) (B) Sympathetic nerve from chick-embryo intestine, cultivated in saline solution directly on glass, without a clot. This drawing is from a fixed and stained preparation. (M. R. Lewis and W. H. Lewis, 1912a, Fig. 23.) (C) Human brain cell cultivated on a plasma-coated cover glass insert in a roller-tube culture. A fixed and stained preparation. (Redrawn from I. Costero and C. M. Pomerat, 1951, Fig. 17.) The similarity in pattern between the cells of frog, chick, and human, grown under modern and under earlier conditions, is evident.

But he had devised the method only to solve a particular problem, and once this was done he made no attempt to develop it further. Two years later Burrows studied with Harrison and introduced the idea of substituting blood plasma for lymph in the cultivation of chick cells (1910). He also appears to have coined the term *tissue culture*. He subsequently joined Carrel, and together these two developed the use of embryo extract as a growth-promoting nutrient and elaborated the methods for growing a great variety of animal tissues (Carrel and Burrows, 1910; Carrel, 1911, 1912a, 1912b, 1913b). These methods, with minor modifications, remained standard for the next 30 years and are still widely used.

Simultaneously with Carrel's first work (1911, 1912a, 1912b), Warren and Margaret Lewis, likewise under Harrison's influence, began a careful study of the effects both of individual nutrient constituents including salts and carbohydrates and of total osmotic value and similar factors, on the short-term growth of animal cells in vitro (M. R. Lewis and W. H. Lewis, 1911a, 1911b, 1911c, 1912a, 1912b). This approach, while less productive of immediate spectacular results in terms of prolonged growth and observable differences in developmental pattern, was in theory more likely to lead to an ultimate understanding of the physiological processes involved. It was ahead of its time, since the roles and even the existence of many of the vitamins, amino acids, respiratory intermediates, enzymes, and the like were then unknown. It did not lead at that time to important results, though it forms the point of departure of much more recent work.

From 1910 to 1920 "tissue culture" consisted largely of a survey to determine how many "tissues" of how many different animals could be grown for more or less prolonged periods. This has continued, but in about 1920 a number of other approaches began to develop. The introduction of the Carrel flask in place of the hanging drop (Carrel, 1923) greatly reduced the amount of routine work required to maintain strains and to grow appreciable masses of tissue. It also permitted a more quantitative approach to many of the problems involved. One natural consequence was the opening up of the possibility of studying in earnest many nutritional problems. This was undertaken by Carrel and his co-workers, Ebeling and Baker. By analyzing tissue juices by simple methods such as filtration, dialysis, precipitation, and differential extraction, these workers made a number of contributions in this direction between 1923 and 1939 (Baker and Carrel, 1926, 1928; Baker, 1936; Baker and Ebeling, 1939; Carrel and Baker, 1926; Ebeling, 1924). Harrison (1928), in reviewing the first 20 years of tissue culture, cited 11 major contributions during that period. Only 3 of these, his own demonstration of the origin of nerve fibers (1907), Burrows' proof of the myoblastic origin of the heartbeat (1912), and Carrel's demonstration of the potential immortality of the dividing animal cell (1912a, 1924), have stood the test of time as

FIGURE 5. The founders of cell culture:

being both valid and unique; the other 8 either still lack full proof or are natural derivatives of Carrel's contribution. Carrel retired in 1939 and his laboratory was disbanded.

Parallel with these there was developing independently a quite different type of investigation of animal materials, introduced by Fell (Fig. 6) (Strangeways and Fell, 1926; Fell, 1928a, 1928b, 1931, 1953) in England. Whole embryonic "organules" (Fischer's term, 1922) such as bones, teeth, eyes, and glands were grown in relatively large volumes of nutrient in simple watch glasses and their metabolism was studied. The approach is an important one, quite different from Carrel's single-tissue pure-line studies.

At about the same time that the development of the Carrel flask gave a powerful impetus to cell-culture studies on animal materials, work was renewed in the parallel plant field. In spite of the efforts of a series of Haberlandt's students—Bobilioff-Preisser, Lamprecht, Thielmann, Czech, Börger, and others—this latter field was still no more of a reality than it had been in the days of Haberlandt's brilliant theoretical exposé of 20 years before. In 1921 Molliard attempted with some success to cultivate fragments of plant embryos. In 1922 Kotte (1922a, 1922b), a student of Haberlandt, and, independently, Robbins (1922a, 1922b), in the United States, succeeded in growing excised plant roots for some weeks in a nutrient solution. Kotte dropped the work, but Robbins, with a co-worker, Maneval, published two more papers in the next 2 years which showed clearly that considerable, but apparently not indefinite, growth of certain roots could be obtained (Robbins and Maneval, 1923, 1924). Robbins also turned to other problems and did not return to this one for 12 years (Robbins et al., 1936).

The field of plant-tissue culture was definitely opened up in 1934 by two workers, White and Gautheret. White (1931) had surveyed the past history of the field and had pointed out some of the reasons for earlier failures, and the directions which future work might profitably take. He

---

Gottlieb Haberlandt, 1854–1946, Director, Pflanzenphysiologisches Institut, the University of Berlin, Germany. First to formulate, in clear fashion, the idea of cultivating isolated cells in vitro as a method of studying problems of organization and cellular interrelationships. First to make planned studies of the cultivation of cells.

Ross G. Harrison, 1870–1959, Sterling Professor of Biology, Osborn Zoological Laboratory, Yale University, New Haven, Connecticut. First successfully to cultivate isolated cells as a means of solving a specific morphogenetic problem.

Alexis Carrel, 1873–1945, Member, The Rockefeller Institute for Medical Research, New York City. Responsible, more than any other individual, for developing and perfecting the techniques of cell culture.

Albert Fischer, 1891–1956, Director, Biological Laboratories of the Carlsberg Foundation, Copenhagen, Denmark. Chief European proponent of the cell-culture method as developed by Carrel.

Warren H. Lewis, 1870–   , and *Margaret R. Lewis,* 1881–   , Emeritus Associates, the Carnegie Laboratory of Embryology, Johns Hopkins School of Medicine, Baltimore, Maryland. First to study in detail problems of cellular nutrition in vitro.

FIGURE 6. Some present-day tissue-culture leaders:

had emphasized the suitability of the Kotte-Robbins root-tip method for study of the nutritional aspects of the problem, and had called attention to the theoretical weakness of Haberlandt's approach and to difficulties in the way of obtaining results by means of Molliard's method. This theoretical discussion was followed by a series of factual papers (1932a, 1932b, 1933a, 1933b) presenting experiments, mostly with excised root tips, which culminated in 1934 in the demonstration of the possibility of growing excised roots of tomato in vitro for periods which had no theoretical limit (White, 1934a) (Fig. 7). These were the first successful plant "tissue," or, perhaps better, "organ" cultures. The strain of roots started at that time is still growing today after 28 years and more than 1,600 passages.

In the same year Gautheret, under the direction of the great French cytologist Guilliermond and influenced by Molliard's earlier work and White's contemporary papers, after making somewhat less successful experiments with root tips, turned to an intensive study of the cultivation of cambial tissues, beginning with those of willow and poplar (Gautheret, 1934, 1935, 1938). These at first proved refractory. Their study was continued, however,[2] and in 1939 Gautheret (1939) in Paris,

[2] There is a story connected with Gautheret's doctorate which is worth repeating for the light which it throws on those traits which characterize and mold a great scientist. Roger Gautheret was the only son of a well-to-do French businessman and as such was in a position to indulge his own wishes to a considerable degree. After he had completed his "licenciate" he went to Professor Guilliermond, under whom he intended to take his doctorate, and said to him, "My Professor, I want to take a doctorate under your direction. I have both money and time. I do not need a position. I can devote all my time to research. I do not care how long it takes to get my degree, or how much it costs, but I do want it to be worth something. What problem can you suggest which would really be worthwhile?" Professor Guilliermond

Honor B. Fell, 1900–   , Director, the Strangeways Research Laboratory, Cambridge, England; Fellow of the Royal Society. Investigator of the in vitro development and function of animal organs.

Margaret R. Murray, 1901–   , Professor of Surgery, College of Physicians and Surgeons, Columbia University Medical Center, New York City. Senior author, A Bibliography of the Research in Tissue Culture (Murray and Kopech, 1953). Developed the use of cell cultures in the classification and diagnosis of tumors, particularly neuromas.

Roger J. Gautheret, 1910–   , Professeur de Botanique, Université de Paris; Membre de l'Institut. One of the first to cultivate normal plant tissues in vitro. Founder of the European school of plant-tissue culture.

Philip R. White, 1901–   , Senior Staff Scientist, the Roscoe B. Jackson Memorial Laboratory, Bar Harbor, Maine. First to establish continuous cultures of plant organs and of plant tumor tissues. First to develop fully defined maintenance nutrients for both plant and animal cells.

Wilton R. Earle, 1902–   , Principal Cytologist, the National Cancer Institute, Bethesda, Maryland. Developed quantitative methods for the maintenance and study of animal-cell cultures.

George O. Gey, 1899–   , Finney-Howell Professor of Surgery, Johns Hopkins School of Medicine, Baltimore, Maryland. Developed the roller-tube method for simple cultures of animal cells.

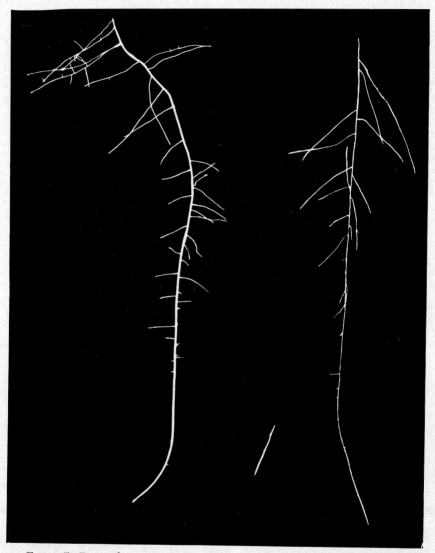

FIGURE 7. Roots of tomato grown in vitro as isolated members. At the center, a piece about 15 mm. long used as inoculum; at the left, a root grown in vitro from such an inoculum for ten days, the photograph representing a member of the strain at the end of 1 year of cultivation, that is through 23 passages; at the right, ten days' growth of the same strain after 27 years of cultivation, through 1,402 passages. (Photos at left and center from White, 1934a; photo at right by White, 1960.) The root at the left was grown in a nutrient containing 0.01 per cent of yeast extract. This was replaced in 1943 by known constituents, so the root at the right has been grown for 17 years in a completely defined nutrient.

Nobécourt (1937, 1939) in Grenoble, and White (1939a) in Princeton published independently, within a period of six weeks, descriptions of the successful cultivation for prolonged periods of cambial tissues of carrot and tobacco. All three of these strains of tissue are still growing (Fig. 8). They represent the first true plant-tissue cultures in the strict sense of prolonged cultures of unorganized materials. Together with White's

FIGURE 8. One of Gautheret's cultures of carrot tissue. This culture is about two months old and is representative of a strain which has been in cultivation since 1937. (Gautheret, 1948b, Fig. 3.)

earlier studies on root nutrition, these papers are to plant-tissue culture what the papers of Harrison in 1907, Burrows in 1910, and Carrel in 1910 to 1913 were to the animal field.

Problems of nutrition are basic to sound progress in all aspects of tissue management. Carrel had not carried the solution of these problems beyond the level of the organic complexes represented by serums and embryo extracts. The corresponding questions with regard to plant tissues had been brought to a fairly high level of precision during the decade from 1933 to 1943 by White, Gautheret, and others. In 1943, at the suggestion of Warren Lewis, White turned his attention from plants to problems of animal-cell nutrition. Departing radically from the approach developed by Carrel, he adopted initially the techniques of Gey (1933; Gey and Gey, 1936), the type of thinking which had motivated the

gave him two problems, one of them the cultivation of plant tissues. Gautheret accepted the challenge with enthusiasm. The first years were years of frustration for both Gautheret and Guilliermond. When positive results finally began to emerge, both were grateful—the pupil for having a master who could formulate such far-reaching and important goals, and the master for having found so tenacious and brilliant a student!

Lewises 30 years before, and the factual background contributed by the heterogeneous accumulation of recent rapid advances in the understanding of such substances as vitamins, protein constituents, respiratory intermediates, enzymes, and trace-element catalysts in their bearing on the nutrition of micro-organisms and of higher animals, including man. On this basis he developed a tentative fully synthetic nutrient capable of supporting prolonged survival of animal cells but without significant growth (1946, 1949). At about the same time, Fischer (1941; Fischer *et al.*, 1948), with a similar general aim but quite different methods, resumed the studies begun in the 1920's by Carrel, Baker, and Ebeling and began analyzing by more modern methods the serum, plasma, and embryo juices which constitute the classic Harrison-Burrows-Carrel nutrient.

Subsequently others, especially Parker in Toronto (Morgan, Morton, and Parker, 1950), Morgan in Ottawa (Morton, Pasieka, and Morgan, 1956), Waymouth in Bar Harbor (1956b), and Earle in Bethesda (Evans *et al.*, 1956a), undertook the elaboration of synthetic nutrients based on those of White and of Fischer. By a series of refinements the embryo extract was first eliminated, the serum concentration was reduced (White, 1955), the serum was then replaced by peptone or other defined protein products (Waymouth, 1956b), and these were finally eliminated to provide fully defined synthetic nutrients capable of supporting rapid and unlimited growth of animal and human cells. In the hands of Morgan and Parker (Morgan, Morton, and Parker, 1950; Healy, Fisher, and Parker, 1955) and of Earle (Evans *et al.*, 1956a, 1956b) these nutrients have been extremely complex and rather costly (60 ingredients in Parker's "Solution 1086," 69 in Earle's "NCTC 109"). Waymouth (1956b, 1959), on the other hand, working in White's laboratory, has developed much simpler formulas (35 to 40 ingredients), which are equally effective, more stable, and less expensive.

Today all the basic techniques are under scrutiny and revision. Ever since the International Tissue Culture Conference which was called in October, 1946, by the Committee on Growth of the National Research Council, the field has undergone a rejuvenation. This was evident at the Decennial Review Conference on Tissue Culture called by the same agency in 1956 (White, 1957). The preparation, standardization, and evaluation of such important vaccines as those of Salk and Sabin would have been gravely handicapped without means of cultivating, in the laboratory and in large quantities, tissues of human and primate origin. The field of human genetics and especially the genetics of constitutional disease owes much to the possibility of examining the chromosomes in rapidly dividing cells of skin or of blood grown in tissue cultures. Our understanding of the chemical control of differentiation, both as it is expressed in normal ontogeny and as it can be used to modify development, depends on taking the body apart without losing the thread of its natural processes. Embryology has found itself up against a blind wall but for the introduction of means of dissecting the living embryo and examining its unfolding in segments. Anatomy and histology have turned to the study of how cells and tissues come to possess the characteristics which we see at different stages of development, function, senescence, and death. These methods are being developed in many directions by new workers and are bringing to fuller realization the potentialities of the discipline of cell culture.

"Ἄλλα δὲ ἐξ ὧν ταῦτα φλοιὸς ξύλον μήτρα, ὅσα ἔχει μήτραν. πάντα δ' ὁμοιομερῆ. καὶ τὰ τούτων δὲ ἔτι πρότερα καὶ ἐξ ὧν ταῦτα, ὑγρὸν ἴς φλὲψ σάρξ· ἀρχαὶ γὰρ αὗται· πλὴν εἴ τις λέγοι τὰς τῶν στοιχείων δυνάμεις, αὗται δὲ κοιναὶ πάντων. ἡ μὲν οὖν οὐσία καὶ ἡ ὅλη φύσις ἐν τούτοις.

"AGAIN there are the things of which such parts (root, stem, leaf) are composed, namely, bark, wood, and core (in the case of those plants which have it), and these are all 'composed of like parts.' Further, there are the things which are even prior to these, from which they are derived—sap, fibre, veins, flesh; for these are elementary substances—unless one should prefer to call them the active principles of the elements; and they are common to all parts of the plant. Thus, the essence and entire material of plants consists in these."

THEOPHRASTUS (320 B.C.).

Chapter 2

THE MATERIALS

Cells, Tissues, and Organs Suitable for Cultivation

The prime objective of most if not all cell culture is the precise definition of those external and internal factors which control the formation, development, and behavior of the cells, tissues, and organs of which metazoa and metaphyta are constituted. For obvious reasons non-cellular protozoa, protophyta, and bacteria, which do not make up organized "societies," fall outside this terrain. The objective is approached by isolating the cell, tissue, organ, or organism from its fellows and following its development in vitro. Any member which can be so isolated and grown is proper material for "tissue culture."

A number of considerations will obviously limit the choice of material. Hair and fingernails of animals, or corky bark of trees, will not be usable, since they are not alive. The cells to be used must not only be living; they must be capable of growing, either as a primary function, as in animal eggs or plant meristems, or by resumption of growth, as in amphibian limb blastemas or plant wound callus. Let us consider those materials in the two kingdoms which satisfy these requirements.

In either plants or animals the fertilized egg is in certain theoretical respects the ideal subject for cell culture. It is a single cell which clearly possesses all the potentialities of all those cells which we find in the adult organism. All factors which determine the course of events by which those potentialities are evoked and segregated during development are of consequence to us. The vogue of experimental embryology of such oviparous metazoa as worms, coelenterates, and amphibians bears witness to the interest of the subject. But oviparous embryology is not cell culture, and the eggs of viviparous organisms have proved unusually refractory objects for in vitro study. The physical conditions which surround the egg during its early development, protect it from untoward influences, and direct its unfolding are extraordinarily complex.

To date it has not been possible to follow in tissue or cell cultures and as a consecutive process all the stages of egg production, fertilization, and

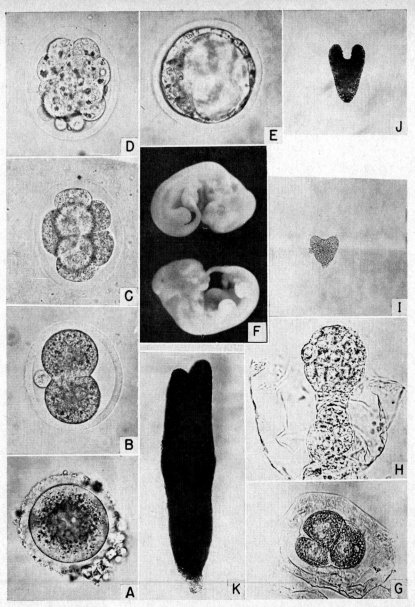

FIGURE 9. Early development of animal and plant embryos: (A) Single-celled mouse egg with its surrounding pellicle. (B) Two-celled stage. (C) Eight-celled stage; this is the stage most suitable for the initiation of in vitro cultures. (D) About 32 cells. (E) Early blastula; the cells are now all oriented on the outside of a sphere, leaving the center filled with fluid. (F) Mouse embryos at about 10½ days postfertilization. (G) A three-cell complex of the daffodil, probably representing an egg and two sister-cell synergids, before fertilization. (H) Early embryo of purslane (*Portulaca oleracea*), a common weed—about 60 cells, with stalk. (I) Heart-shaped embryo; this is about the earliest stage which has been successfully explanted and grown in culture. (J) An older embryo with the cotyledons well initiated. (K) Young but complete embryo (compare Fig. 46). (A–E from Lewis and Wright, 1935; F–G photos by White, 1960; H–K from White, 1932a.)

24

development. Nevertheless many segments of this process have been so studied. Gaillard (1957) has excised rat ovaries and followed the development of oocytes in organ cultures. The transplantation of bits of ovary into castrated animals (Robertson, 1945; Stevens, 1957) and the subsequent fertilization of the foreign eggs so provided are routine procedures in some laboratories (Stevens, Russell, and Southard, 1957). Lewis was early able to observe in vitro the first few divisions of fertilized eggs of monkeys and of mice (Lewis and Wright, 1935) (Fig. 9). Whitten has carried these to the blastocyst stage (1956, 1957), and such blastocysts have been successfully reimplanted to give viable adults (McLaren and Biggers, 1958). This is a field of investigation of great current interest, to which tissue-culture techniques and nutrients have given a powerful impetus.

A parallel picture has emerged for plant materials. Following a technique introduced by Nitsch (1949, 1951), Maheshwari's group has grown a variety of ovaries (Sachar and Kanta, 1958; Sachar and Baldev, 1958; Maheshwari and Lal, 1961), anthers (Vasil, 1957), and ovarian tissues (Ranga Swamy, 1961) and have followed the development of egg cells, pollen cells, and adventive (nucellar, parthenocarpic) embryos therein. It has not as yet been possible to excise the egg cells and grow them, but by isolating ovaries after pollenation it has been possible to observe fertilization and early embryo development in such organ cultures. And the embryos themselves, once they have reached the torpedo stage have been excised and grown to maturity (Tukey, 1934; Nickell, 1951; Maheshwari, 1958). This material is also ripe for further exploitation.

An interesting variant of this approach is one initiated by La Rue in which cells derived from the endosperm of maize and the male gametophytes of *Ginkgo, Larix*, and other plants have been cultivated in vitro (La Rue, 1953; Straus, 1954; Straus and La Rue, 1954; Tulecke, 1953, 1957). These tissues, although triploid (maize) or haploid (gymnosperms), nevertheless behave quite like corresponding diploid sporophyte tissues.

Beyond the pro-embryo stage both plant and animal embryos take on characteristics sufficiently adult to make it best to treat them as adults. Here we must deal with plants and animals separately.

Plant Tissues

Plants grow continuously from germination until death. They do not, however, grow continuously in all their parts. An adult plant can be separated into perhaps four categories of cells. First there are the meristems, regions which characteristically grow uninterruptedly although seasonal factors may at times reduce their growth level to a minimum. These are the primary growing points: stem apexes, root apexes, lateral cambiums, buds, and the intercalary meristems of grasses, some mints, lianas, and the like. Excised fragments containing any of these meristems may be expected to grow without any lag period if they are provided with a proper nutrient. Of these root apexes, which can be excised by a single straight cut with a minimum of trauma, are the simplest. They served for the first successful plant-tissue (organ) cultures (Robbins, 1922a, 1922b; Kotte, 1922a, 1922b; White, 1934a) and for most of the basic studies on tissue nutrition. Stem apexes are equally suitable, theoretically, but somewhat more difficult to divest of their enclosing wrappings. They were grown with some success by White (1933a) and Loo (1945) and more recently by Ball (1946) and others. The intercalary meristems of grasses, vines, and the great kelps, which can be excised with two straight cuts, should be almost as satisfactory but have not been studied extensively. The lateral cambiums require for excision the exposure of traumatized surfaces on all six faces of a cuboidal fragment. They were at first avoided for this reason (White, 1931). Experiments by Gautheret with cambiums of *Salix* and other trees (1934, 1935, 1938) removed some of the objections to their use. Subsequently, in the hands of Gautheret (1939), White (1939a), and Nobécourt (1939), they became the basis for the first true plant-tissue cultures as distinct from organ cultures. Their use, as developed by Morel, Gioelli, Riker, Steward and others, has now become routine. The axillary gemmae of *Marattia* represent an example which has, so far as this writer knows, not been investigated.

The secondary meristems—phellogens, intercalated cambiums, medullary ray parenchymas, pericycles, etc.—are closely related to these but essentially distinct in character. These secondary meristems are capable of intermittent growth without preliminary dedifferentiation but do not normally grow with any continuity. The pericycle, which gives rise to lateral roots, is an excellent example. The lag period which intervenes between excision of a bit of non-apical root tissue and the emergence of lateral roots therefrom represents the time required for new root primordia to form in the pericycle. Another striking example appears in the cultivation of callus derived from medullary ray tissue excised adjacent to the pith in 50-year-old linden trees (Barker, 1953). These cells had been reproductively quiescent for half a century yet provided living material capable of normal growth. The leaf-notch meristems of *Bryophyllum* are another example (Naylor, 1931). The carrot-phloem cultures of Caplin and Steward (1948, 1949) fall into the same category, as do many of the cultures originating in tuber tissues (Gautheret, 1959). It should be noted that such potential meristems lie scattered through almost all living portions of adult plants and that as a consequence there are probably few living parts of adult plants from which it should not, theoretically, be possible to isolate tissue cultures, difficult though this may prove to be in practice.

There exists, also, over and above these, a very large group of tissues which, while already differentiated for other functions, are capable under suitable treatments of undergoing a dedifferentiation and reacquisition of meristematic potencies. The cortical parenchymas, certain types of epidermal cells, above all and most spectacularly the megaspore and microspore mother cells, tapetum and endosperm, and the lining of the ovarian wall which gives rise to apogamous embryos in the dandelion and grapefruit are examples of this category. So also are those pith tissues from which Gautheret and Skoog have evoked growth by auxin treatment as in the case of the artichoke (Gautheret, 1959), tobacco (Skoog and Tsui, 1948; Skoog, 1951), and the potato tuber tissue investigated by Steward and Caplin (1951).

There is, finally, a large group of cells which, while living and theoretically capable of growth, are nevertheless so highly differentiated and specialized either structurally or physiologically as to be refractory to treatment. Stomatal guard cells, glandular hairs, trichomes, storage sclerenchymas such as those of the date seed, stone cells, wood tracheids, tannin cells, and the like belong to this group. Interestingly enough, it was with precisely this category of cells that Haberlandt (1902) and his students wrestled unsuccessfully for nearly 20 years—sufficient reason for the three decades' delay in achieving a successful culture!

The cultures of flowers and fruits carried out by Nitsch (1951); those of seed primordia by White (1932a); and the excised leaves cultivated for special physiological purposes, for example, the tobacco leaves grown by Dawson (1938) and Vickery et al. (1937) in studies of nicotine metabolism, although important, do not fall naturally into any of these groups, since they are organ rather than tissue or cell cultures.

Animal Tissues

In plants there is no normal replacement of deep-seated cells but a more or less continuous marginal (terminal and lateral) growth and formation of new cells in specialized and local regions. In animals, on the contrary, there are throughout life a constant destruction of worn-out cells and a replacement of them throughout the body. This is most rapid in young animals, in exposed regions such as the skin, or in very active organs such as the intestine. But it occurs in almost all tissues. The muscles of the heart and the neurones of the central nervous system appear to be exceptions, but even these sometimes resume replacement growth under special pathological conditions. For these reasons explants from any organ of the animal body, at any age, should be capable of growth as tissue cultures. The limitations are technical, not biological.

Practice, in fact, shows this to be true. Cultures of skin, epithelium of the eye, kidney, liver, thyroid, ovary, and other glands, bone, nerve cells, connective tissue, skeletal muscle, tooth primordia, bone marrow, white blood cells, and many others have been grown. Tissues taken from embryos in the early stages, of which the chick embryo before the eighth day of incubation may be taken as an example, will grow, that is, show active migration and mitotic proliferation, without noticeable lag. Tissues from older animals may be more sluggish.

There is, however, one difficulty in the establishment of cultures by the classic plasma–serum–embryo-extract method, which is probably technical rather than biological. There is a tendency for the "fibroblasts" or "histiocytes" to overrun and replace all other types of cells. No matter with what one starts, if it is a mixed culture, one will under these conditions usually end with a pure line of fibroblasts. It is possible to establish other types of cells on a plasma substrate only either by establishing pure lines from the beginning, that is, by some method of cloning (see Chapter 7) or initial selection, or else by cultivation on modified nutrients designed to favor differentially the growth of cells other than histiocytes. Pure cultures of epithelium can be obtained from the margin of the iris by direct isolation. Many authors have, it is true, reported the transformation of histiocytes or of epithelial cells into macrophages and vice versa, under the influence of special nutrients (Fischer, 1925; M. R. Lewis and W. H. Lewis, 1926). Frédéric (1951) has reported the derivation of macrophages from liver epithelium treated with choline in massive quantities (M/100 = ca. 0.12%). Of special significance here are the work of Wilde and that of Fell. Taking cells from the early blastulas of amphibians and growing them in nutrients whose constitution differed only with respect to the single amino acids, glutamine and alanine and their analogues, Wilde (1959) was able to direct development at will into either pigmented epithelial cells or striated muscle. Similarly, using later tissues of potential cartilage, nasal mucosa, or skin epithelium, Fell and Mellanby (1952, 1953), by altering the nutrient levels of vitamin A, were able to obtain at will sound bone or degenerate masses of chondroblasts on the one hand and ciliated secretory epithelium or hard keratinized skin on the other. Although not entirely impossible, there seems little probability that in any of these cases there has been a selective stimulation of already distinct cell types from a mixed population; these appear to be true "modulations," that is, transformations, and indicate that the potentialities of cells may be far wider than is normally expressed, subject to evocation by appropriate stimuli. They support the evidence discussed on pages 4 to 5 and lend credence to the concept that all cells of a given organism are, in fact, totipotent and interconvertible within the limits of species specificity. These questions will be answered definitely when such transformations are observed or induced in single-cell clones. A beginning has already been made in this direction in the studies of Sanford *et al.* (1954) and of Puck and Fisher (1956) showing that mutations do occur in clonal strains.

Suffice it to say that any animal tissue—and we must include any human tissue—with the exception of heart muscle, liver parenchyma, and perhaps adult nerve, can be "grown" in cell culture. Even these can be maintained for long periods and caused to migrate, alter their form, and extend their dimensions, though perhaps without the formation of new muscle or nerve cells.

INVERTEBRATE TISSUES. Blood cells of marine invertebrates were among the first of the materials to be studied in tissue culture (Lewis, 1916). Trager, in 1935, undertook a detailed investigation of the possibility of cultivating insect tissues and succeeded in maintaining cells alive for some weeks and in cultivating the grasserie virus in such cells (1935). Active and continued growth was not obtained. Wyatt (1956), by the use of a complex nutrient based on an analysis of insect hemolymph and containing twenty-two amino acids, had somewhat better success. This nutrient was further improved by Grace (1958a, 1958b) by the addition of nine vitamins of the B group. Medvedeva (1960) has had some success with nutrients modified from those of Wyatt. Apparently fully successful cultures of insect tissues, with the establishment of rapid growing and continuous strains, have been carried out in China (Liu, Schick, and Gaw, 1958; Gaw, Liu, and Zia, 1959). These papers are in Chinese and are not readily accessible to western readers.

Most recently Grace (1962) has reported the establishment of four strains of tissue from the eucalyptus moth (*Antheraea eucalypti*) which have been maintained through repeated subcultures and for long enough periods to be considered permanent. This has been accomplished by the addition of heat-treated pupal blood to his earlier nutrient. The field of invertebrate-tissue culture thus appears to be firmly established. The methods, however, are so new and so little tried that it seems best at this time to refer the reader to the original papers rather than to try to present them in detail here. The preparation of Grace's nutrient is described at the end of Chapter 4. This is an important segment of the field of cell culture which will merit future intensive study.

"[My] ʀᴏᴏᴍ was generally hung round with Guts, stomachs, bladders, preparations of parts and drawings. I had sand furnaces, Calots, Glasses and all sorts of Chymical Implements . . . Here I and my Associates often dined upon the same table as our dogs lay upon. I often prepared the pulvis fulminans and sometimes surprized the whole College with a sudden explosion. I cur'd a lad once of an ague with it, by fright. In my own Elaboratory I made large quantitys of sal volatile oleosum, Tinctura Metallorum, Elixir Proprietatis and such matters as would serve to put into our Drink."

> Diary of Mr. Wm. Stukeley, 1707, describing his rooms at Cambridge where he and his fellow student, Mr. Stephen Hales, planned and carried out some of the first real experiments in plant and animal physiology.
>
> (Cʟᴀʀᴋ-Kᴇɴɴᴇᴅʏ, 1929)

Chapter 3

THE LABORATORY

Facilities and Equipment for the Cultivation of Cells

A cell-culture laboratory must satisfy the same general requirements as must the space required for any detailed microculture work. It must provide: (1) facilities for the preparation, sterilization, and storage of nutrients and for the cleansing of used equipment; (2) a place for the aseptic manipulation of tissues; (3) facilities for the maintenance of cultures under carefully controlled conditions; (4) facilities for examination and study of cultures in whatever way may be desired; and (5) a place for the assembling and filing of records. It will seldom be possible to carry on all these procedures in a single room with any degree of effectiveness, but the degree of complexity introduced into the organization of the laboratory will depend on the particular needs and the facilities available for any given work. The ideal organization will allow a separate room for each of the above functions: a media room, an operating or transfer room, one or more culture rooms, a laboratory, and an office. All of these requirements except the culture rooms will be essentially the same for either plant or animal studies (Fig. 10).

The Media Room

The cleaning of glassware, preparation and sterilization of nutrients, and storage of supplies in readiness for use are services of the utmost importance for satisfactory cell-culture work. The room in which these services are to be maintained, and its facilities, must therefore be given very careful consideration. The room need not be large nor elaborate, but it must be adequate. The "media room" at the Mount Desert Island Biological Laboratory (Fig. 11), providing these services for a summer personnel of ten workers, was only 9×12 feet. This is too small to be fully satisfactory, but a room twice this size can be excellent. It is possible to include these facilities within a larger laboratory, but a separate room is to be preferred. Moreover this room should, if at all possible, be re-

31

served for cell-culture work, since sharing it with bacteriologists, mycologists, or pathologists involves risk of contamination, both biological and chemical.

Adequate light and ventilation will be the first requirements. The room must contain: (1) a sink for washing glassware, with adequate

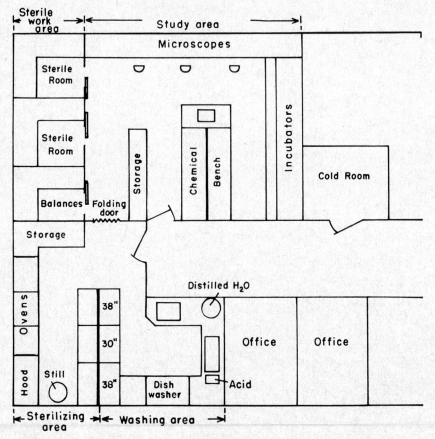

FIGURE 10. Plan of a compact cell-culture laboratory unit, modified from portions of the plan of the Roscoe B. Jackson Memorial Laboratory, Bar Harbor, Maine.

facilities for drainage, drying, and storage; (2) an oven for dry sterilization of glassware; (3) an autoclave for steam sterilization of heat-stable nutrients and of certain special equipment; (4) a muffle furnace for baking filter candles; (5) one or more stills or deionizing units for providing pure water for the final cleansing of glassware and for making up nutrients; (6) a good stove or hot plate for carrying on the many operations, such as cleaning rubber stoppers, filters, and the like, which require boiling; (7) vacuum for filtrations; and (8) tables of both standing and sitting height at which such operations as wrapping glassware, preparing cotton plugs, and the like can be carried out. A chemical hood for handling fuming or otherwise dangerous materials must be available but will be used so rarely that it need not necessarily be housed in the cell-culture department.

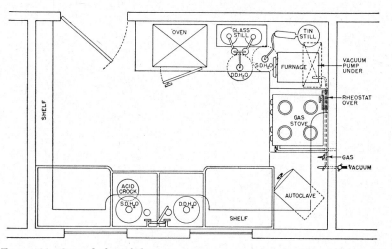

FIGURE 11. Ground plan of the preparation room used at the Mount Desert Island Biological Laboratory, Salisbury Cove, Maine: In a space of 9 × 12 feet this room includes all the important services required for cleaning and sterilizing equipment and supplies and for preparing nutrients for a laboratory of ten workers in the field of cell culture.

Washing Glassware

One of the most important and exacting procedures involved in cell-culture work is the cleaning of glassware. It is also one of the least standardized aspects of the subject; each laboratory has its own preferences.

In order that proteinaceous materials may not become dried onto the surface, all glassware should be placed immediately after use in a vessel containing metaphosphate (Alconox) or another inorganic detergent, or Clorox. If the cultures are maintained on colloidal substrates such as agar, gelatin, or plasma, where the cells are not in direct contact with the glass, subsequent washing may be with any standard detergent followed by thorough and repeated rinsing in hot water. Detergents, however, are extremely difficult to remove from the surface of glassware and may be highly toxic to cells. Where cells are to be grown in monolayers directly on the glass without an intervening detoxifying colloidal layer, experience has shown that much more thorough treatments will be necessary. Special attention must be paid to the facilities for this purpose. We have found the dishwashing units on the market satisfactory only for the rinsing phases of these operations.

Parker for many years followed the practice of Carrel, boiling his glassware in white-soap solution, rinsing it thoroughly in water and then in 95 per cent alcohol, allowing it to dry, and finally wrapping and dry sterilizing it (1950). More recently (1961) he has turned to cleaning by ultrasonics; units for this purpose are expensive and not likely to be available to all workers. Vogelaar and Erlichman (1939) recommend washing in sodium pyrophosphate solution. Another method is to boil in metaphosphate (Alconox), rinse, then boil in dilute hydrochloric acid, rerinse in water, then in 95 per cent alcohol. Earle (1943a) boils his glassware in 80 per cent sulfuric acid containing a trace of nitric acid, then washes with water. This requires a hood and special Duriron kettles which are very costly. Hanks (Scherer *et al.*, 1955) uses an ingenious and thoroughly logical procedure which deserves further investigation. He starts from the premise that his cleaning procedure should contribute nothing which is not characteristic of the experimental environment of the cells. Soaps, strong acids, alkalies, and organic detergents are therefore not acceptable. But sodium metasilicate (water-glass) satisfies this requirement. Hanks first rinses thoroughly with water or with a detergent; when protein residues are present he digests them with trypsin. He then places the glassware, mouths up, in a series of containers, a separate one for each size or type of flask or tube; each is covered with a stainless wire-mesh cover, clamped on. Plastic containers are quite satisfactory. The containers are filled with a dilute solution of water-glass, 0.1 per cent in tap water. This is prepared as follows: 40 g. of calcium metaphosphate (Calgon) are dissolved in 3 l. of water, heating if necessary. Three hundred and sixty g. of water-glass are suspended (they will not fully dissolve) in 1 liter of water. The two are then mixed, filtered, and used as a stock, which is diluted 1 : 100 for use. The glassware is boiled for 20 minutes in this solution. A hose is then inserted down to the bottom of the container and the water-glass washed out from the bottom so that the scum which sometimes forms on the surface is washed away at the top and does not come in contact with the glass. The containers are inverted to pour out the solution in the glassware, rinsed repeatedly but briefly with tap water, and allowed to drain thoroughly. Normal hydrochloric acid is added to neutralize the alkali residue, allowing 0.25 ml. per liter of container volume, and water is flowed in until the vessels are full. They are allowed to stand for 15 minutes, again decanted, rinsed twice with distilled water, and inverted to drain overnight. The covers are then unclamped and the glassware is emptied out on a wire mesh. At no time is the glassware touched by the operator's hands before it is thoroughly dry, since even brief contact is presumed to contribute oily contaminations which would "creep" over the wet surfaces.

The result is certainly beautifully clean glassware. Probably what really happens is that a monomolecular layer of sodium silicate (glass!) is deposited on all exposed surfaces. The procedure, requiring as it does separate containers for the many different types of vessels used in a cell-culture laboratory, is not simple. It is, however, highly effective and theoretically irreproachable and might conceivably be simplified.

We have tried many methods of cleaning in our own laboratory. We have always returned to the use of a sulfuric acid–sodium dichromate cleaning solution in spite of all that has been said by others against it. We use a large plastic sink (Durcon 5) with lead splash- and drainboards. A 4-gallon lead-lined, covered tank is placed at the right-hand side of the sink, and a stainless-steel or polyethylene tray $14 \times 24 \times 2$ inches is propped up on a wooden strip on the right-hand drainboard, sloping toward the tank. The tank is filled to about 3 inches from the top with cleaning solution. This is prepared by combining 100 ml. of a saturated solution of sodium dichromate with each gallon of concentrated sulfuric acid. Be sure to pour the acid into the solution, not the reverse! The glassware to be washed is first freed of all visible residue by brushing under tap water. It is then placed in the tank, being handled with acid-proof rubber gloves with long gauntlets (see Appendix III). Care must be taken that no air is occluded in the flasks or tubes. We have designed special carriers for handling Carrel flasks in quantity (Fig. 12) which have proved highly effective; with slight modifications they might be adapted for use with other types of culture vessels. During the handling of glassware it is best to have a few inches of water in the sink.

Glassware is allowed to remain in the acid for a minimum of four hours. It is then removed with rubber gloves, superficially drained into the tank, and set up in the tray for further draining. Subsequently the sink is filled with warm tap water and the glass is immersed therein piece by piece.

From this preliminary rinsing on, two procedures are possible. If a laboratory glassware washer of either the Heineke or the Fisher type is available, the glassware may be transferred thereto and a normal cycle of rinsing started. In the Heineke machine or in an electrically operated Fisher unit there should be a final rinse in distilled water. In the steam-operated Fisher unit (Fig. 13) the final steam treatment will take the place of the distilled water. If a mechanical washer is not available, the rinsing operations must be carried out by hand. Miscellaneous glassware is rinsed in running, hot tap water at least ten times, twice in single-purified water, once in double-purified water, and set aside to drain.

Culture tubes can be assembled in plastic jars, covered with non-corrosive wire-mesh covers, and filled and emptied en masse.

For routine glassware the above procedure is sufficient. For culture tubes, Carrel flasks, pipettes, etc., which come in direct contact with living tissues or with nutrients for long periods, we add as a final step a

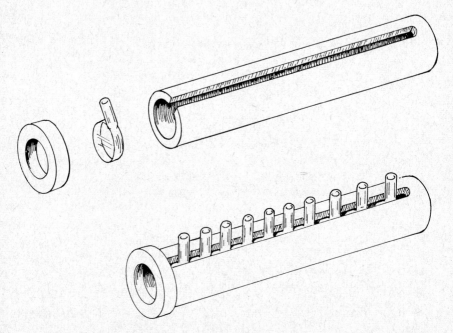

FIGURE 12. A polyethylene carrier useful in handling Carrel flasks through the acid and water treatments necessary in cleaning.

half-hour in the autoclave immersed in double-distilled water. This will remove any traces of heavy metal ions which might have escaped the previous treatment. Glassware so handled has given us complete satisfaction over many years of experience with the most exacting cultures maintained directly on the glass, without detoxifying colloids and in defined, synthetic nutrients.

The procedure described is tedious, and the handling of large quantities of acid has its hazards. We believe, nevertheless, that it is simpler than many others, and more saitsfactory.

Pipettes are washed by a similar procedure but rinsed in an automatic pipette washer. Cover glasses are dropped one by one into a beaker of boiling metasilicate solution and simmered for 20 minutes with glass beads. They are rinsed for five minutes with a jet of water entering the container at the bottom and of sufficient force to "tumble" the glasses. The tap water is then replaced by distilled water, shaken, and drained, and clean absolute alcohol is added. The cover glasses are finally removed singly with a cover-glass forceps, placed on a linen-covered wood block, polished with a second similar covered block (Fig. 14), and assembled in a small Petri dish for sterilization.

FIGURE 13. A dishwasher which carries out efficiently all the rinsing processes in the cleaning of laboratory glassware.

We have found it best to place soiled glassware to the left of the sink, that in the process of drainage, etc., to the right. Distilled water is piped to a point above the sink, or two 20-l. Pyrex carboys may be placed on a shelf, one for single-purified water, the other for double-purified water to be used for final rinsing. The outlets are protected from actual contact with glassware and from lateral splash by glass "filling bells." No adequate precaution can be taken against direct vertical splash, but if the outlets are hung quite high, only a little below face level, they will be reasonably safe. It is not advisable to drain graduates over such a washing sink.

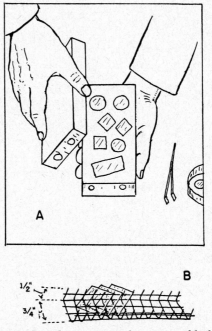

FIGURE 14. (A) Method of drying cover glasses on a block covered with linen or silk over a loose pad of blotting paper. (B) A wire rack for cover glasses made from ¼-inch-mesh wire screen.

Water

The question of pure water is a perennial problem in all laboratories and is important enough to justify special attention. Modern deionizers are capable of supplying water of extremely low specific conductivity, hence of high physical quality so far as content of inorganic ions is concerned. But it should be remembered that deionizers do not eliminate un-ionized volatile materials, oils, organic gasses, or large molecules, and that the deionizing bed may even serve as a culture substratum for many sorts of bacteria which may produce specific toxic products, the so-called pyrogens. Such water is not necessarily *biologically* pure. Pyrogen-free water can be guaranteed only by reliably controlled distillation. And proper distillation can of itself provide all the protection given by deionizers, plus its own unique contributions. One may use two stills in tandem. Perhaps the ideal combination uniting simplicity and effectiveness is to pass the water first through a deionizer and then through a good still. Such combination units are available. Those on the market, however, generally include tin-lined copper heat exchangers; copper is extremely toxic to most cells, and the product of such stills is not free from suspicion. For the preparation of nutrients, water from such a still should be redistilled from Pyrex, Vycor, quartz, or some non-toxic metal such as nickel. The Bellco Glass Company has recently (1960) introduced a Pyrex still which is very efficient; it is, however, provided with a stainless-steel immersion heating unit to which theoretical objections might be raised. These objections may prove in practice to be groundless. In our laboratory we use a deionizing unit followed by a still having a pure nickel heat exchanger. This gives a product which uniformly shows a specific resistance of approximately 2 million ohms and which can be used for all purposes without further treatment. Whatever the source, the distillate should be delivered into Pyrex or polyethylene containers protected from contact with the air and should at no time come in contact with metal or with soft glass.

Water of this quality will be satisfactory for all except certain special types of work. It should be remembered, however, that water stored in Pyrex cannot be used for studies involving questions of boron deficiency, since Pyrex is a borosilicate of a solubility sufficient to provide the minimum boron requirements of some plant tissues. Moreover, any contact with rubber, even the purest available, may vitiate experiments on sulfur or zinc requirements. For such purposes special sources of pure water may have to be provided.

Sterilizing Equipment

The equipment for sterilization of nutrients and supplies is second in importance only to the dishwashing equipment and that for preparing pure water. The general theory and practice of sterilization are treated thoroughly in Underwood's textbook of sterilization (1941) and in Parker's text (1961). Equipment for the purpose will consist of three items, intended, respectively, for "dry" sterilization of glassware (flasks, tubes, pipettes, filters, etc.), for "wet" sterilization of heat-stable solutions (items of equipment like rubber, cellophane, or other partly heat-labile materials must be included here), and for filtration of solutions which are heat-labile to such an extent that they cannot be autoclaved, as is the case with some protein materials, vitamins, carbonate solutions, and the like. The first two of these functions can sometimes be combined by the use of an autoclave equipped for use as a gas sterilizer

Dry sterilization will be carried out in an oven, preferably an electric one. We have found the Boekel [1] 31- $\times$ 31- $\times$ 21-inch type satisfactory. For either dry or wet sterilization, materials should be placed in special containers or wrapped, care being taken to allow free circulation of air to all surfaces requiring sterilization (Fig. 15). Most items requiring

---

[1] Where specific brand names and catalog numbers are given, they are intended merely as examples without any implied preference over similar products of other manufactures.

wrapping can be enclosed in Patopar paper,[1] sealed with Scotch[1] sterilizer tape, which records the completion of sterilization by a color change. For oven drying a temperature of 160° C. is generally recommended; we have found, however, that if glassware wrapped in muslin, paper, or foil is so arranged as to allow reasonably free penetration of heat and is left for at least four hours at a temperature of 140° C. (timing should begin only *after* this temperature has been reached), sterilization will be ade-

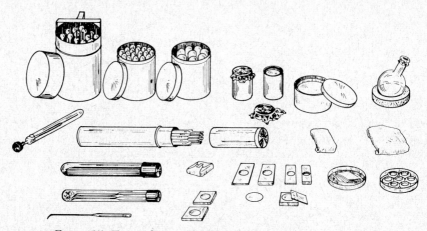

FIGURE 15. Types of materials which can be sterilized by dry heat.

quate and there will be less charring of cotton or paper. Charring is to be avoided since distillation of cellulose products, unless they are highly purified, may result in the formation of tars which are extremely toxic to living cells. It is for this reason that kraft paper is to be avoided. Bits of charred cotton may fall into solutions and seriously affect cultures. Schopfer and Rytz (1937) have shown that cotton contains significant amounts of certain vitamins which may affect the growth of cultures if nutrients have come in contact with such materials. Cotton should be avoided wherever possible. Cotton plugs, where it is necessary to use them for tubes and flasks, are made of non-absorbent cotton covered with fine bandage muslin which prevents fibers from pulling loose and either sticking to the glass or falling into solutions. Plastic foam plugs are now available. For many uses the Norton stainless-steel caps, or heat-stable plastic caps, are better than plugs. Cotton must still be used to plug pipettes and filter columns.

A wad of glass wool wrapped in glass cloth is placed in the bottom of pipette cans to prevent breakage. Standard 10-cm. Petri dishes are dry sterilized in regular Petri-dish cans sold for the purpose, or they can be wrapped in paper, muslin, or foil in groups of three or four. The smaller ones (60 mm.) can be stacked in cans such as the 70×100-mm. ones used for fruit juices, capped with aluminum foil (do not use cans lined with plastic!). Balloon flasks and other items requiring dry sterilization are likewise capped with foil. Standard pipettes are placed in metal cans. Inoculating pipettes are usually sterilized in large test tubes capped with Norton caps. Culture tubes are first autoclaved, mouth up, in double-distilled water, in stainless steel dressing jars. The jars are then opened, inverted to pour off the water, and allowed to drain, and the tubes dried

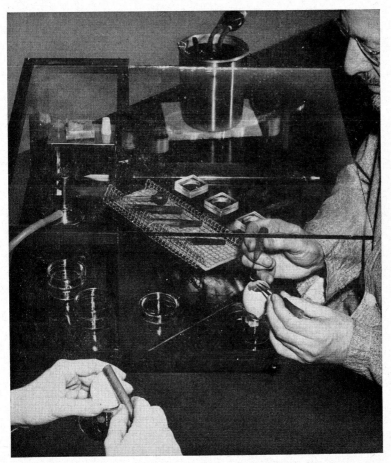

FIGURE 16. A plastic shield which protects from falling dust tissues exposed during the various manipulations of dissection. Here chick embryos are being removed from the eggs for the preparation of cultures. This picture also shows the use of a beaker and immersion heater for sterilizing instruments, a wire rack for instruments, the use of paired Columbia watch glasses as recipients for tissues and organs during the stages of dissection and washing, and the "buttonhook" with which chick embryos are removed from the egg.

in the oven. Instruments may be placed in suitable containers and sterilized in the oven or autoclave, or they may be boiled in water (Fig. 16). Some workers dip instruments in alcohol and then flame them, but heat so applied risks affecting the temper; for most purposes we prefer boiling. The small-size (#18) Renwal instrument sterilizer is excellent for this.

The autoclave, like the oven, must be adequate in size. A 20- × 30-inch cylindrical or a 16- × 16- × 24-inch rectangular one is excellent for routine large-scale work. It should be of the double-jacket type which permits vacuum drying of stoppers and the like as well as the usual steam sterilization. This may be usefully supplemented by a smaller autoclave, since there will be many routine operations of small volume but requiring immediate attention.

Rubber stoppers can be placed in Petri dishes, small end down. A sheet of hard (qualitative) filter paper should be placed between the stoppers and glass to prevent sticking. A 10-cm. Petri dish will hold about 50 No. 00, 30 No. 0, or 7 No. 4 stoppers. The dishes may be wrapped in paper, muslin, or foil (Fig. 17).

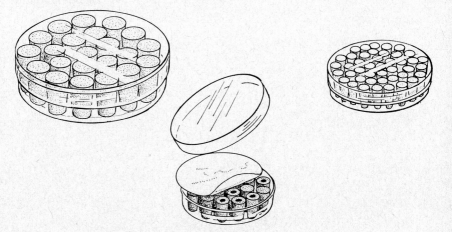

Figure 17. Stoppers are autoclaved in Petri dishes.

Operating Rooms

Tissues under operation, implements, culture vessels, etc., must be protected from contamination at all times. The classic method of attaining this end is through the use of special operating or transfer rooms equipped with ultraviolet sterilizing lamps—where surgical gowns and masks are worn; disinfecting sprays, baths, swabs, etc., are used; large numbers of interchangeable instruments are provided; complete silence is maintained in the culture rooms; and similar expedients are in effect. While it may be nice to have stainless-steel operating rooms, skylights, gray walls, steam jets, etc., and to wear black gowns and masks if one is so inclined, none of these things are necessary and some are actually to be avoided. We will proceed, therefore, from the complex to the simple.

The operating and transfer room will ideally be an inside room, not larger than 8×10 feet with an 8-foot ceiling. The walls should be of smooth finish: steel, Carrara glass, tile, enamel paint, or simply waxed asbestos board (Transite). It should be free as far as possible from all fixtures which might catch dust. A dark gray color is best, but light gray or green is good; white is likely to give poor contrast and to be distracting. There should be no heating unit of the usual type in the room, since radiators are constant sources of dirt and of convection currents. Ventilation should be provided by an air-conditioning unit. A small unit consisting of a fan and filters, such as are sold to hay fever sufferers for installation in or below a window, can be placed above the door, forcing filtered air into the room. Rooms provided only with such ventilation are likely to overheat because of the accumulation of heat from the bodies of the operators and from the gas flames or boiling vessels used for sterilizing instruments. For this reason a full air-conditioning and cooling system is to be preferred, but the small total air volume involved makes small household units quite satisfactory for the purpose. The door should have a glass and should slide rather than swing. It should *not* fit tightly. If filtered air is blown into the room under positive pressure and escapes around the door, there will be little danger of contaminating dust getting in even when the door is opened. Light is best provided by a skylight, but well-placed windows and recessed overhead lighting provide a good substitute. The only stipulation is that all windows be absolutely airtight and be so placed as to require no curtaining at any time. If outside windows are used, they should be double. This is to reduce the temperature drop and consequent convection currents which cold glass will create; this is one reason for preferring an inside room without windows. Electricity and gas should be provided, and, if possible, water, vacuum, and compressed air. A table-height shelf 30 inches wide should be built along two sides of the room. This should be hung from brackets, with no legs running to the floor, since legs are always a source of accumulated dirt and get in the way of the operator's knees. There should also be a small movable table, about 2×2 feet, which, when attached against the side shelf, provides a T-shaped unit where two operators can face one another while the fixed shelf furnishes a place for additional equipment within easy reach. Table tops should be of black Formica, wood, or slate. They should never be of stainless steel, which gives a reflecting surface against which it is impossible to see white or transparent objects well and has a surface so smooth that the least moisture causes glass objects to stick to an objectionable degree. The floor should be of linoleum, tile, or some other easily cleaned surface. We do not recommend ultraviolet sterilizing lamps for such a room; they are certainly unnecessary and represent an added complication, a possible source of toxic ozone, a source of radiation from which both tissues and operator must be scrupulously shielded, and a general nuisance.

Such a room provides an aseptic atmosphere and permits free movement and manipulation. Nevertheless the operator will bring some contaminations in with him unless he wears the classic sterile surgeon's gown, hood, and mask, and unless he reduces movement and conversation to a minimum. These are annoying and unnecessary restrictions. They may be obviated by placing on the table one or the other of two types of shield. The simpler and most widely used type consists of a 20-inch square of ¼-inch Plexiglas held in a frame 9 inches above the table, the frame being so built that the front and most of the two sides and back are open (Fig. 16). This is so placed that the front edge of the shield projects an inch or so beyond the edge of the table. Dissections and manipulations can be made freely under this shield completely protected from falling dust, from the breath of the operators, and from any, except fairly violent air currents. Hoods and masks are unnecessary; they have not been used in our laboratory in almost 30 years of successful tissue cultures. We have, in fact, found that all but the most prolonged operations can safely be carried out under such a shield placed in a regular laboratory room, without the need of a special transfer room. Similar protection is provided in a somewhat less flexible form by the double-glass table tops (one glass about 8 inches above the other) installed in the laboratories of the Department of Surgical Pathology at the Columbia University College of Physicians. A somewhat more elaborate hood has

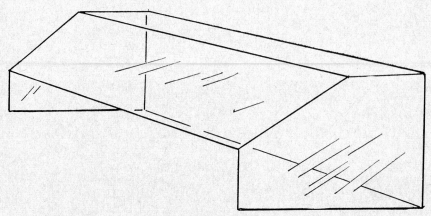

FIGURE 18. An enclosed plastic shield for handling tissues in an ordinary laboratory where a sterile air-conditioned room is not available.

proved valuable in making aseptic weighings and mass transfers of plant tissues. This is made of Plexiglas. It is 38 inches wide, 24 inches deep, and 12 inches high at the back. The front is open to a height of 6 inches, above which the face slopes back at a 45° angle, leaving a flat top 12 inches wide. Back, ends, and top are closed, the bottom and front being open (Fig. 18). This provides complete protection from dust and from air currents while permitting free manipulation and complete visibility. We have set a precision balance inside such a hood, with a microburner alongside for flaming tubes, and have made thousands of weighings of exposed cultures with almost no contamination. For most purposes such a hood can be used without a transfer room.

Implements and Glassware

The varieties of paraphernalia which have been used in making cell cultures in one laboratory or another are legion and if brought together in one place might well frighten the uninitiated. New items are being added daily. It seldom happens, however, that a single laboratory will carry on all types of cultures or make extensive use of all techniques. The equipment actually needed in any one laboratory will not be great.

Every laboratory must of course have a basic supply of graduates, bottles, filters, and the like. We use Pyrex or polyethylene serum bottles of 4-, 9-, and 20-l. capacity in making up, sterilizing, and storing large volumes of solutions. Our stock solutions of salts for plant cultures, for example, are stored in 4- or 9-l. serum bottles made of non-actinic plastic or painted black to exclude light. In making up quantities of not more than 2 l. we prefer balloon flasks rather than Erlenmeyers, since they can be stirred and rinsed out more effectively and, if need be, can be heated more safely over a flame. We therefore keep a supply of short-necked Pyrex balloon flasks of 200-, 500-, 1,000-, and 2,000-ml. capacity, with cork rings on which to set them. The only special item used in making up nutrients is the Mudd filter column (Fig. 19, left) supplied by A. H. Thomas, which we find superior to any other vessel for receiving sterile filtered fluids. The columns need not, however, be graduated. Bellco Glass, Inc., now provides a variety of sizes of these columns (Fig. 19, right). For sterile filtrations the sintered glass filters manufactured by Corning are effective and rapid, and being glass are irreproachable from a biological point of view. They are, however, expensive and rather fragile and have the added disadvantage of not permitting high-temperature cleaning. We have not had uniformly satisfactory results with Millipore filters. We therefore prefer the $\frac{1}{2}$- $\times$ 4-inch Selas porcelain candles. These are effective, very uniform, rugged, and can be freed of organic residues by baking at 600° C. followed by simple rinsing with water. We have developed special equipment which makes this washing largely automatic (Fig.

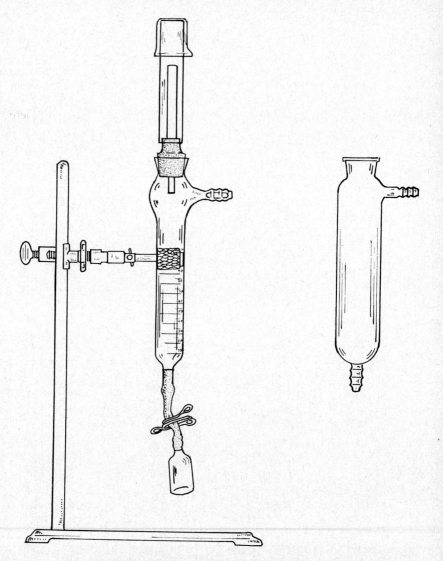

FIGURE 19. A Mudd filter column and Selas porcelain filter set up for the preparation of sterile fluids containing heat-labile substances. At the right Bellco's somewhat larger version. (Courtesy A. H. Thomas, Bellco Glass, Inc., and The Selas Corp. of America.)

20). The handling of these filters will be detailed later. We use pipettes of 10- and 5-ml. capacity graduated to 0.1 ml. and of 2- and 1-ml. capacity graduated to 0.01 ml. We also use special inoculating pipettes which will be considered later. These are all plugged with cotton and sterilized in standard metal pipette cans or large test tubes. Beyond these items all

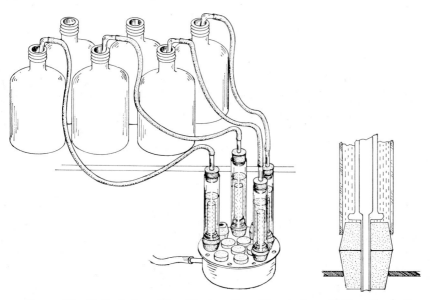

FIGURE 20. Method of washing filter candles: The steel manifold at the bottom will take up to 12 candles. Each candle has its own reservoir of water so that known quantities can be passed through in each washing cycle even though the effective flow may differ as candles become clogged. Candles can be inverted for "back-washing." The doubled stoppers by which the candles are inserted into the manifold or the filter column (Fig. 19) are shown at the right.

glassware used in preparing nutrients is standard and is found in every well-equipped microbiological laboratory.

Special Glassware

CULTURE VESSELS. Culture vessels consist of various types of (1) slides; (2) flasks, bottles, and special chambers; (3) tubes; and (4) watch glasses.

Slides. Ordinary 1- $\times$ 3- and 2- $\times$ 3-inch plane slides are standard and will be used for many purposes. In addition, hollow-ground slides of the deep Rockefeller Institute type will sometimes be used. The shallow-depression slides of the sort used by protozoologists are valueless for tissue cultures. Pierced slides, of both 1- and 2-inch width, of either glass, plastic, or metal, and of both 2- and 5-mm. thickness, will be desirable for phase-contrast work and for "sitting-drop" cultures (Fig. 21).

Flasks. Standard 125-ml. Erlenmeyer flasks are used for root cultures, for growing relatively large masses of plant tumor and cambial tissues on agar, and for certain types of animal-cell cultures where volume is impor-tant (Maitland and Maitland, 1928; deBruyn, 1955). Six-ounce flat medi-cine bottles (Blake bottles) have been used for both animal and plant

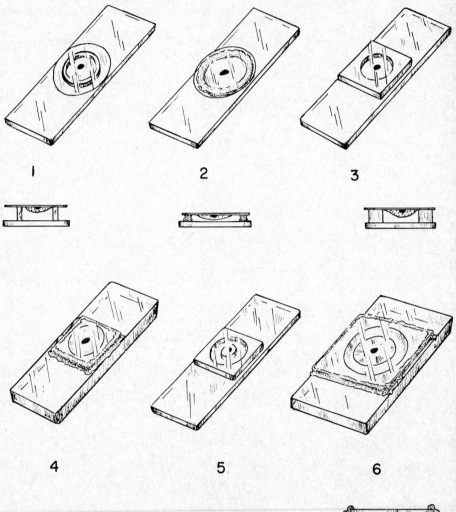

FIGURE 21. Types of slides: (1) Plane slide with glass ring (Van Tiegham cell, A. H. Thomas No. 7052). (2) Plane slide with ring of Vaseline-paraffin (1 : 3), as used by Lewis. (3) Plane slide with drilled glass plate (A.H.T. No. 7050). (4) Depression slide of Rockefeller Institute type (A.H.T. No. 7047). (5) Plane slide provided with pierced glass plate as in (3) but with an additional disk of glass or Plexiglas which permits the culture drop to establish contact with both upper and lower plate; this is the only type of drop culture which is suitable for study by phase-contrast optics without sacrifice of the free air circulation which is essential for some sorts of cells, particularly plant cells. (6) Maximov double-cover-slip culture over a deep depression slide (A.H.T. No. 7048-C).

cultures. Milk-dilution bottles are of better optical quality and have been employed for the maintenance of stocks. A variety of disposable plastic flasks and Petri dishes have recently been introduced. Plastic flasks certainly support beautiful monolayer cultures of animal cells and are especially good for shipping cultures, and the Petri dishes have proved good for some types of plant cultures; they have not, however, been adequately

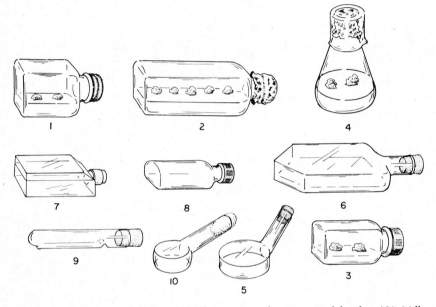

FIGURE 22. Types of flasks: (1) Three-ounce pharmaceutical bottle. (2) Milk-dilution bottle (A.H.T. No. 2246). (3) One-ounce French square bottle (A.H.T. No. 2207-K). (4) One hundred twenty-five–ml. Erlenmeyer flask. (5) Carrel flask. (6) "T-flask" (after Earle) (Kontes No. K-88250). (7) Falcon plastic flask. (8) One-half-ounce pharmaceutical bottle. (9) Leighton tube (Bellco No. 14-1950). (10) Porter flask (Kontes No. K-88225). Numbers (1) and (3) have been used to date only for plant cultures on agar; numbers (5)–(9) are most suitable for animal cells; numbers (2) and (4) have been used for both plant and animal cultures; numbers (7) and (8) are most suitable for shipping animal-cell cultures.

tested to date. Like so many aspects of the cell-culture regimen, the choice of containers is presently in a state of flux, and we may expect many useful innovations in the coming years (Fig. 22). Besides those mentioned above, the flasks in most general use are the Carrel D-3.5 flask and the "T-flask" designed by Earle. An expensive but very useful item for maintenance of stock cultures is the spinner flask (Fig. 23) introduced by McLimans (McLimans *et al.*, 1957a, 1957b) and now available in several forms and sizes. A balloon flask provided with a Teflon-covered magnet activated by an exterior rotating element makes

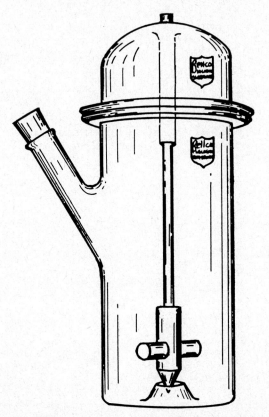

FIGURE 23. Spinner flask for the continuous cultivation of stock cultures in quantity: Growth of the culture is facilitated by the circulation and aeration provided by the magnetically activated stirrer. Nutrient can be added and cells withdrawn through the side tube. (Bellco Glass, Inc.)

a good substitute. These spinner flasks have proved to be too violent for plant-cell cultures, but a more satisfactory rotation of fluid can be obtained by placing Erlenmeyer flasks on a mechanical shaker.

Tubes. A 25- × 150-mm. Pyrex lipless test tube has proved to be a very satisfactory container for many plant tissues other than roots and embryos. Gautheret (1959) and his group use these tubes in a vertical position with a single culture per tube (Fig. 24). We slope the tubes sharply, exposing a greater area of agar; this permits growing two or three cultures in each tube. Sloped tubes can also be used with a liquid nutrient with a filter paper insert in place of agar (p. 88). Sloped tubes are easier to inoculate than vertical ones.

Such a tube is too large for satisfactory animal-cell cultures, but a standard 16- × 150-mm. tube such as those used by bacteriologists has

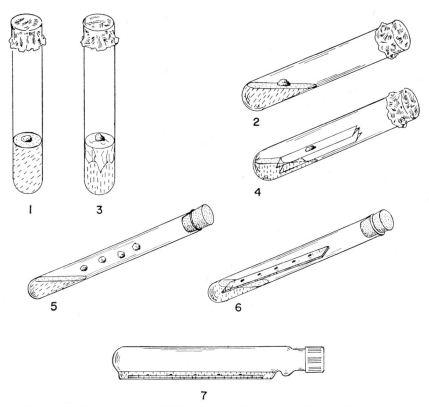

FIGURE 24. Types of tubes: (1) Vertical agar base as used by Gautheret. (2) Agar slant used by White. (3) A filter paper support in a liquid medium, designed by Heller. (4) Folded paper support in liquid nutrient with sloped tube (White). (5) Roller tube with cultures attached to the wall of the tube. (6) Roller tube with "flying cover slip" insert carrying the cultures; this can be removed for examination under the higher powers of the microscope, for washing, and for renewal of nutrient without interrupting growth. (7) Leighton tube with cover-slip insert. Numbers (1), (3), and (4) have been used only for plant cultures, numbers (6) and (7) only for animal cells. Number (5), although chiefly used for animal cells (Gey and Gey, 1936) has been used by White (1953) for plant cells. Number (2), although principally used for plant cultures, has been used by a number of workers, notably by Wallace and Hanks (1958), for some types of animal-cell cultures.

proved suitable for the roller-tube method. These tubes are sterilized and stored in either stainless-steel or "tin" cans.

Closures. Free circulation of air is important for many plant cultures. The vessels are therefore usually closed with cotton plugs wrapped in muslin. These have the disadvantage of allowing rather too free evaporation of the culture fluid. They also permit the entry of mites and, in damp weather, of mold hyphae and are rather messy in general. For short-term cultures the vessels may be closed with rubber stoppers, but this reduces the air supply too drastically to be tolerated if the tubes are to remain closed for more than a week or so. For many routine experiments we have found closure with aluminum foil, without a plug, satisfactory. The steel or plastic caps recently introduced may well prove to be still better. Screw-capped bottles may be used and the caps left loose; be careful, however, that the caps are not Bakelite, which sometimes releases volatile and toxic phenolic residues. Polyethylene caps or liners are acceptable (Fig. 25).

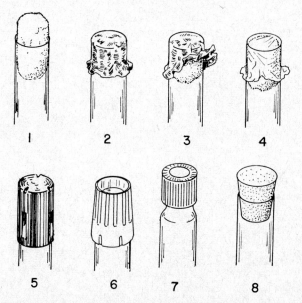

FIGURE 25. Tube closures: (1) Cotton. (2) Aluminum or tin foil (White). (3) Foil over cotton (Gautheret). (4) Pliofilm over cotton (Morel and Wetmore). (5) Norton stainless-steel cap (courtesy Bellco Glass, Inc.). (6) Autoclavable plastic cap. (7) Screw cap. (8) Rubber stopper. Numbers (1)–(6) allow free air circulation and are suitable for plant cultures, for closure during autoclaving, or for animal cultures when maintained in a special CO_2 incubator. Numbers (7) and (8), being airtight, are suitable for animal cells in an open incubator but are unsatisfactory for plant materials except for short periods.

Animal cells, unlike plant cultures, generally require an airtight closure, since any gas exchange permits carbon dioxide to escape, with resultant rise in pH unless special buffers are used or the culture vessels are incubated in special gas-conditioned incubators. For this reason animal cultures must also have their air supply renewed at frequent intervals. The usual closures for animal cells are of rubber, yet both natural and synthetic rubbers often contain toxic substances which may constitute a hazard if fluids condense on them and flow back into the flask; the West

Company, of Phoenixville, Pennsylvania, has developed a special rubber, "Formula 124," which is relatively non-toxic. These are available in several sizes, S-43 corresponding to No. 00 for Carrel flasks and S-41 to No. 0 for 16-mm. tubes. The West Company also makes more expensive pure-silicone stoppers which, however, we have found unsatisfactory because they lack resilience and are so smooth that they tend to slip out of the tubes.

Watch Glasses. The so-called Columbia embryological watch glass has proved most satisfactory for dissections. These are placed face to face in pairs, separated by a sheet of hard, chemically inert paper, so that one glass serves as a cover for the other, wrapped in foil or paper, and sterilized. This type has not been used as a culture dish although it might prove useful for any purpose for which the deep-depression slides are employed (Fig. 26 [4]). Fell uses a standard chemical watch glass of about 5 cm. diameter for the cultivation of embryonic femurs and the like, placing the watch glass in a larger Petri dish with an inlay of moist cotton to maintain humidity (Fig. 26 [1] [2]) (Fell, 1928a, 1928b). Gaillard (1948) and Wolff *et al.* (1953) use for this pur-

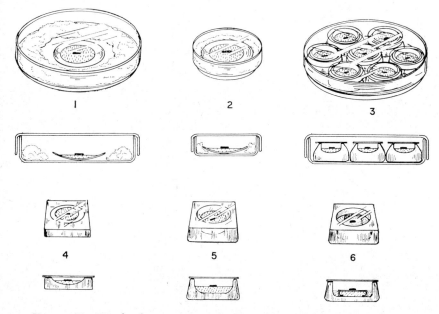

FIGURE 26. Watch glasses: (1), (2) Chemical watch glasses in Petri dishes (Fell). (3) Syracuse watch glasses (A.H.T. No. 9850) with individual covers. (4) Columbia watch glasses (A.H.T. No. 9851). (5) Embryological watch glasses (A.H.T. No. 9842) as used by Gaillard and Martinovitch for cultures on a plasma clot. (6) Watch glass with metallic wire-mesh support permitting use of a liquid nutrient as suggested by Shaffer (1956) and Trowell (1959).

pose standard embryological watch glasses ("salt cellars") charged with nutrient, covering the dishes with standard square covers (Fig. 26 [5]). In our laboratory we have used the small (27-mm. outside, 20-mm. cavity) Syracuse watch glass designed for the United States Department of Agriculture and available from A. H. Thomas (Fig. 26 [3]). Seven such glasses can be placed in a single 10-cm. Petri dish, and each can be covered individually with a round 25-mm. cover glass. These are ideal for the cultivation of various types of plant embryos, algal sporelings (Davidson, 1950), Entomostraca, and the like. They should be equally effective for animal-organ cultures.

Watch glasses may be charged with a plasma clot (Fell, Gaillard), an agar substratum (Wolff), or a liquid nutrient (Martinovitch, Shaffer). If a liquid nutrient is used, the culture must be supported. Martinovitch (1953) lays the culture on a series of glass rods. Shaffer (1956) accomplishes the same end somewhat more reliably by preparing minute tables made by folding strips of fine stainless-steel or tantalum gauze to the right dimensions (Fig. 26 [6]). If a square of rayon-acetate voile is laid on such a table, it can be transferred with its culture or removed for fixation without disturbing the tissue, or the nutrient can be renewed with a pipette, whereas cultures on plasma or agar must be lifted out of the matrix.

Pipettes. Inoculating pipettes are of three types. That used in many laboratories is the so-called Pasteur pipette. It consists of a piece of 4-mm. hard glass tubing drawn out to a long point 1 mm. in diameter and bent at a right angle for the terminal 5 mm. The tip is sealed as it is drawn out so that the interior is sterile. This tip is broken off immediately before use; the tissue or nutrient is manipulated with a hemacytometer mouth tube; and the entire pipette is discarded after use. This is obviously wasteful of glass and in our experience is unnecessary. The type of pipette used by Gey is equally effective and seems to us more sensible. A piece of 6-mm. Pyrex tubing is cut to about 20 cm. in length, drawn out to a diameter of about 2 mm. at the middle, and then cut in two. The drawn-out tips are lightly fire polished and then bent at about a 60° angle for a length of about 7–8 mm. These pipettes are plugged with cotton and sterilized in large test tubes. They can be manipulated with either a mouth tube or standard rubber bulbs, and can be cleaned and used repeatedly. They are very satisfactory, especially in working with roller-tube cultures. Such pipettes can now be purchased at a reasonable price. We use in our laboratory a pipette which has certain advantages. The tip is essentially identical with the Gey type. The shaft is shorter, about 20 cm. in over-all length. The wide end is provided with a bulb about 3 cm. from the end, and above this is a constriction to prevent the cotton plug from being forced into the bulb. The bulb permits the manipulation of fairly large quantities of fluid without danger of wetting the plug and without the need for the greater length of the Gey type. The bulb is also of such a diameter and at such a distance from the tip that a single pipette will rest in a 16- $\times$ 150-mm. test tube with the tip about $\frac{1}{2}$ cm. from the bottom. Pipettes in such tubes are sterilized in a can or jar. The pipette and its tube can be handled without exposing the tip, can be examined to select a suitable tip, and can be returned to the tube with a minimum risk of contamination. While such pipettes are fairly expensive, their evident advantages would seem to justify the cost.

Miscellaneous. In addition to the items listed above, a few hypodermics will be needed. Those of 1-ml. capacity with No. 22 needles $\frac{3}{4}$ inch long will be used to measure out small amounts of such trace nutrients as insulin, thyroxine, vitamin C, etc. They are also used in many laboratories for dispensing serum, plasma, and nutrients to hanging-drop cultures, where small volumes are needed. Those of 20-ml. capacity, without a needle, will be used for trituration of embryos, the embryo being forced through the syringe into a 15-ml. conical centrifuge tube. Those of 30-ml. capacity, with No. 18 needles 2 inches long, will be used to draw blood from the hearts of cockerels or rabbits.

This covers most of the equipment and space needed for setting up tissue, organ, and cell cultures. Some of the equipment will be discussed in more detail later. It is impractical to outline in detail the design of laboratories, storage rooms, and offices, since these will differ with each type of problem and with each organization.

"Round about the cauldron go;
In the poison'd entrails throw.
Toad,[1] that under a cold stone
Days and nights has thirty-one
Swelter'd venom sleeping got,
Boil thou first i the charmed pot.[2]
Fillet of a fenny snake,
In the cauldron boil and bake,
Eye of newt and toe of frog,
Wool of bat and tongue of dog,[3]
Adder's fork and blind-worm's sting,
Lizard's leg and howlet's wing,[4]
Scale of dragon, tooth of wolf,
Witches' mummy; maw and gulf,
Of the ravin'd salt [5] sea shark,
Root of hemlock digg'd i the dark,
Liver [6] of blaspheming Jew,
Gall of goat, and slips of yew
Shiver'd in the moon's eclipse,
Nose of Turk and Tartar's lips,
Finger of birth-strangled babe [7]
Ditch-deliver'd by a drab,
Make the gruel thick and slab;
Add thereto a tiger's chaudron,
For the ingredients of our cauldron,
Cool it with a baboon's blood,[8]
Then the charm is firm and good!"

SHAKESPEARE, *Macbeth*, Act IV, Scene I.

[1] Harrison (1907) started tissue culture with "lymph of frog."

[2] One sees such pots in Earle's wash room (Earle, 1943a).

[3] While Doljanski (Doljanski and Hoffman, 1943) recommended adult tissue, the usual practice has been to employ embryo juices. Chick embryo is most commonly used (Carrel, 1913b), but beef (Gey and Gey, 1936) or dog serves equally well.

[4] Chicken-wing blood is also often used (see Cameron, 1950).

[5] Doubtless the salts of Tyrode solution (1910).

[6] Liver extract has been used by Baker and Carrel (1928) as a substitute for embryo juice.

[7] Many laboratories still use human placental-cord serum. It can be purchased from Difco (*Difco Manual*, 10th Ed., 1959) and from Microbiological Associates.

[8] A fibrin clot serves equally well (Porter, 1947), as does chick plasma (Burrows, 1910).

Chapter 4

THE NUTRIENTS

What One Feeds to Cells

Clotted lymph from a frog was the first tissue-culture nutrient (Harrison, 1907). This was replaced by chicken plasma in 1910 (Burrows). These provided both mechanical support and nutrition and were excellent for short-term cultures but would support neither rapid nor unlimited growth. Carrel greatly improved the nutritional conditions by adding an extract of chick embryos (1913b). From these basic ingredients have been developed most of the complex media still often used for animal cells. The so-called synthetic nutrients of Baker (1936; Baker and Ebeling, 1939) and of Fischer (1941; Fischer *et al.*, 1948) are outgrowths of this approach.

At about the same time that Carrel was developing the use of embryo extracts, the two Lewises (M. R. Lewis and W. H. Lewis, 1911a *et seq.*; W. H. Lewis, 1929) began a study of the effects of particular substances, especially inorganic salts, on the growth of animal cells. Out of this approach have come the salt solutions of Gey and Gey (1936), Hanks and Wallace (1949), and others, and by projection the synthetic nutrients of White (1946, 1949), of Morgan, Morton, and Parker (1950), of Evans *et al.* (1956a), and of Waymouth (1956b, 1959), and the semidefined nutrients of Eagle (1955a, 1955b).

As we have already seen, the tissue-extract approach did not prove workable in dealing with plant tissues, for which synthetic nutrients were from the start the only ones which were effective. For this reason the development of satisfactory nutrients for plant tissues had to await the accumulation of an adequate knowledge of nitrogenous and vitamin nutrition. As a result plant-tissue nutrients, while historically latecomers, are nevertheless simpler and in general more precisely defined than are those for animal tissues. Hence, they will be dealt with first.

Nutrients for Plant Tissues

For any tissue, plant or animal, the nutrient must supply all the *essential* materials available in vivo in the tissue juices. There are two of these juices in plants, conveyed in, and diffusing from, the xylem on the one hand and the phloem on the other. The xylem "sap" moves upward from the soil toward the leaves in the so-called transpiration stream. Its major constituents, quantitatively at least, are the inorganic salts. This is in most important respects equivalent to a "good" soil solution, only modified by a certain amount of differential absorption and exclusion at the root surface. Based on this fact a series of excellent nutrients for plants (not plant-cell cultures) were developed more than a century ago, beginning with the work of Woodworth (1699) and Duhamel (1758). The formula of Knop (1865) has long been used by Gautheret (1935, 1959) as an inorganic base for plant-tissue culture nutrients. The Pfeffer solution, employed by Robbins (1922a, 1922b) for this purpose seems to be merely Pfeffer's formula for Knop's solution as improved by Knop in his later (1884) publications. White (1932a, 1932b, 1933b, 1937d, 1938a, 1943b) used as a base the solution of Uspenski and Uspenskaia (1925) because of its greater stability over a wide pH range. Trelease and Trelease developed a complex salt solution for the same reason (1933). The most complete solution was probably that of Hoagland and Snyder (1933). Heller (1953) re-examined the problem in detail and introduced a new solution which has largely replaced the earlier Knop solution in Gautheret's laboratory. In practice all of these are effective. They are compared in Table I.

The second "sap" characteristically moves downward through the phloem, from the leaves to the root. It contains materials manufactured in the photosynthetic tissues and elsewhere in the plant, and is characterized by a low inorganic and high organic content. Its chief constituents (again quantitatively) are sucrose (or dextrose) and asparagine (Borodin, 1878; Murneek, 1935) or glutamine (Vickery *et al.*, 1936; Archibald, 1945). Attempts to establish nutrients for plant-cell cultures by adding asparagine and dextrose to a Knop solution, as Kotte did (1922a, 1922b), failed and many years of research intervened before it was realized that although carbohydrates and amino acids are the ingredients of phloem sap most in evidence quantitatively, there exist certain things called "vitamins," which, although not so evident, are of equal and crucial importance.

This discovery was indirect. Kotte (1922a, 1922b) had found a digest of Liebig's meat extract to be a partially effective supplement for a Knop-dextrose-asparagine nutrient. Robbins (1922b) had used a yeast autolyzate with equal, but still only partial, success. White showed (1934a)

Table I

Salt Solutions in Common Use for Plant-Cell Cultures

Salts	White, 1934a, 1943a, 1943b	Gautheret, 1942b, (Knop, 1865)	Steeves and Sussex, 1952 (Knudson, 1925)	Heller, 1953, Gautheret, 1959	Torrey, 1957
	Milligrams per liter				
1 KCl	65			750	60
2 CaCl$_2$·2H$_2$O				75	
3 KNO$_3$	80	125			85
4 Ca(NO$_3$)$_2$·4H$_2$O	300	500	1000		240
5 NaNO$_3$				600	
6 MgSO$_4$·7H$_2$O	720	125	250	250	40
7 NaSO$_4$	200				
8 (NH$_4$)$_2$SO$_4$			500		
9 K$_2$HPO$_4$			250		
10 KH$_2$PO$_4$		125			20
11 NaH$_2$PO$_4$·H$_2$O	16.5			125	
12 Fe$_2$(SO$_4$)$_3$	2.5	50			
13 FeCl$_3$·6H$_2$O				1	2.5
14 Fe-citrate			2		
15 MnSO$_4$·4H$_2$O	7	3		0.1	4.5
16 ZnSO$_4$·7H$_2$O	3	0.18		1	1.5
17 H$_3$BO$_3$	1.5	0.05		1	1.5
18 KI	0.75	0.5		0.01	
19 CuSO$_4$·5H$_2$O	0.001[*]	0.05		0.03	0.04
20 MoO$_3$	0.0001[*]				
21 Na$_2$MoO$_2$·2H$_2$O					0.25
22 AlCl$_3$				0.03	
23 NiSO$_4$		0.05			
24 NiCl$_2$·6H$_2$O				0.03	
25 CoCl$_3$		0.05			
26 BeSO$_4$		0.1			
27 Ti(SO$_4$)$_3$		0.2			
28 H$_2$SO$_4$		1			

[*] Added by Boll and Street (1951)

that, by substituting sucrose for dextrose (1940a, 1940b, 1943a) and utilizing a non-autolyzed yeast extract, a fully adequate nutrient could be provided. The yeast was then analyzed (1937a) and its effects were shown to be due to its content of amino acids (1937b), especially glycine (1939c), on the one hand, and of vitamins, especially thiamine, on the other (1937c; see also Robbins and Bartley, 1937; Bonner, 1938). Robbins and Schmidt (1938a, 1938b, 1939a, 1939b) then added pyridoxin and nicotinic acid to the list of substances which are beneficial though not essential, in the sense of being synthesized in minimum but suboptimum quantities by the tissue itself (see also Bonner and Bonner, 1938; Bonner and Devirian, 1939). Morel (1946) and others have since added biotin, panthothenic acid, choline, inositol, and other constituents as being essential for certain tissues (Gautheret, 1948a, 1950, 1959). At present a great many nutrient formulas are available for plant tissues. The most widely used are modifications of those of White and of Gautheret. These we will present in detail.

White's standard nutrient solution for plant tissues (1943a, 1943b), modified in current practice, consists of four parts: an inorganic salt solution, a carbohydrate, a vitamin supplement, and a pH indicator. Stocks for the preparation of this nutrient are commonly made up in quantity as follows:

1. Set out four 1-l. flasks of double-purified water (I, II, III, IV).

To I add	$Ca(NO_3)_2 \cdot 4H_2O$	12.0 g.
	KNO_3	3.2 g.
	KCl	2.6 g.
To II add	$MgSO_4 \cdot 7H_2O$	30.0 g.
	Na_2SO_4	8.0 g.
To III add	$NaH_2PO_4 \cdot H_2O$	0.76 g.
To IV add	$MnSO_4 \cdot 4H_2O$	0.20 g.
	$ZnSO_4 \cdot 7H_2O$	0.12 g.
	H_3BO_3	0.06 g.
	KI	0.03 g.
	$CuSO_4 \cdot 5H_2O$	0.0004 g.[*]
	MoO_3	0.00004 g.[*]

[*] These two may be added by making up a concentrated solution consisting of 40 mg. $CuSO_4 \cdot 5H_2O$ and 4 mg. MoO_3 in 100 ml. of water and adding 1 ml. of this stock to flask IV.

When the four are quite dissolved, they are mixed slowly to provide stock 1, which should be stored in the dark or in black or nonactinic bottles.

2. In 100 ml. of water, dissolve 300 mg. glycine, 50 mg. nicotinic acid, 10 mg. thiamine, and 10 mg. pyridoxine. Sterilize by filtration; draw off into test tubes; and store frozen in the refrigerator.

3. Dissolve 100 mg. chlorophenol red in 25 ml. N/100 NaOH; then add water to make 250 ml. Adjust to pH 6.0, filter, and store in tubes in the refrigerator.

Stocks 1 and 3 will keep indefinitely if not allowed to become contaminated; stock 2 should not be kept longer than 60 days unless frozen ($-15°$ C.).

One liter of nutrient is prepared by taking 889 ml. of water, dissolving therein 20 g. sucrose and 2.5 mg. $Fe_2(SO_4)_3$, and adding 100 ml. stock 1 (salts), 1 ml. stock 2 (vitamins), and 10 ml. stock 3 (indicator). The nutrient should have a pH of about 5.5 as indicated by a pink color; if it is too yellow, it can be adjusted with N/1 KOH. When complete, it is distributed to culture flasks, bottles, or tubes, autoclaved, and allowed to cool. It is now ready for use in the cultivation of roots or other tissues. For tissues requiring a semisolid substratum (p. 17), the same procedure is followed except that only 389 ml. of water are used. Five grams of agar (Difco "Noble" agar or its equivalent) are dissolved in 500 ml. of hot water. When thoroughly liquefied, the two are combined, distributed, and autoclaved. This basic nutrient is suitable for many sorts of tissues and will be subject to many modifications to be considered later.

Heller's solution, which many continental Europeans consider superior to the above, is prepared in seven stocks.

1.	KCl	100 g.	water 1,000 ml.
2.	$NaNO_3$	100 g.	water 1,000 ml.
3.	$MgSO_4 \cdot 7H_2O$	100 g.	water 1,000 ml.
4.	$NaH_2PO_4 \cdot H_2O$	10 g.	water 1,000 ml.
5.	$CaCl_3 \cdot 2H_2O$	10 g.	water 1,000 ml.
6.	$FeCl_3 \cdot 6H_2O$	1 g.	water 1,000 ml.
7.	$ZnSO_4 \cdot 7H_2O$, 1 g.; H_3BO_3, 1 g.; $MnSO_4 \cdot 4H_2O$, 10 mg.; $CuSO_4 \cdot 5H_2O$, 30 mg.; $AlCl_3$, 30 mg.; $NiCl_2 \cdot 6H_2O$, 30 mg.; KI, 10 mg.;		water 1,000 ml.

In preparing nutrients, add to 962 ml. of water 20 g. dextrose, 7.5 ml. stock 1, 6 ml. stock 2, 2.5 ml. stock 3, 12.5 ml. stock 4, 7.5 ml. stock 5, 1 ml. stock 6, and 1 ml. stock 7. Gautheret and Heller give no general formula for vitamins or other growth substances to be included in their nutrients but provide these according to special formulas for each particular tissue. Most of their nutrients contain 1 mg. of thiamine per liter.

Although many tissues can be grown on relatively simple nutrients of the types described above, others have proved more refractory and a great many methods of overcoming this have been examined. It will be recalled that the first successful cultures involved the use of yeast extract (Robbins, 1922b; White, 1934a). Torrey and Shigamura (1957) have found this useful for pea-root callus. A suitable preparation is furnished by boiling 100 mg. of dried brewer's yeast such as "Difco Bacto-yeast" in 500 ml. of water for 30 minutes, centrifuging for 10 minutes at 1,000 G, decanting, and using this supernatant to make up 1 l. of nutrient. The effects are largely, if not entirely, attributable to the vitamins and amino acids extracted. Casein digests have been similarly used by Nickell and others. Another still less clearly defined supplement is coconut milk, first used by van Overbeek, Conklin, and Blakeslee (1941). This has proved to be highly effective as a stimulant and seems to be most beneficial when added at about 15 per cent by volume. It is usually prepared by filtration but may be boiled. The milk of young coconuts is more uniformly satisfactory although that of ripe fruits has sometimes given good results. In spite of extensive studies, especially by Steward and Schantz (1954, 1955), there is no clear evidence of the nature of the effective constituent or constituents. It is stable to boiling at acid, neutral, and alkaline reactions; it is dialyzable; and all attempts at fractionation have only resulted in the separation of a large number of fractions all of which have some effect and are additive in various combinations. Since coconut-milk factors are not *essential* for any known tissue once its growth is well established but merely aid in the initiation of growth, our laboratory has preferred not to use them, although they have found wide acceptance elsewhere. Similar stimulating materials have been obtained from malt extract and malt steep liquor, tomato juice, orange juice, and various tissue extracts. None of these seem to be of general importance.

A little more clear-cut but nevertheless impossible to generalize are the results with a large number of chemically defined growth substances of the auxin type. Most normal plant tissues require one or more of these. The most commonly used is indoleacetic acid, which is employed at concentrations of from 10^{-5} to 10^{-10}. Naphthaleneacetic acid can be used at somewhat higher concentrations, 2,4-dichlorophenoxyacetic acid (2,4-D) usually at somewhat lower ones. More recently kinetin, gibberellic acid, DNA, and a number of the vitamins including inositol, biotin, folic acid, choline, pantothenic acid, and others have come into use. These likewise are effective at concentrations of the order of 10^{-7} to 10^{-12}. In many cases their action is synergistic. Thus Steward and Caplin (1951) found both 2,4-D and coconut milk necessary to initiate growth of potato-tuber tissue. Similar synergisms seem to exist between indoleacetic acid and kinetin (Skoog and Tsui, 1948; Skoog, 1951). Sometimes special materials must be employed for special purposes. Thus, the tissues of many trees, particularly the conifers, may be limited in their growth in culture by the presence of powerful phenol-oxydase systems. Jacquiot (1947) tried with some success to inactivate these by addition of caffein or ascorbic acid to the nutrient. The use of tyrosine and of reducing agents such as cysteine may be beneficial, but they must be used with prudence, since they are quite toxic if supplied at too high a concentration (Reinert and White, 1956).

This aspect of the nutrition of plant tissues is at present in a state of active development and cannot be presented effectively in detail in a general text. For the sake of completeness we will say that, if these accessory substances—biotin, Ca-pantothenate, indoleacetic acid, 2,4-D, etc.—are dissolved each at the rate of 10 mg. in 1 l. of water and these stocks are sterilized by filtration and introduced into the nutrients at the rate of 10 ml. per liter, they will give final concentrations of 10^{-7}. This is a suitable tentative concentration and can be adjusted after preliminary tests.

The nutritional requirements of plant tissues have thus been definitely established in a general way and only require further refinement in detail. Until very recently the same could not be said of animal tissues, and even now it is best to present a much less finished picture and to proceed from the complex to the simple.

Nutrients for Mammalian Cells

The nutrients for animal tissues consisted first of clotted lymph (Harrison, 1907), then of serum diluted with a salt solution (Burrows, 1910, 1911), and finally of a variety of mixtures of plasma, serum, embryo extracts and other tissue juices, and salts. Lymph has entirely disappeared from use, but the other complexes, although rapidly being replaced by better-defined materials, still find wide usage, especially in dealing with tissues which have not previously been grown and whose behavior is unknown. Therefore, all these nutrients must be discussed. Fortunately, commercial sources of most of these ingredients are available. For workers who do not have access to such sources, or who for other reasons prefer to prepare their own, it will be best to outline at least briefly the necessary procedures.

BLOOD PLASMA AND SERUM. The serum and plasma of the domestic fowl, because of their relative transparency, uniform texture, high fibrin content, and low level of proteolytic enzymes, have proved superior to all others for general use. Blood may be obtained in large quantity by bleeding from the carotid artery. This method has been widely used. It has the great disadvantage, however, of requiring a great deal of equipment and personnel and of killing the bird at the second bleeding so that uniform samples cannot be obtained week after week from a single bird. We have never used the method and will not describe it in detail. The interested reader may refer to the texts of Cameron (1950), Paul (1960), and Parker (1961). A continuous supply of blood of reliable uniformity can be obtained by bleeding repeatedly from the same bird but in smaller quantities. This can best be done either from the wing or direct from the heart. Paul (1960) gives an excellent description of bleeding from the wing. We prefer the heart. While a procedure for doing this is outlined in the accounts of Lewis (1928) and of Buchsbaum and Loosli (1936), we have found it difficult to follow their directions. Our own procedure will therefore be described.

The equipment required consists of

Two 30-ml. syringes provided with No. 18 needles 2 inches long and with two extra needles in reserve

Four 15-ml. conical centrifuge tubes coated with silicone, in ice,
   stoppered
One vial of heparin solution 1 : 1,000
Alcohol, with cotton
A board for holding the chicken, with tie tapes

A young, healthy cockerel about one year old is kept without food,
but with adequate water, for 24 hours. He is then brought in and tied
loosely to the board with the right side down, head to the left. The left
wing is tied back and the feathers removed from the flank. Lewis (1928)
gives an elaborate description of the landmarks for locating the heart.
In our experience, if the little finger of the right hand (assuming a
moderate-sized or small hand!) is placed on the hip bone of the fowl and
the hand allowed to rest in a relaxed position, the thumb will describe
an arc which passes over the heart (Fig. 27). Similarly, if the same finger
is placed at the point where this arc passes over the spine, the thumb will
again describe a second arc crossing the heart. Where these two arcs
intersect should be very close to the proper point of entry. The place is
recognizable as a soft triangle, the rearward of two such triangles. The
spot is sterilized with alcohol. A sterile syringe is taken and the inner
walls of the needle moistened with heparin by drawing solution from the
vial into the syringe and then returning it to the vial. The amount
remaining on the walls will be sufficient in quantity and in concentration
to prevent coagulation of 20 ml. of blood when drawn.[1]

The needle is then inserted into the bird's side at the previously
marked spot and is directed slightly rearward and under the sternum.
When the needle has been inserted to about half its length, it should be
possible to feel the beat of the heart against it. If this is not felt, the
needle should be partly withdrawn and the angle altered until the proper
point is found. With a little practice the place should be found immediately. Pierce the heart with the needle, being careful not to go too far
and pass through the heart. The blood will flow freely into the syringe,
forcing the plunger out. It should not be necessary to use more than a
minimum of suction at any time. When about 20 ml. have been drawn,
the syringe should be removed from the needle without withdrawing the
latter, and a new syringe should be attached. Force the blood from the
syringe slowly into two of the centrifuge tubes, 10 ml. per tube, and
return the tubes to the ice. When a full supply has been accumulated

[1] Once the operator becomes expert, heparin can be dispensed with entirely. Its
use can also be avoided, if desired, by using a 1-ml. syringe as "guide," discarding
this syringe with the first milliliter of blood drawn and replacing it with a fresh,
chilled 30-ml. syringe. In this way any juice from tissues injured in inserting the
needle will be discarded and no prothrombin will be drawn with the final blood
supply.

centrifuge the tubes briefly, five minutes at 700 G. Draw off the super-natant plasma with a chilled and siliconed pipette, being careful not to disturb the packed erythrocytes, and transfer it to small paraffined or siliconed storage tubes, usually not more than 5 ml. per tube. Store these in the refrigerator. Such plasma should keep for months. Lyophilized plasma, which can be purchased commercially, is satisfactory for most cell cultures but, according to Fell and Mellanby (1952) and Carpenter (1942), cannot be used satisfactorily for organ cultures, which seem to require freshly prepared plasma.

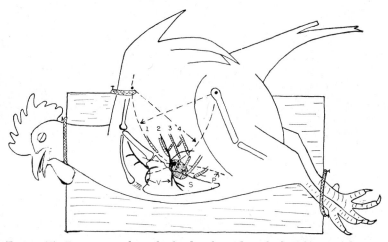

FIGURE 27. Diagram to show the landmarks and method of locating the point of entry for drawing blood from a fowl by direct heart puncture.

During the early part of the bleeding operation the bird will not struggle, but, after about 30 ml. have been drawn, there will be a mo-ment when he is likely to react violently. If he is held firmly at this moment, no harm will be done and the convulsion will not be repeated. Another 10 or 20 ml. can safely be drawn. If the bird is not firmly held, however, the heart may be torn and the bird will die.

If this operation is successfully carried out, the bird can be returned to his cage and fed immediately and will suffer no serious injury. We had one cockerel which was bled in this way at two-week intervals for more than a year, that is, through more than 25 bleedings, before he was finally killed in a fight with another bird. During this time we had a constant supply of blood, more than a liter in all, which, in all those qualities which are of hereditary origin, was entirely uniform. Serum can be prepared by adding enough thromboplastic material such as tissue extract to bring about clotting and then breaking up the clot with a sterile glass rod, after which the supernatant serum can be drawn off.

We have used rabbit serum in our laboratory with excellent results. The animals are bled to death from the carotid, directly into a collecting vessel, with no special precautions except reasonable cleanliness, and the blood is allowed to clot. The serum separates by syneresis. The clots are broken up with a glass rod and the serum is decanted. It is then centrifuged, decanted, and finally filtered through an 03 Selas candle. The sterile serum is collected and stored in the refrigerator at −15° C. It seems to keep indefinitely under these conditions, at least for a year. We have never encountered any evidence of toxicity in any samples which had not become contaminated with bacteria. A variety of special serums—horse, ox, calf, lamb, pig, etc.—are available on the market and are sometimes specified for particular strains of cells. They will not be necessary or even desirable for most work.

Many investigators whose laboratories are attached to large hospitals prefer to use human placental-cord serum. Blood is either drawn from the umbilical vein with a hypodermic or allowed to drain directly from the cut cord into a suitable container. It is allowed to clot, and the supernatant serum is drawn off after syneresis, filtered to render it aseptic, and stored in the refrigerator. It should be remembered, however, that the use of anesthetics or antibiotics, or even the ingestion of fat shortly before delivery may render the serum toxic or otherwise unusable, and that the mixing of serum from more than one patient, as busy delivery nurses may do, adds to the unreliability of this source. It is not generally to be recommended.

Embryo Extracts and Other Tissue Juices. The use of embryo extracts has largely disappeared. It is nevertheless sometimes recommended and its preparation should be described. For most purposes chick embryos will be the ones most readily available. A group of 10- to 12-day eggs are opened (p. 95), and the embryos are removed into a sterile dish. Five to seven embryos are dropped into a 20-ml. syringe, heads and all, and the plunger inserted. Earle (Evans *et al.*, 1951) and Hanks (Scherer *et al.*, 1955) insert a fine-mesh stainless-steel screen in the syringe; we find this unnecessary, though perhaps it gives a finer pulp. The mouth of the syringe is inserted into a 15-ml. centrifuge tube and the plunger pushed down. The embryos will be forced through the opening and will be finely triturated without excessive destruction of the cells. About 4 ml. of juice will be obtained from each embryo. An equal volume of salt-dextrose solution (Tyrode, Gey, Earle, Hanks) is added, the whole mixed thoroughly with a sterile glass rod and set aside overnight. The brei is then centrifuged at 1,000 G for ten minutes and the supernatant decanted and either filtered or stored immediately in the refrigerator. We find this method more satisfactory than any of the grinding or chopping methods described elsewhere. It is certainly simpler, involving less manipulation and, hence, less danger of contamination. A still more active preparation can be obtained if the raw juice is frozen and thawed once or twice before centrifuging. Some workers prefer to incubate the brei and salt-dextrose solution together at 37° C. for 10 to 24 hours before centrifuging. Embryo extract, either liquid or lyophilized, can be purchased commercially. Moreover Earle (Evans *et al.*, 1957) finds that if whole unembryonated eggs are filtered they provide an "extract" which is just as effective as that prepared from embryos.

Each batch of embryo extract, and of blood serum as well, should be tested bacteriologically before being used.

Unfortunately embryos of mice, rats, rabbits, pigs, beef, and other mammals, while physiologically quite satisfactory, are too fibrous to be treated by passing through a syringe. They must either be ground in a tissue grinder, cut up with knives or scissors, or divided in some other way. Special grinders with glass barrels and Teflon pistons are available for use with small embryos. Beef embryos can be obtained from a slaughterhouse, with the amniotic sac intact, and brought to the laboratory in sterile saline. An embryo about 5 or 6 inches long will be suitable. In the laboratory the sac is opened and the embryo cut up. This can then be ground briefly in a Waring blender. If grinding is stopped soon enough, this gives a fairly satisfactory result. Too prolonged grinding may result in a milky suspension which cannot be cleared by centrifugation. One 5-inch beef embryo will provide several hundred milliliters of clear juice, enough for many weeks work in the average laboratory.

Lewis and Lewis (1911b) and, more recently, Hoffman, Dingwall, and Andrus (1951) have shown that bouillons from adult tissues provide fairly satisfactory nutrient materials. Chicken leg or breast muscle, veal muscle, beef heart, etc., are cut into pieces a centimeter or less cube and boiled and the fluid decanted and used as a nutrient. Such bouillons should be as nearly fat-free as possible, since fatty materials are generally growth-inhibiting.

For cultures in which the purity of the cell strain is important it will be necessary to filter all tissue juices and serums, to make certain that living cells are not carried over from the nutrient sources. Many experiments have been ruined by such carryover of viable foreign cells, a possibility which long went unrecognized. As prepared, embryo extracts tend very rapidly to clog any suitable filter. This can, however, be prevented by first treating the extract, immediately before filtration, with hyaluronidase at such a strength as to give a final concentration of 0.01 per cent by volume. The extract is then passed through an 03-porosity Selas candle or its equivalent.

SELAS FILTERS AND THEIR USE. A description of the use of these filters seems not out of place here. The Selas porcelain filter is of the same general type as the Berkefeld or Chamberland candle, but because of its special method of manufacture the pores are all within a narrow range of diameters. The filters, hence, do not require standardization and are free of possible leaks. Although made in several sizes and pore diameters, the $\frac{5}{8}$- $\times$ 4-inch candle of ultrafine (03) porosity is the one most commonly used in cell-culture work. This is sold with a special double-ended rubber stopper of a size about equivalent to a No. 7, and a Pyrex mantle which permits its effective use down to about 3 ml. of fluid. The stopper can be placed directly in a standard filter flask of the Erlenmeyer type. We prefer the "Mudd column" originally designed for filtering bacteriological preparations. The Selas stopper is too small to fit this column satisfactorily but is rendered snug by covering it with a double thickness of Gooch-crucible tubing.

We found it unsatisfactory to sterilize this equipment assembled. We use the following procedure: The filter candle is inserted in the stopper, candle up, and the Gooch tubing added. This is laid on the corner of a 10- $\times$ 10-inch piece of paper or muslin and the corner folded around it once. The glass mantle is then laid alongside, the wrapping completed, and the whole sealed with sterilizer tape. The upper mouth and side tubulations of the collecting column are closed with cotton plugs, the side plug being snug enough so as not to be easily forced out by changes in air pressure. The outlet is provided with a piece of pure-gum tubing about 3 inches long into which is inserted a small filling bell. The bell is likewise plugged with cotton, the tube bent so that the bell lies alongside the column, and the whole wrapped in paper and sealed. Both column and filter are sterilized by autoclaving at 15 pounds' pressure for 10 minutes followed by drying under vacuum, as in handling all equipment containing rubber.

When it is to be used, the collecting column is unwrapped and set up in a standard burette support, without removing the protecting plugs. The filter mantle is unwrapped and taken in the left hand, and the unwrapping is continued to expose the candle; this is picked up with the right hand; grasping the stopper with the sterile paper, the filter is inserted in the mantle and then quickly introduced into the top of the column. The vacuum tube is attached, being sure that an adequate trap is introduced between the column and the vacuum source (this is especially important if a water pump is used as the source of vacuum); a pinch clamp is placed on the rubber outlet tube; and the apparatus is ready for use (Fig. 19). The material is poured into the mantle and the vacuum started.

In practice we find it almost impossible to control the rate of change from atmospheric pressure to vacuum and back again directly at the vacuum source (water pump, vacuum pump, vacuum line) gradually enough to prevent the protective plug in the side tubulation from being forced either into the vacuum line or into the column, either of which would destroy the sterility of the system. To obviate this we place in the vacuum line a T-tube the stem of which is provided with a soft rubber tubulation and a screw clamp. The vacuum is started with this tubulation open, and the screw clamp is then closed gradually. Vacuum should be maintained below 250 mm. mercury to avoid boiling, particularly when filtering solutions containing bicarbonate. After filtration is complete, this tubulation is again opened gradually with the vacuum still on, the latter being shut off only after the system has been fully opened.

Vitamin solutions, bicarbonate, salts, sugar, and the like will filter very quickly; viscous preparations such as serum or embryo extract will be much slower unless treated with some agent such as hyaluronidase.

The procedure for cleaning filters must also be described. The candles are removed from their stoppers as soon as they have been used, rinsed thoroughly in tap water, and then stood stem up in a 500-ml. HT polyethylene beaker of dilute hypochlorite solution (Clorox). They should not be allowed to dry out. When a number have been accumulated, the fluid is poured off and the beaker and filters are filled with concentrated sulfuric acid containing a trace of sodium nitrate or nitric acid. This is simmered in a water bath under a hood for a half-hour. The acid is then decanted and the filters rinsed thoroughly in tap water. They are then set up as for filtration but attached to a water pump, and about a liter of distilled water is passed through each filter. We have developed a manifold and continuous feed mechanism which makes this washing largely automatic (Fig. 20). This procedure removes most soluble residues from the pores of the candles. The candles are then removed, all water is shaken out, and they are placed in a drying oven to remove all moisture. They are then placed in a shallow metal tray in a muffle furnace where they are brought to 600° C. and held there for a minimum of one-half hour. They should be allowed to cool slowly to avoid cracking. This treatment will completely incinerate any insoluble organic residues. The candles are then again attached to the vacuum line, and a liter of single-purified water, followed by 500 ml. of double-purified water, is flushed through each, after which they are ready to be dried, wrapped, and sterilized for use again.

Although this procedure is tedious, it is technically simple and highly effective, and the results are irreproachable. Seitz filters may be objectionable because of the constituents of the filter pads. We have not had uniformly good results with Millipore filters. Sintered glass filters are fragile and cannot be incinerated. Berkefeld and Chamberland filters are uneven in quality and prone to leaks and irregularities. The Selas filter has none of these objections.

SALT SOLUTIONS. The older tissue-culture nutrients were all built around the salt solutions of Ringer (1886), Locke (1895), or Tyrode (1910). The reader is referred to Parker's book for a full and adequate discussion of their preparation (1961). These solutions, however, were not originally designed for this purpose and bear little resemblance to the ionic composition of body fluids. Theoretically better solutions have been developed. Salt solutions in most general use today are those of Earle, Hanks, Eagle, and Waymouth, all of which are commercially available. The formulas for these and other solutions are compared in Table II.

SYNTHETIC OR DEFINED NUTRIENTS. The first tissue-culture nutrients, except for their salt content, were made up largely of biological products of unknown constitution. Vogelaar and Erlichman (1933), Baker (1936), and Baker and Ebeling (1939) described reasonably effective nutrients made up largely of "defined" materials, which they designated as "synthetic." These, however, all contained small amounts of blood serum and other unknowns and were therefore not truly defined. The same is true of Eagle's more recent formulas (1955a, 1955b), which when used for prolonged cultures are supplemented with serum or serum dialysate. Fischer (1941; Fischer et al., 1948) went a step further in reducing the unknowns by employing plasma, serum, and embryo extract which had been subjected to prolonged dialysis against a dextrose-Ringer solution until they no longer supported cell proliferation when used alone or diluted with salt-dextrose solution. These were considered to be "biologically inert." They were still unknowns, however, and the work of White and Lasfargues (1949), Barski et al. (1951), and Harris (1952, 1954) cast doubt on the biological basis of their inertness. Harris (1954) showed that mere addition of sodium bicarbonate restored much of their effectiveness. In this work no attempt was made to *build up* complete nutrients without the use of organic supplements.

In 1946, White (1946, 1949) initiated a new approach to the problem. Making use of the mass of accumulated data on the vitamins, amino acids, purines, hormones, and similar defined chemicals which are known to play important roles in the nutrition of animals, plants, and microorganisms, and proceeding from the assumptions that blood serum and tissue extracts contain not only nutrients but also products of catabolism which may be of no nutritional value, and that synthetic nutrients should therefore be *simpler* than serums, he first established a formula which

Table II

Salt-Dextrose Solutions in Common Use for Animal-Cell Cultures

grams per liter

Ingredients	Fell, 1931; Tyrode, 1910	Simms "Z"; Simms and Sanders, 1942	Earle, 1943b	White "W_1" 1946	Hanks and Wallace, 1949	Morgan, Morton, and Parker, #199, 1950	Wolff, 1955	Healey, Fisher, and Parker, #858, 1955	Eagle, 1955a	Waymouth, MB 752/1, 1959
1 Glucose	1.00	1.00	1.00	8.50	1.00	Identical with Earle, 1943b.	1.00	Identical with Earle, 1943b.		5.00
2 NaCl	8.00	8.00	6.80	7.00	8.00		8.00		5.85	6.00
3 KCl	0.20	0.20	0.40	0.40	0.40		0.20		0.37	0.15
4 $CaCl_2$	0.20	0.15	0.40		0.14		0.20		0.11	0.12
5 $CaCl_2 \cdot 2H_2O$										
6 $Ca(NO_3)_2 \cdot H_2O$										
7 $MgSO_4$										
8 $MgSO_4 \cdot 7H_2O$			0.10	0.20	0.20					0.20
9 $MgCl_2 \cdot 6H_2O$	0.10	0.20		0.30			0.10		0.10	0.24
10 KH_2PO_4	0.05			0.03	0.06		0.05			0.08
11 $NaH_2PO_4 \cdot H_2O$			0.125						0.14	
12 Na_2HPO_4		0.02			0.06					0.30
13 $Na_2HPO_4 \cdot 12H_2O$				0.15						
14 $NaHCO_3$	1.00	1.00	2.20	0.55	0.35		1.00			2.24
15 $Fe(NO_3)_3 \cdot 9H_2O$				0.0014		0.0001		0.001		
16 Phenol red			0.002	0.005	0.02	0.02		0.02		0.005

71

supported prolonged survival and function of a variety of animal tissues, but without growth (1946, 1949). Rapid growth could be obtained when such a solution was supplemented with a small percentage (as low as 0.1 per cent) of serum, without embryo extract (White, 1955). Morgan, Morton, and Parker (1950) subsequently introduced a similar but more complex formula, "solution 199," which soon came into wide use in the cultivation of viruses. This also required a small amount of serum to support continuous and rapid growth. Morgan (Morton, Pasieka, and Morgan, 1956, "solution M 150"), Parker (Healy, Fisher, and Parker, 1955, "solution 858"), and Evans et al. (1956a, 1956b, "solution NCTC 109") elaborated on Parker's solution 199, producing finally true "synthetic" nutrients which would support slow but continuous growth of a limited variety of cells in the complete absence of organic complexes. These formulas were, however, extremely complex, Parker's No. 858 containing 62 and Evans and Earle's No. 109 containing 69 ingredients. They were also expensive and somewhat unstable. In the meantime, Waymouth, starting from White's 1946 formula and from Fischer's work, had progressively replaced the embryo extract and serum with a peptone and finally replaced the peptone; by further refinements much simpler formulas were arrived at which eliminated all complexes yet provided for continuous rapid growth (Waymouth, 1956b, 1959). Waymouth's fully synthetic nutrient MB 752/1 contains 40 ingredients and supports for indefinite periods growth of certain mouse cells, especially a number of sublines of the L-strain, at levels of 20-fold increase per passage of one week.

Solutions 199, 858, Eagle's nutrient, NCTC 109, and Waymouth's MB-752/1 are all available commercially. For the sake of those who must, or who prefer to, prepare their own, we will give detailed instructions for preparing Eagle's solution and for Waymouth's MB 752/1.

Eagle's Solution (Eagle, 1955). This is prepared in nine stocks.

1. NaCl .... 5.85 g.　Water, 1,000 ml. This can be auto-
   KCl .... 0.37 g.　claved or filtered.
   CaCl₂ .... 0.11 g.
   MgCl₂·6H₂O .... 0.10 g.
   NaH₂PO₄·H₂O .... 0.14 g.
   Phenol red .... 0.02 g.

2. L-Arginine .... 1.74 g.　Water, 1,000 ml. This is best fil-
   L-Histidine .... 0.32 g.　tered, although it can probably
   L-Lysine .... 1.46 g.　safely be autoclaved.
   L-Leucine .... 1.31 g.
   L-Isoleucine .... 2.62 g.
   L-Methionine .... 0.75 g.
   L-Phenylalanine ...... 0.83 g.
   L-Threonine .... 1.19 g.
   L-Tryptophane .... 0.20 g.
   L-Valine .... 1.17 g.

3. L-Tyrosine .... 1.80 g.   Dissolve in N/10 HCl, then make
   L-Cystine .... 0.48 g.   up to 1,000 ml. with water. This
                                         must be filtered.

4. Choline .... 0.139 g.   Water, 100 ml. This must be fil-
   Nicotinamide .... 0.123 g.   tered.
   Pantothenic acid ...... 0.220 g.
   Pyridoxal .... 0.205 g.
   Riboflavin .... 0.038 g.
   Thiamine .... 0.337 g.

5. Biotin .... 0.024 g.   Dissolve in 100 ml. of water to
   Folic acid .... 0.044 g.   which phenol red is added to
                                         bring to the necessary shade of
                                         color; then adjust to pH 7.2 with
                                         N/2 NaOH. This must be fil-
                                         tered.

6. Glucose ....   Add 1.0 g. of glucose to 100 ml.
                                         of stock 1. This should be fil-
                                         tered.

7. NaHCO₃ .... 1.4 g.   Water, 100 ml. This must be fil-
                                         tered.

8. Na-penicillin G. ...... 200,000 units   Water, 100 ml. Filter.
   Streptomycin sulfate ... 0.5 g.   This should be stored at −15° C.

9. L-Glutamine ....   Add 1.46 g. L-Glutamine to 100
                                         ml. of stock 1. This should be
                                         filtered and stored at −15° C.

From the above general stocks a "working stock" is prepared each
week by combining 10 ml. of each of stocks 2, 3, 5, 6, 8, and 9 with 1 ml.
of stock 4.

One hundred milliliters of nutrient are prepared when needed, by
combining 84 ml. of stock 1, 6.1 ml. of the working stock, and 10 ml. of
serum (horse, rabbit, chicken, human, or any other indicated) and adding enough of stock 7 (sodium bicarbonate) to bring the final solution
to the desired pH of 7.2–7.4. This gives a medium containing 10 per cent
of serum. Other combinations can be prepared as desired. This is an
effective nutrient for many tissues and is widely used. It is *not*, however,
a defined nutrient.

Waymouth's Defined Nutrient MB 752/1. This is prepared from five
stocks.

1. NaCl .... 12.00 g.   Water, 1,000 ml.
   KCl .... 0.30 g.   Filter or autoclave.
   CaCl₂·2H₂O .... 0.24 g.
   MgCl₂·6H₂O .... 0.48 g.
   MgSO₄·7H₂O .... 0.40 g.

2. Na₂HPO₄ .... 0.60 g.   Water, 1,000 ml.
   KH₂PO₄ .... 0.16 g.   Filter.
   NaHCO₃ .... 4.48 g.

3. Glucose .... 10.00 g.   Water, 1,000 ml.
    Ascorbic acid .... 0.035 g.   Filter.
    Choline·HCl .... 0.50 g.
    Cysteine·HCl .... 0.18 g.
    Glutathione .... 0.03 g.
    Hypoxanthine .... 0.05 g.
    Glutamine .... 0.70 g.

4. Thiamine HCl .... 40 mg.   Water, 100 ml.
    Ca Pantothenate .... 4 mg.   Filter.
    Riboflavin .... 4 mg.
    Pyridoxine HCl .... 4 mg.
    Folic acid .... 1.6 mg.
    Biotin .... 0.08 mg.
    m-Inositol·2H₂O .... 4 mg.
    Nicotinamide .... 4 mg.
    Vitamin B₁₂ .... 0.8 mg.

5. L-Cystine .... 150 mg.   Water, 1,000 ml.
    Glycine .... 500 mg.   NaOH, to *p*H 7.4
    L-Phenylalanine .... 500 mg.   Filter.
    L-Glutamic acid .... 1,500 mg.
    L-Aspartic acid .... 600 mg.
    L-Tyrosine .... 400 mg.
    L-Lysine·HCl .... 2,400 mg.
    L-Methionine .... 500 mg.
    L-Threonine .... 750 mg.
    L-Valine .... 650 mg.
    L-Isoleucine .... 250 mg.
    L-Leucine .... 500 mg.
    L-Tryptophan .... 400 mg.
    L-Arginine·HCl .... 750 mg.
    L-Histidine·HCl .... 1,500 mg.

Nutrient is made up by combining 12.5 ml. water, 25 ml. 1, 25 ml. 2, 25 ml. 3, 2.5 ml. 4, and 10 ml. 5, to make 100 ml.

This nutrient, without supplement, has been found to be adequate for continuous rapid growth of a number of strains of mouse cells. It is less effective for human materials but will support growth of HeLa cells if supplemented with 1 per cent serum; we have used rabbit serum.

Although many other formulas are in uses these two will serve as working examples.

NUTRIENTS FOR ANIMAL ORGANS. One other type of formula for mammalian tissues should be mentioned. For short-term cultures of organs, where differentiation rather than rapid growth is the objective, much simpler nutrients will serve and may even be necessary. Et. Wolff and his collaborators (1953), especially Emilienne Wolff, have developed a series of these. Their basic substratum consists of a dextrose-Tyrode solution coagulated with 0.5 per cent agar, to which either serum and embryo extract or synthetic replacements therefor are added. A simple solution which provides the basic requirements for short-term survival, growth, and differentiation of, for example, the fowl syrinx is prepared as follows. There are four stocks.

1.	Agar	30 g.	Autoclave or filter.
	NaCl	40 g.	
	KCl	1.5 g.	
	$CaCl_2$	1.0 g.	
	$MgSO_4 \cdot 7H_2O$	0.2 g.	
	$MgCl_2 \cdot 6H_2O$	0.8 g.	
	Water	1,000 ml.	

2.	$NaHCO_3$	2.7 g.	This must be filtered.
	$NaH_2PO_4 \cdot H_2O$	0.1 g.	
	Na_2HPO_4	0.45 g.	
	KH_2PO_4	0.1 g.	
	Water	1,000 ml.	

3.	Glucose	5 g.	Filter or autoclave.
	Water	1,000 ml.	

4.	L(+) Arginine (base)	0.314 g.	Filter.
	DL-Methionine	0.114 g.	
	DL-Histidine HCl	0.135 g.	
	L(+) Lysine 2HCl	0.664 g.	
	L(−) Cysteine HCl	0.132 g.	
	Water	1,000 ml.	

Solutions 1, 3, and 4 can be autoclaved, but solution 2 should be filtered, and we prefer to filter all four. They can be kept for months in the refrigerator. In preparing final nutrients, solution 1 is brought to liquefaction on a water bath. Then equal quantities of 1, 2, 3, 4, and water are combined aseptically in the culture dish, usually a watch glass; mixed thoroughly; and allowed to cool. Penicillin may be added in the water portion if desired. This is Wolff's "minimum nutrient 46" (1957b). More complete and effective nutrients are prepared by adding to this minimum a group of either vitamins or additional amino acids in place of the water fraction designated above. These are prepared as follows:

5.	L(+) Glutamic acid	0.620 g.
	Glutathione	0.022 g.
	DL-Aspartic acid	0.260 g.
	Ornithin 2HCl	0.220 g.
	DL-Phenylalanine	0.308 g.
	L(−) Asparagine	0.220 g.
	DL-Serine	0.550 g.
	Glycine	0.110 g.
	L(−) Tryptophan	0.230 g.
	Water	1,000 ml.

6.	CaPantothenate	0.040 mg.
	Riboflavin	0.400 mg.
	Folic acid	0.400 mg.
	m-Inositol	0.400 mg.

Para-aminobenzoic acid .... 0.400 mg.
Thiamine .... 0.400 mg.
Ascorbic acid .... 4.000 mg.
  Water .... 1,000 ml.

Solution 6 will usually be made up to 100 times this strength and diluted 1 : 100 before use. Solutions 5 and 6 must be filtered; both are *probably* stabile in the refrigerator.

Wolff's nutrients have been used successfully over periods of a month in studies on growth and differentiation of bones, gonads, and other organs, especially the syrinx of chickens and ducks.

One point should be noted. The solutions of Hanks, White, Wolff, and Fell all contain much less NaHCO₃ than do those of Parker, Earle, and Waymouth. Solutions with high bicarbonate levels will, if exposed to the air, rapidly lose CO₂ and become alkaline. They can be maintained at a pH suitable for the maintenance of cells only if they are kept either in closed vessels (Carrel flasks, roller tubes) or in CO₂ incubators

(Puck's method). By reducing the bicarbonate level, it becomes possible to maintain *p*H in open vessels. Although the organ cultures of Wolff and Gaillard are generally maintained in closed watch glasses, Fell's method requires their exposure in open watch glasses protected only by enclosure in a Petri dish. This would be impossible if nutrients of high bicarbonate content were used. This matter should be given proper attention in planning experiments.

Tissues of lower vertebrates, especially of fish, have been successfully grown in nutrients designed for mammalian cells (Wolf *et al.*, 1960).

NUTRIENTS FOR INVERTEBRATE CELLS. Grace's nutrient (1962) for the cultivation of insect tissues is prepared from seven stocks.

A₁. MgSO₄·7H₂O .... 2,780 mg.   Dissolve in H₂O to make 100 ml.
    MgCl₂·6H₂O .... 2,280 mg.
    KCl .... 2,240 mg.
    NaH₂PO₄·2H₂O ..... 1,140 mg.
    NaHCO₃ .... 350 mg.

A₂. CaCl₂ .... 1,000 mg.   Dissolve in 100 ml. H₂O.

B. L-Arginine .... 700 mg.   Dissolve in H₂O to make 100 ml.
    L-Aspartic acid ..... 350 mg.
    L-Asparagine .... 350 mg.
    L-Alanine .... 225 mg.
    β-Alanine .... 200 mg.
    L-Cystine HCl ...... 25 mg.
    L-Glutamic acid .... 600 mg.
    L-Glutamine .... 600 mg.
    L-Glycine .... 650 mg.
    L-Histidine .... 2,500 mg.
    L-Isoleucine .... 50 mg.
    L-Leucine .... 75 mg.

L-Lycine HCl ...... 625 mg.
L-Methionine .... 50 mg.
L-Proline .... 350 mg.
L-Phenylalanine ..... 150 mg.
DL-Serine .... 1,100 mg.
L-Tryptophan ...... 100 mg.
L-Threonine .... 175 mg.
L-Valine .... 100 mg.
L-Tyrosine (dissolve
   in N/1 HCl) ..... 50 mg.

C. Sucrose .... 26.68 g.   Dissolve in H_2O to make 100 ml.
  Fructose .... 0.40 g.
  Glucose .... 0.70 g.

D. Malic acid .... 670 mg.   Dissolve in 100 ml. H_2O. Neutralize
  α-Ketoglutaric acid .. 370 mg.   with KOH.
  Succinic acid .... 60 mg.
  Fumaric acid .... 55 mg.

E. Penicillin G, sodium   Dissolve in 100 ml. H_2O.
   salt .... 30 mg.
  Streptomycin sulfate.. 100 mg.

F_1. Folic acid .... 20 mg.   Dissolve in 100 ml. H_2O. Dilute
  Biotin .... 10 mg.   1 : 1,000 to make stock F_1.

F_2. Thiamine HCl ...... 20 mg.   Dissolve in 100 ml. H_2O. Dilute
  Riboflavin .... 20 mg.   1 : 1,000 to make stock F_2.
  CaPantothenate ..... 20 mg.
  Pyridoxin HCl ..... 20 mg.
  Para-aminobenzoic
   acid .... 20 mg.
  Niacin .... 20 mg.
  i-Inositol .... 20 mg.
  Choline chloride .... 200 mg.

To prepare 100 ml. of nutrient, combine 10 ml. of each of these stocks. Adjust the *p*H to 6.5 with KOH; then make up to 100 ml. and sterilize by filtration. One milliliter of heat-inactivated pupal blood (60° C. for five minutes) is added to each 19 ml. of the above basic nutrient at the time cultures are prepared. The optimum temperatures for insect cells appear to be 27–30° C.

Chapter 5

THE CULTURES

In What Ways Are Cells Commonly Grown?

Cultures of plant, animal, and human cells and tissues will all fall into five main types: (1) hanging drops, (2) flask and bottle cultures, (3) test-tube cultures, (4) watch-glass cultures, and (5) Petri-dish cultures (Fig. 28).

Hanging-Drop Cultures

These are the simplest in point of equipment required. If suitably prepared, they also permit the greatest precision of optical study by use of oil-immersion, phase-contrast, or interference objectives. But they have the serious drawbacks of very poor control of nutrient variables and extreme tedium in the long-term maintenance of cultures, owing to the need for very frequent subculturing. Hanging-drop cultures are made on glass, mica, or plastic covers suspended over hollow-ground slides, pierced slides, van Tiegham cells, or small watch glasses.

In the simplest procedure a series of 22- $\times$ 22-mm. No. 1 cover glasses, scrupulously clean and sterile, are laid out on a sheet of black glass or plastic on the culture table (Fig. 29[A]). A single drop of nutrient, either synthetic or containing plasma, is placed at the center of each glass and spread over an area not to exceed one-half the diameter of the cavity of the slide. Bits of tissue (animal tissues, root tips, cambiums, sporelings, mammalian eggs, limb primordia, etc.) are then placed in the nutrient drops. If embryo extract is to be added, it is added at this time and the whole is quickly mixed with the end of the pipette, with a glass rod, or with a platinum spatula. Two drops of Vaseline are applied with a glass rod, brush, or piece of stick, at the two sides of the cavities of an equal number of slides. A slide is then inverted over each cover glass and pressed down firmly. The cover glasses will be attached to the slides, which are then carefully lifted and placed on a suitable rack or tray (Fig. 29 [D], [E]) to wait while other cultures are being prepared.

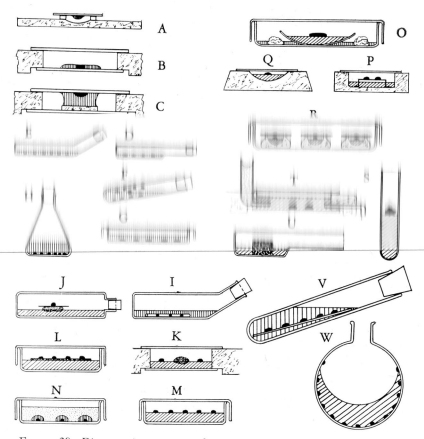

FIGURE 28. Diagramatic summary of most of the types of cultures commonly encountered (White, 1959): (A) Hanging drop over depression slide (Harrison). (B) "Sitting drop" (Gey). (C) Continuous drop suitable for phase contrast and interference microscopy (Gautheret). (D) Porter flask. (E) Carrel flask. (F) Roller tube (Gey). (G) Petri dish with liquid nutrient (Puck). (H) Erlenmeyer flask with liquid nutrient (deBruyn). (I) Carrel flask with cells in capillary tube for isolation of clones (Sanford). (J) Plant-callus culture on agar with filter paper overlay and microculture on the paper, for isolation of clones (Muir). (K) Plant-callus culture on agar with microcultures surrounding the primary mass (Torrey). (L) Animal cells plated on agar onto a monolayer which has been inactivated by radiation, used in isolating clones (Puck). (M) Cells plated onto dilute agar to reduce diffusion (Puck). (N) Cells grown in microdrops under mineral oil (Dulbecco; Marshal and Mazurier; Jones). (O) Chemical watch glass (Fell). (P) Watch glass with metal-mesh support and liquid nutrient (Shaffer). (Q) Embryological watch glass (Gaillard). (R) Syracuse micro-watch glasses (White). (S) Vertical test-tube culture on agar (Gautheret). (T) Perfusion chamber (Rose). (U) Leighton tube with sponge insert. (V) Roller tube with flying cover glass (Pomerat). (W) Agitated flask (Earle).

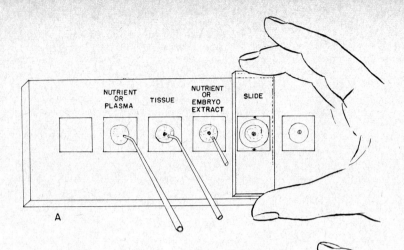

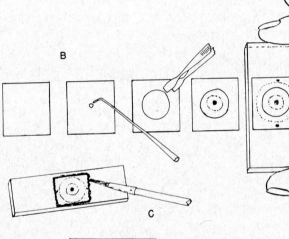

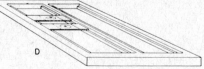

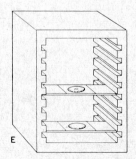

FIGURE 29. (*Explanation on opposite page.*)

During this time the culture will become firmly attached to the glass, and, in the case of plasma cultures, the plasma will coagulate. The slides can then be inverted by a quick centrifugal motion which does not disturb the drop of nutrient, and the covers are sealed with a hot paraffin-Vaseline mixture (3 : 1) applied with a brush (Fig. 29[C]). The slides are then ready for observation or for the incubator.

When cultures are to be observed for not more than a day or two, this procedure provides satisfactory results. It is, however, difficult to remove such a cover slip from the slide without cracking the cover, disturbing the drop, or otherwise deranging the culture. If the nutrient is to be renewed, or subcultures or microchemical tests are to be made, the double-cover-slip method of Maximov (1925) is superior (Fig. 29[B]). Here large cover slips, usually 30- × 35-mm., are laid out; a drop of sterile distilled water or balanced salt solution is applied to each; and a 20-mm.-round or a 16-mm.-square cover glass is placed on this drop. The quantity of fluid is gauged to be just sufficient to hold the second cover to the first firmly, by capillarity. The culture is then placed on the smaller slip. The rest of the procedure is the same as before. In transferring or otherwise manipulating these cultures, the small slip may be floated free merely by adding an excess of sterile water or saline at the side.

Both of these methods, depending as they do on hollow-ground slides, have the optical disadvantage imposed by the curvature of the cavity. This may be obviated by the use of flat slides bearing metal or glass rings, or pierced glass, metal, or plastic slides. One of the most satisfactory is a pierced slide with both top and bottom routed out around the opening to take a square cover glass at a level slightly below that of the slide (White, 1943a, Fig. 27). A No. 2 cover slip is attached with Vaseline to the lower side of the slide, forming an optically flat bottom to the closed chamber. The culture is set up exactly as described for use

Figure 29. Preparing hanging-drop cultures of animal tissues: (A) Single-cover-slip method. Six clean 22- × 22-mm. cover slips are laid on a block of glass or plastic. A drop of nutrient or plasma is placed on each glass and is spread to a uniform circle about 7–10 mm. in diameter. A bit of tissue is then placed in each drop. If plasma has been used, a drop of embryo extract is added and stirred in thoroughly but without spreading the drop further. Two drops of Vaseline are placed at opposite margins of the cavities of six depression slides and the slides are inverted over the cultures, pressing down firmly; the Vaseline will attach slide and cover. The slides are then inverted and the covers sealed with paraffin-Vaseline mixture (C). They are then transferred to a tray (D) or storage rack (E), either with the cover down so as to permit the cells to settle onto the glass, an important stage for liquid cultures, or with the cover up, which gives a more satisfactory result with plasma cultures. (B) Maximov double-cover-slip method. This differs from the simple hanging drop only in that the culture is prepared on a small detachable cover slip (usually a 20-mm.-round one) which is attached by means of the capillary action of a small drop of water to a larger, rectangular glass which, in turn, rests on the slide. For this, 35- × 40-mm. covers are usually employed.

on a hollow-ground slide. By removing the bottom cover glass, one can open the cavity without disturbing the slip carrying the culture, so that nutrient can be changed or subcultures made. For especially precise optical studies, with phase-contrast or interference optics, the pierced slide can be made thin enough so that the culture drop will make contact with both top and bottom glass, thereby providing a continuous optical medium at the same time that the margins of the drop, in contact with the air, provide the necessary aeration. This is what Gey terms a "sitting drop" culture. Such a drop must be handled carefully to prevent the drop's slipping sideways and coming in contact with the edge of the cavity. This may be prevented by placing a small bit of plastic or glass, such as a small cover glass, on top of the lower cover slip, to which it is attached by capillarity, as one does with a Maximov preparation; the culture drop will then conform to the dimensions of this "table" and will not slip beyond the limits so provided (Fig. 28[C]).

In place of pierced or hollow-ground slides, Lewis has used low metal rings dipped in paraffin and applied to plane slides; or one can purchase the more expensive "van Tiegham rings" sold for making cultures of fungi.

Hanging drops such as have been described are regularly employed for short-term studies of animal cells of all sorts. They also served for many of the long-term cultures of Carrel, Fischer, and their followers, particularly before the development of the Carrel flask. Plant materials such as embryos, root and stem tips (White, 1932a, 1933a), intercalary meristems, and algal sporelings have also been grown by this method. Its chief drawbacks are its relative tediousness where the nutrient must be changed, and the rapid and uncontrollable changes in total concentration, pH, oxygen tension, ionic levels, and the like, to which a small drop of fluid is inevitably subject when exposed with a large surface area in contact with both a glass surface and even a saturated atmosphere.

TRANSFERRING SLIDE CULTURES. It is difficult to subculture hanging-drop preparations of animal cells in liquid nutrients. With plasma clots, however, subcultures can be made; in fact, this method served Carrel and Ebeling for their 30-year cultivation of chick fibroblasts. The cover slip carrying a well-grown plasma-clot culture (usually about ten days old) is placed clot up on a raised block, and the fluid supernatant, if any, is withdrawn. The thin edges are trimmed off and discarded. For this, Parker (1961) recommends cataract knives, which are expensive. Bits of razor blade held firmly in a hemostat, or Bard-Parker knives, can be used. The important thing is not to tear or crush the culture, hence the knife must be very sharp. With a cataract knife the cut should be made with the knife laid across the culture, with the handle low and the blade tilted at a slight angle (about 10°) from the perpendicular. A quick but very slight forward-backward motion will cut without tearing, after which the knife should be lifted, not drawn, away. The same applies to razor blades in hemostats. With Bard-Parker knives a small round-edged blade should be used and the blade rocked across the culture. Any of these methods will make a clean cut. The edges are trimmed by four such cuts, leaving a square of dense growth with the original explant in the center (Fig. 30).

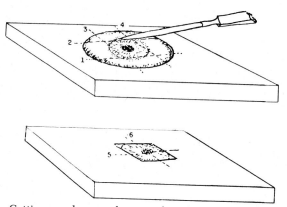

FIGURE 30. Cutting up plasma cultures such as hanging drops in preparing four pieces for subculturing. The numbers designate the sequence of cuts required to trim and separate four subcultures from an old culture (see text).

This square may then be divided into two or four pieces, depending on how well it has grown. It should not be divided into more than four pieces, since, in subculturing, smaller bits will seldom grow satisfactorily. These bits should be picked up on the knife blade, transferred to a new cover slip, laid out flat without rolled edges, and then covered with fresh plasma. All these operations must be carried out in such a way that the tissue will not dry out, and with as little crushing as possible.

Flask and Bottle Cultures

Tissues are maintained in flasks either in liquid media or on solid or semisolid substrata. For purposes of discussion, cultures in which the cells are attached to the glass, even though submerged in liquid, will be considered to fall into the latter category, the glass being equated with a solid substratum. Excised roots are grown floating on a liquid nutrient (White, 1934a, 1943a). One hundred twenty-five–milliliter Erlenmeyer flasks are usually employed, with 50 ml. of nutrient. A bit of root about 10–15 mm. long is inoculated into the flask with a bacteriological loop. It will float on the surface of the liquid and grow. It can be cut into pieces after an acceptable period, usually a week, and the desired subcultures can be made by simple transfer. For cutting, Heyman nose-and-throat scissors are excellent. Such root cultures have been maintained for more than 30 years. Roots have also been grown in Petri dishes (Bonner and Addicott, 1937), which are difficult to handle without slopping, and in 25- × 100-mm. test tubes in which no more than 20 ml. of nutrient can be supplied.

DeBruyn (1955) has used Erlenmeyer flasks for the routine maintenance of human cells, particularly those strains which grow well directly on the glass, in liquid nutrient. A 125-ml. flask is charged with 10 ml. of nutrient, a suitable suspension of cells from a growing culture is introduced and distributed, and the cells are allowed to settle. This gives excellent results, but these cultures can be studied only on an inverted microscope (Fig. 31), a disadvantage for many laboratories.

Animal viruses have been grown in Erlenmeyer flasks or in bottles by a method originated by Maitland and Maitland (1928), perfected by Li and Rivers (1930), and recently revived in various forms for the cultivation of poliomyelitis and other viruses (Enders, 1952; Enders *et al.,* 1949). A "nutrient" is prepared by cutting a suitable host tissue such as rabbit testicle or monkey kidney into small bits and suspending them in a salt-dextrose solution such as a Hanks solution. Virus is then supplied by transfer of a small amount of fluid from a previous culture. The tissue does not "grow" or increase in amount but gradually breaks down. It serves for some days, however, as a living substratum on which the virus can multiply, and from which transfers can be made to fresh containers at weekly intervals (Feller, Enders, and Weller, 1940). Interest here rests not in the tissue but in the virus, and this method, carried out in test tubes, flasks, or bottles, has been very useful. A somewhat comparable method has been used by Osgood (Osgood and Brooke, 1955) and others for relatively short-term cultures of blood cells and bone marrow.

If, however, the primary interest lies in long-term cultivation and observation of living cells, more specialized methods must be used. Carrel flasks, although expensive and somewhat clumsy, are still the best containers for this purpose, although Earle's "T" flasks, the recently introduced plastic flasks, and a variety of small prescription bottles are replacing them to some extent. Cultures in flasks can be made directly on the glass without coating of any kind, on a plasma clot, or an agar gel, or on or under cellophane. Since agar liquefies at about 40° C., only a few degrees above the usual incubator temperature for animal cells, it is generally not suitable for flask cultures except where they are to be studied on an inverted microscope. In preparing primary cultures on glass, the tissue fragments or dissociated cells should be placed in the flask with just enough fluid to spread them and keep them from drying

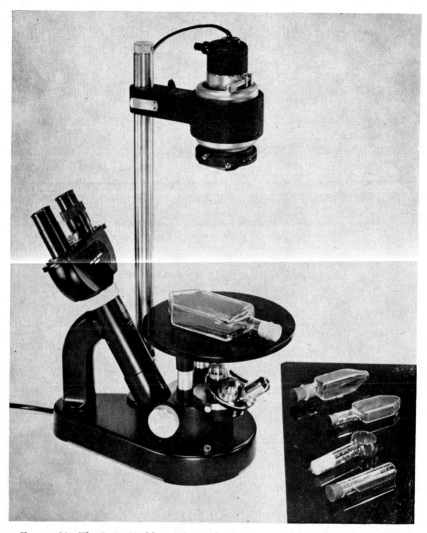

FIGURE 31. The Leitz-Waldman inverted microscope used by deBruyn and others. This has the advantage of having much greater maneuverability than do most of the other, heavier models of inverted microscopes. (E. Leitz & Co.)

out; the fluid transferred with the inoculum will usually suffice. They are allowed to stand for about ½ hour to permit the cells to attach themselves to the glass; culture fluid is then added carefully so as not to wash the implanted tissue loose. The flasks can then be placed in the incubator, and within 48 hours the cells will be firmly attached.

The preparation of plasma cultures in Carrel flasks is very well discussed by Parker (1961), and the reader is referred to his book. Briefly, about 0.5 ml. of chick plasma and 0.5 ml. of embryo extract are pipetted into the flask (a 1-ml. hypodermic is better than a pipette) and spread over the entire bottom. From one to three pieces of tissue are then quickly inserted and oriented as desired. The plasma will clot within a few minutes, and an additional 1 ml. of fluid nutrient can be added on top of the clot. In washing cultures, it is this last 1 ml. which is removed and replaced. In making subcultures, the entire clot is freed from the glass, using a platinum spatula. The clot is rolled and slid out onto a sterile glass plate; the culture is cut out and divided into two or four pieces, as was described for slide cultures (Fig. 30); and these pieces are transferred to fresh clots as inocula.

The plasma method has, it seems to the author, only one advantage. Cultures grow radially outward from the implant at a rate which is relatively uniform on all sides and in which the margin of the culture is fairly clearly defined. This permits one to estimate growth rates with considerable precision by means of planimetric measurements of total area (Ebeling, 1921). This cannot be done with the scattered and loosely distributed growth which occurs directly on glass.

Most established strains and many primary explants will grow directly on glass if the flasks have been adequately cleaned. Some which are still refractory can nevertheless be established without plasma by inoculation under cellophane by the methods developed by Evans and Earle (1947). Disks of a special perforated cellophane (obtainable from Microbiological Associates) are cut to a diameter slightly larger than the bottom of the flask. The cellophane must be thoroughly cleaned before use, since, as sold, it is coated with a waxy plasticizer. Parker (1961) recommends reflux extraction in hot acetone in a Soxhlet extractor. We have found this helpful but not sufficient. In practice, we reflux overnight in acetone. The extractor is then opened, and the cellophane disks (100–200 at a time) are removed and passed through two changes, ten minutes each, of ether, absolute alcohol, and, finally, distilled water. They are then inserted into the flasks, 1 ml. of distilled water per flask is added, and the flasks are capped with Norton caps and autoclaved. The water is then discarded (p. 103), and the caps are replaced with rubber stoppers. In setting up cultures under cellophane, the nutrient is pipetted into the flasks before inoculation. The tissue to be used is washed in Gey, Earle, or Hanks salt-dextrose solution by transferring two or more times to fresh dishes of solution.

In setting up such cultures, Earle recommends the use of rather large inocula, 2×5 mm. We prefer to cut the tissue quite fine, preferably not more than 0.1 mm. in diameter. The resulting brei is taken up in a straight pipette and inoculated under the cellophane. If larger pieces are used, they should be transferred with a platinum spatula. After inoculation, the cellophane is pushed down with the pipette or spatula to spread the inoculum, after which the flasks, stoppered with No. 00 stoppers, are ready for the incubator. Growth occurs largely between the cellophane and the glass, although some cells will pass through the perforations and grow on top. In a classic serum-embryo-extract nutrient, growth from a primary inoculum of embryonic tissue should cover the bottom of the flask in about three to four weeks.

In making subcultures from such flasks, a curved pipette is used. The cellophane is lifted, and both glass and cellophane are scraped thoroughly with the end of the pipette to loosen the cells. A uniform suspension can be obtained by drawing the fluid into the pipette and ejecting it several times. Earle obtains a still more uniform suspension by passing it through a series of stainless-steel wire screens of progressively finer mesh (Evans et al., 1951), but this is unnecessary for most purposes. When thoroughly mixed, the entire suspension is taken up and distributed in approximately equal parts to a series of fresh flasks. These may be two, three, up to ten in number, depending on the density of the original colony. Care must be taken not to use too small an inoculum in subculturing, for there is a minimum density characteristic of each cell strain and of each nutrient, below which cultures do not re-establish themselves satisfactorily.

Many strains of cells require neither plasma nor cellophane, for initiating cultures or for maintaining them, but will grow well from the start directly on glass. These can all be treated in much the same way. The "L"-strain of mouse fibroblasts is a good example. A flask containing a ten-day-old culture of "L" cells is opened and the floor scraped thoroughly. We prefer a platinum spatula for this purpose. A "rubber policeman" has also been used. The contents are then drawn up into a 1-ml. pipette (about 0.9 ml. can be drawn off), ejected repeatedly to mix, and then distributed in 0.1-ml. aliquots to nine new flasks, each previously charged with 1 ml. of nutrient. A still more complete separation of the cells can be obtained by treating the culture with trypsin or with Versene. Although first introduced more than 40 years ago by Rous and Jones (1916), this method became practicable only as a result of the elaborations of Moscona (1952) and of Melnick et al. (1955). The nutrient is removed from a series of flasks as if for renewal. A corresponding amount of 0.25 per cent trypsin (250 mg. Difco 1/250 trypsin in 100 ml. balanced salt solution) or of Versene (20 mg. Na-ethylene-diamine-tetra-acetate in 100 ml. of a buffered salt solution made up without calcium and magnesium ions) is then added to each flask. After incubation for ten minutes, the cells will separate and the resulting suspension can be pipetted off and either used directly as inoculum or else diluted to stop digestion, using a nutrient free of trypsin or Versene, after which it is centrifuged for five minutes, washed, and resuspended in nutrient. Some experiment may be necessary to establish the optimum time of exposure and the concentration suitable for particular strains. The same method is important in the preparation of many primary cultures, since it gives a uniform inoculum of discrete cells. Trypsinization is also necessary if the growth of cultures is to be measured with a high degree of accuracy.

A number of alternative methods have been developed for routine maintenance of cells in quantity. For the production of viruses and vaccines, cells are often grown in prescription bottles. The square bottles sold for milk-dilution studies are optically somewhat better and have been used for routine cultures of both plant and animals cells. Greater masses of cells can be grown if, instead of being spread over a limited surface on the walls of a vessel, they are suspended in a fluid nutrient. This requires that the nutrient be agitated quite violently in some way (Owens *et al.*, 1954; Kuchler and Merchant, 1956). One method is by placing ordinary culture flasks or bottles on a shaking mechanism. This method has been used by Earle *et al.* (1954) for the production of animal cells for chemical studies (Fig. 28[W]), and by Hildebrandt and Riker (1953) for similar studies of plant cells. Steward and Caplin (1954) have used a more complicated tumbling mechanism which, however, provides results quite similar to those obtained on a simple shaker. Various methods of stirring the nutrient without shaking the flask have been tried. One is by bubbling air through the nutrient (Melchers and Engelmann, 1955). Probably the best for animal cells is the "spinner flask" (Fig. 23) developed by McLimans *et al.* (1957a, 1957b), which makes use of a suspended rotor turned by an external magnetic field. Such a flask provides a continuous source of cells, the nutrient being replenished and samples drawn off at will through lateral tubulations. An ordinary balloon flask provided with a "magnetic flea" makes a reasonably satisfactory substitute for the more complicated and expensive spinner flask. A single flask, so long as it does not become contaminated, can provide a rapidly growing supply of cells indefinitely. This idea has been enlarged and elaborated in the so-called chemostat originally designed by Novick and Szilard (1950) for the production of quantities of bacteria but now sometimes used for both plant (Nickell and Tulecke, 1960) and animal (Graff and McCarty, 1957; Ziegler *et al.*, 1958) cells. In all of these methods, samples can be drawn off for microscopic examination at any time; growth cannot, however, be studied *in situ* or continuously; for this, the best means are still the hanging drop or the Carrel flask.

Tube Cultures

Pyrex test tubes 25 × 150 mm. and charged with 15 ml. of agar nutrient have been largely used for plant-callus cultures. These are either stored vertically (Fig. 24[1]) (Gautheret, 1942b, 1959) or sloped (Fig.

24[2]) (White, 1943a). They permit greater numbers to be maintained in a small space than with flask cultures, and they are easier to manipulate. Unlike animal cultures, these tubes not only do not need to be hermetically sealed, but they should not be so sealed for long periods. They have usually been closed with cotton plugs (Fig. 25[1]), which, especially with sloped tubes in which a large surface of nutrient is exposed, permit rather rapid desiccation of the agar unless cultures are maintained in a room with controlled high humidity. To obviate this, Gautheret caps the tubes with pieces of tin foil over cotton plugs (Fig. 25[3]) (1942a, 1959). We have used aluminum foil without plugs with excellent success (Fig. 25[2]). Our best results have been with 2- $\times$ 2-inch squares of foil. The cotton plug with which the tube has been autoclaved is discarded; the tube mouth is flamed lightly; and the culture is inoculated. A square of aluminum is then placed over the mouth and bent down tightly around the tube. The aluminum can then be flamed more thoroughly on the outside. Enough air will circulate under the cap to provide adequate respiration. Morel and Wetmore (unpublished) have used vinyl plastic sealed on with tape (Fig. 25[4]). This must be sterilized before application. We have tried "Pliofilm" (a paraffin-rubber film) but without complete satisfaction. "Norton caps" of stainless steel provide an excellent but expensive substitute (Fig. 25[5]). The recently introduced plastic caps may prove useful (Fig. 25[6]).

Cultures of plant callus, or of tumors, are usually placed on top of an agar substratum as a means of exposing them to the air (Fig. 24[1][2]) (White, 1939a, 1939b, 1953). While agar is non-nutritive, it is not physicochemically inert, introducing as it does adsorptive factors and other elements which cannot easily be estimated. To obviate this objectionable feature, Heller and Gautheret (1947) have tried replacing the agar with glass wool or glass tape, both of which are unsatisfactory because of the extremely large glass surface exposed to the solvent action of the nutrient, which introduces factors at least as objectionable as the agar. A better substitute, also devised by Heller (1949, 1953), is an inverted cup made by folding a disk of ash-free filter paper over a mandrel in the form of a glass tube of slightly smaller diameter than that of the culture tube. Once formed, this cup can be slipped into the culture tube in the inverted position and pushed down far enough so that it dips into, and remains saturated with, the liquid nutrient. The culture can then be placed on the cup, which serves as a support (Fig. 24[3]). This is effective only when the tube is kept in a vertical position. For sloped tubes we have folded 5-cm. squares of filter paper into narrow strips a little wider than the diameter of the culture tube. With the tip of such a strip immersed in the nutrient and the culture placed on the upper part, this has proved very satisfactory (Fig. 24[4]). The various shakers provide effec-

tive but expensive and in some ways awkward substitutes for these procedures.

These plant cultures have two important differences from animal cultures. Plant cultures have their optimum pH at about 5.4, which is essentially the point at which an unbuffered aqueous solution is in equilibrium
with the CO_2 of the air. They therefore need not be sealed and are in
fact better not sealed. The optimum pH for animal cells, on the other
hand, is between 7.2 and 7.6. This can only be maintained by use of
powerful buffers, of which those most commonly used contain sodium
bicarbonate. But, if such a solution is left unsealed, it rapidly loses CO_2
and becomes alkaline, which is as injurious to animal cells as it is to plant
tissues. Animal-cell cultures maintained in poorly buffered nutrients or in
nutrients buffered with bicarbonate must therefore be sealed or else
maintained in special CO_2 incubators. Further, while no method has yet
been devised for persuading plant cultures to limit their growth to the
immediate surface of a solid or semisolid substratum, which would be a
great advantage for microscopic observation, such a habit is a fairly
universal feature of animal-cell growth. In an undisturbed flask, animal
cells other than definite discrete organ explants grow as monolayers on
the bottom of the flask. In order to obtain adequate oxygenation, the
covering layer must be very thin—never more than 2 mm. thick. These
two facts preclude the use of simple, unsealed, fixed tubes for any animal-
cell cultures except the virus cultures mentioned above. Yet tubes have
certain advantages over all the various types of flasks so far devised,
especially as regards cost, ease of cleaning and of handling, and space
requirements. This has led to the introduction of other methods. An
especially useful one is the roller-tube method, suggested by a number of
workers, particularly Carrel (1913c) and Loewenstadt (1925), but first
made practical by Gey (1933) and Lewis (1935).

The roller-tube method, in its simplest form, makes use of a standard
16- $\times$ 150-mm. test tube. Cultures may be placed directly on the glass,
usually four or five per tube, allowing the tubes to stand as described for
Carrel flasks to permit the cells to become fixed to the glass before introducing the nutrient; or the tube may be lined with a thin plasma clot and
the cultures implanted thereon. After the cultures are properly in place,
each tube is charged with either 1 or 2 ml. of nutrient (the choice is a
matter of personal preference; the author uses 1 ml.) and closed with a
No. 0 stopper. The tubes are then placed in a drum (Fig. 32) which
is so sloped as to permit the liquid to cover the lower side of the
tube to about half its length and which is slowly rotated. By this means
the cultures are immersed in nutrient for about one minute out of every
ten and exposed to the air of the tube for the remaining nine minutes.
This provides excellent circulation of nutrient, aeration, and removal of

waste products. Nutrient can be removed and replaced at intervals. Cells grow very well in such tubes. The tubes cost about a thirtieth as much as do Carrel flasks; they are easy to handle and to clean; and they require little space. They will permit routine examination with a 16-mm. objective but not with higher powers unless special thin tubes are selected

FIGURE 32. Roller-tube drum for animal or plant cultures. This drum holds 240, 16- × 150-mm. tubes, rotating them at a rate of about once in ten minutes so that the nutrient is constantly circulated.

or special objectives with a long working distance (2 mm. minimum) are employed. The only costly features is the rotor. Serviceable ones are on the market, but all those we have seen have the holes arranged in circular patterns which make any sort of mapping of the drum almost impossible. A rectangular or triangular pattern, with the holes in rows, is much more efficient. A very good one, capable of carrying 200 tubes, can be built for about $150. Much cheaper and simpler ones can be built but will be less sturdy and serviceable.

These tube cultures have had, in common with flasks, one serious disadvantage as compared to hanging drops, namely, that cultures can neither be stained *in situ* for permanent preservation without sacrificing the entire container nor can they be removed for remounting without injury. Brues's pierced flask (Shaw, Kingsland, and Brues, 1940) was an attempt to obviate this disadvantage. A partial solution has been devised by introducing narrow strips of cover glass ("flying cover slips") into the flask or tube (Pomerat, 1951). These are particularly effective in Leighton tubes (Figs. 22[9], 24[6], 24[7]). Cultures are permitted to grow on these strips on a plasma clot (see Chapter 6, Fig. 35). The entire cover slip can then be removed for permanent preservation. Rose *et al.* (1958)

have improved on this method by using water-permeable "Visking" dialysis membrane, without plasma, to attach the cultures to the cover slips. Using special culture chambers, the tissue is laid on the cover glass and a strip of membrane is superimposed and held against the cover by pressure from a rubber gasket over which a second cover glass is clamped by means of a screw clamp. Nutrient is hypodermically introduced into the chamber formed by the two covers. Many tissues grow more satisfactorily and with more "normal" morphology under such membranes. This has been especially true of muscle and nerve. The cultures can be examined under the highest magnifications, and the cover glasses can be introduced into fixatives or stains at will.

Roller tubes can be used for plant as well as animal cultures with some advantage, since they offer another means of eliminating the objectionable adsorptive characteristics of agar (White, 1953).

Watch Glasses

Until recently, most of the cell-culture work the world over was carried out by some one of the three methods described above. There are, however, other methods. One, the watch-glass method, variously developed by Fell, Gaillard, Martinovitch, Wolff, and others, has been of real importance, especially for the study of morphogenesis in massive cultures and for the cultivation of organs and organ parts. Fell uses a standard chemical watch glass about 5 cm. in diameter, set in a Petri dish provided with a ring of moistened cotton which serves both to support the watch glass and to maintain the required humidity (Fig. 26[1]) (Fell and Robison, 1929). A plasma clot is prepared in the hollow of the watch glass, and the organ to be investigated (limb primordium, patella, frontal bone, eye) is placed on the surface of the clot. The Petri dish is closed for incubation but may be opened for observation or manipulation of the culture. This is of course far more accessible than any flask or tube. Gaillard (1948, 1953, 1955) and Martinovitch (1953) have substituted standard deep-molded embryological watch glasses (square "saltcellar" type), each covered with its own square cover glass, for similar cultures of glands such as thyroids and ovaries (Fig. 26[5]). The small Syracuse watch glass made for the United States Department of Agriculture for the cultivation of nematodes and sold by A. H. Thomas should be superior to either in some ways. It is of such a size that seven fit nicely into a 100-mm. Petri dish. Each watch glass can be covered individually with a 25-mm.-round cover glass, which makes an individual moist chamber of each dish. These covers can be removed for manipulation yet do not interfere with general observation (Fig. 26[3]). The author's laboratory has used such watch glasses for cultures of sporelings of algae (Davidson, 1950), hydroids, amphibian eggs and embryos, fish eggs, Entomostraca, and certain types of plant tissue. The chief objections to watch-glass cultures are (1) the difficulty in sealing the container to prevent loss of CO_2 and the consequent rise in pH, which forces one to use nutrients of low bicarbonate content or to supply a sealed CO_2 incubator, and (2) the impossibility of making microscopic examinations except under the dissecting binocular at magnifications not exceeding about 100 diameters. On the other hand, they are ideal for various sorts of chemical studies.

Sponge Matrices

One other method should be mentioned. Cultures in stabile flasks, bottles, tubes, and hanging drops generally take the form of monolayers of great surface area but little volume. They place severe limits on the amount or form of tissue grown in a given space. Cultures grown in agitated fluid on the other hand tend to separate into single cells or into small "pearls" which, again, though in a different way, place severe limits on the degree of differentiation which can be attained. Neither provides conditions even remotely resembling the three-dimensional *structure* of the organism. Cultures in watch glasses permit structured growth but do not permit easy confrontation of new tissue combinations.

These objections have been partially met in the matrix cultures developed by Leighton (1951, 1954). Bits of cellulose sponge are placed on the surface of, or partly immersed in, a nutrient of the usual type in such a way that they become saturated with nutrient (Fig. 28[U]). Cells are then allowed to invade this matrix, as was the case with Arnold's bits of pith in 1887. This provides a three-dimensional scaffold with widely varied surfaces, cavities, faces exposed to the air, etc. These conditions resemble those of the interior of an organism in many respects, only falling short in that there is no circulatory system to improve the metabolic interchanges necessary for normal differentiation and function. This method even provides one advantage over intact organisms: If two different types of cell—muscle and nerve, mouse and human, or healthy and cancerous, for example—are inoculated on opposite sides of such a matrix and allowed to meet in the interior, a unique opportunity is provided for studying cell interactions of wholly new sorts. It does not, of course, permit direct day-to-day observation; the matrix must be fixed and sectioned like any other anatomical preparation. Its advantage lies in its great versatility.

Chapter 6

THE PROCEDURES

Setting Up Cultures

Having organized and equipped the laboratory, prepared the nutrients, and chosen the tissues to be used and the type of culture, we are ready to proceed to the actual setting up of cultures. Here plant and animal materials will require quite different approaches.

Animal Materials

THE CHICK EMBRYO. For the beginner the chick embryo is the classic example and will be universally available. Let us assume, therefore, that we are going to prepare parallel sets of cultures of (1) chick-embryo heart, (2) lung, (3) skin, (4) leg muscle, (5) leg bone, and (6) frontal bone, in Carrel flasks, roller tubes, watch glasses, and sponge matrices, in the classic plasma-type nutrient and in a synthetic nutrient of the Waymouth type. To do all these in a single operation would be quite impossible, yet the preliminary steps will be the same for all types of cultures. Let us, then, prepare our tissues and proceed afterward to the detailed steps. We will need

1 dozen embryonated eggs, incubated large end up for 10 days (If so incubated, without being turned, the embryo will lie under or near the air sac.)

2 half–Petri dishes, 10 cm. (These need not be sterile.)

2 beakers, 50 ml.

6 small Petri dishes, 6 cm., sterile

1 instrument sterilizer (A #18 Renwal sterilizer is excellent, or a 1-l. stainless-steel beaker with a small immersion heater will serve. In this is suspended a 100-ml. Pyrex beaker hung on a wire loop. Use distilled water for boiling; tap water may deposit calcareous material on the instruments.)

2 pairs medium-fine forceps, straight

2 pairs mosquito forceps, straight

2 pairs medium-fine forceps, curved
2 pairs mosquito forceps, curved
2 dissecting needles with right-angle knife-ground tips
1 stainless-steel hook, like a buttonhook
2 cataract knives or Bard-Parker knives, No. 7 handles, No. 10 blades
2 hypodermics, sterile, 20 ml.
1 hypodermic, sterile, 10 ml.
2 #20 or #18 needles, 2-inch, sterile
1 box 10-ml. pipettes, sterile
6 inoculating pipettes, straight and curved, sterile
2 red rubber bulbs
10 pairs Columbia watch glasses, sterile
28 small watch glasses in Petri dishes, sterile
20 cover glasses, sterile, 22-mm.-round
1 piece of steel rod, $\frac{1}{2} \times 6$ inches
1 microburner
1 dissecting shield
1 wire instrument rack
Tubes of salt-dextrose solution, plasma, embryo extract, complete classic nutrient (40 per cent serum : 20 per cent embryo extract : 40 per cent salt solution), and synthetic nutrient
Alcohol, 70 per cent

The work table is wiped clean with a damp cloth; the supplementary "T"-table is set up; and the dissecting shield is set on the table at an angle so that the "T" is at the principal operator's left, the wire instrument rack is under the shield and at the right, and the sterilizer filled with water is at the right hand of the operator. The heater is started, and the coarser forceps and "buttonhook" are placed to boil. When thoroughly sterilized, they are removed and set on the wire instrument rack. The six small sterile Petri dishes are placed under the shield, at the back. The assistant, sitting at the opposite side of the "T," places two eggs upright in 50-ml. beakers, each set in a half–Petri dish. An egg is wiped with a pledget of cotton soaked in alcohol and is cracked all around just below the top with the piece of steel rod. It is then wiped again with alcohol and passed to the principal operator, and a second egg is prepared in like fashion. The operator takes the first egg in his left hand, under the shield, and with a curved forceps held points forward plunges the tip into the cracked shell. Then, turning the egg in the left hand and "snipping" the forceps like a pair of scissors, he cuts off the top of the shell all around (Fig. 33[A]).

If the break has been high enough, the end of the egg will come off just above the air-sac membrane, leaving the membrane intact. Project-

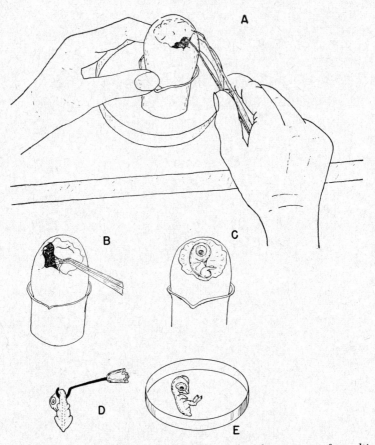

FIGURE 33. Procedures used in preparing chick-embryo tissues for cultivation (see text): (A) Opening an egg above the air sac, using curved forceps. (B) Lifting the air-sac membrane to expose the embryo. (C) The embryo, after removal of the air-sac membrane and rupture of the chorioallantoic membranes. (D) Lifting the embryo with a "buttonhook" inserted under the neck. It is placed (E) in a small Petri dish; its head is removed, and then it is laid on its back, limbs spread. The embryo being held with curved mosquito forceps, a midventral incision is made (F). With the outer layers folded back, the viscera (h, heart; p, lung; l, liver; g, gizzard)

ing bits of shell can be chipped off, down to the membrane. The forceps are returned to the boiling water, and with a second, fresh pair the membrane is lifted off, exposing the liquid interior and the embryo (Fig. 33[B], [C]). The second forceps is placed in the water, and the first, now resterilized, is returned to the rack. With a straight forceps in the left hand and the "buttonhook" in the right, the allantoic membrane is lifted enough so that the hook can be inserted under the embryo's neck, the embryo is gently lifted out (Fig. 33[D]), the adherent membranes are

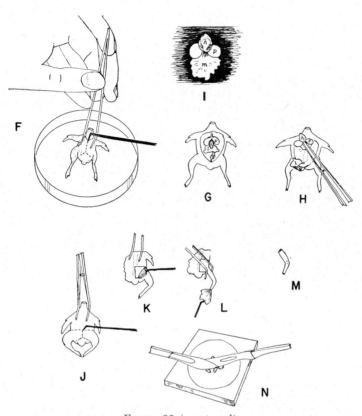

FIGURE 33 (*continued*).

are exposed (G). The digestive organs are pulled downward, and the heart and lungs are carefully separated and pushed forward (H) so that they can be transferred to a dish of nutrient (I). The mesenteries (*m*) are discarded, and the heart and lungs are placed in separate dishes. The body is then turned over; an incision is made down the back (J); the skin is pulled down over the leg (K), (L); and the leg itself is removed (M) and transferred to a separate dish of nutrient, where the bones can be removed. Finally, all tissues, after being washed, are transferred to dry watch glasses and cut up with scalpels (N).

pulled free, and the embryo is deposited in one of the small Petri dishes (Fig. 33[E]). The egg is then discarded and a second is operated on in the same way. All embryos can be placed in a single Petri dish until it is full. We find the "buttonhook" superior to a curved forceps for lifting embryos, since use of the former entails far less danger of damaging or even severing the neck.

When all of the embryos have been dissected out, six pairs of Columbia watch glasses are opened and placed under the shield. Each is charged with about 1 ml. of salt-dextrose solution. The forceps are exchanged for the finer mosquito set, and these and the dissecting knives are sterilized. With two small Petri dishes in front of the operator, the dish of embryos is opened, and, with a curved forceps, the neck of an embryo is severed and the head and body transferred to separate dishes. Then, with a curved mosquito forceps in the left hand and a right-angle knife-needle in the right, the body is laid on its back and its legs and wings are spread. With the points of the forceps laid parallel to the sides of the body, holding it down, a midline incision is made with the needle, extending to the upper end of the sternum (Fig. 33[F]). This is extended as a Y to the base of each wing, and the body is laid open (Fig. 33[G]). The needle is then exchanged for a pair of straight forceps. With this, the heart is lifted gently forward. The intestines, stomach, and liver are then pulled down between the legs. The lungs are thus exposed and can likewise be lifted forward. Then with the forceps in the right hand, points down and held not quite closed against the base of the heart, the mass consisting of heart, lungs, and diaphragm is pushed forward (Fig. 33[H]), torn loose from the neck, and laid in the Petri dish (Fig. 33[I]). The peritoneal membranes are separated and discarded; the heart, with the aortic vessels, is separated from the lungs; and the heart and lungs are placed in separate watch glasses of nutrient solution. Returning to the Petri dish, the body is now turned belly down and is again held with the forceps. With the needle an incision is made down the back, then across above the legs (Fig. 33[J]). Using the needle as a hook, the skin of the leg can now be everted down to the "heel" joint (Fig. 33[K], [L]). The skin is cut free and placed in a third watch glass. The leg is severed at the "heel" with the knife, then again at the "hip"; and the limb, freed of skin (Fig. 33[M]), is placed in a fourth watch glass of salt-dextrose solution. The operation is repeated on the other leg. The head is then grasped with the forceps, and the skin is slit across the brow and pulled back. The tip of a fine forceps can then be inserted through the median suture, and the two frontal bones can be lifted out and placed in a fifth watch glass. This process is repeated until a sufficient number of hearts, lungs, bits of skin, legs, and frontal bones (usually six of each) have been isolated.

The covers of the watch glasses are now inverted and filled with nutrient. The aortic vessels are torn out of the hearts and discarded. Since the hearts will have continued to beat during this interval, they should be reasonably free of internal blood. This method, of transfer to fresh dishes of nutrient, has proved a much more effective method of washing away adherent blood than any number of washings by aspiration with a pipette. The lungs are similarly transferred, depending on peristalsis to free them of occluded amniotic fluid; this will not be complete, and some washing out of fluid will continue for several days. The bones are carefully dissected out of the legs and placed in a sixth dish of nutrient, the muscle being likewise transferred to fresh fluid. This completed, a third series of watch glasses is prepared but without fluid. The tissues—hearts, lungs, leg muscles, and skin, all except the bones—are transferred a few at a time with the forceps to these dry watch glasses, the adherent moisture being sufficient to keep the tissues from drying out.

Before this last operation, the cataract knives or Bard-Parker knives have been placed in the boiling water, sterilized, and set on the wire rack to cool. With a knife in each hand, held together like the blades of a pair of scissors (Fig. 33[N]), the hearts, lungs, and muscles are now cut up. We prefer to cut them quite fine so that no fragments larger than about 0.3 mm. remain. These are now ready for inoculation.

HANGING DROPS—MAXIMOV SLIDES (see Chapter 5, Fig. 29[B]). Lay out 12 clean, sterile 30- × 35-mm. No. 1 cover glasses. Place a small drop of sterile water or balanced salt solution in the middle of each and add a clean 20-mm.-round No. 0 cover glass. The water should be in such amount that it fills the space under the cover glass but does not float the glass free. On six of these, place small drops of plasma, spreading them in a thin layer to within 2 mm. of the edge. To the other six add somewhat larger drops of Waymouth's MB 752/1 nutrient, spreading in like manner. Now, with a fine pipette, place a bit of tissue on each cover, heart on four, lung on four, and muscle on four. To the six plasma drops add an equal amount of embryo extract, and immediately stir with a needle or platinum spatula so as to mix the plasma and extract. Place two drops of Vaseline on opposite sides of the cavities of 12 hollow-ground slides. Invert a slide over each cover glass, pressing down firmly so as to spread the Vaseline. Now, with a quick "flip" invert each slide. Seal the covers to the slides with hot 1 : 3 Vaseline : paraffin with a brush. The slides are now ready to be labeled and placed in the incubator.

ROLLER TUBES. Set out 24, 16- × 130-mm. test tubes. With a curved pipette, run in plasma along the side of 12 tubes, spreading it to form a band about 5 mm. wide and about 50 mm. long. Place these tubes horizontally, with the plasma streak down. To each tube add four bits of tissue—heart, lung, muscle, or bone—placing the bits in rows down the middle of the plasma streaks (Fig. 34). From a hypodermic, add a drop of thrombin solution or embryo extract to each tissue bit to ensure prompt clotting. As soon as clotting is complete, turn all tubes, both with and without plasma, so that the tissue fragments are on the upper side; place the tubes in a sloped rack; and add 1 ml. of nutrient to each, using a 20 : 40 : 40 embryo extract : serum : BSS mixture for six tubes with and without plasma, and MB 752/1 for the corresponding number of each

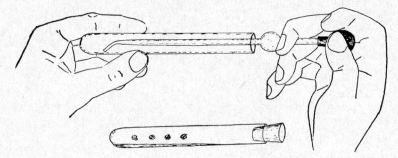

FIGURE 34. Method of inoculating roller tubes: Four (or more) pieces of tissue are placed in a line along the inner surface of the tube. This may be done either with or without a plasma or fibrin clot.

type. Stopper the tubes and place them, in the racks, in the incubator for four hours. This allows time for those cultures without plasma to become attached. At the end of this time the tubes may be transferred to the rotor for continued cultivation. Primary outgrowth will develop directly from the explants. When this outgrowth is well established, secondary masses of fibroblasts and of lung epithelium will wash free and reattach themselves in new positions. Heart muscle extends but does not ordinarily establish new centers of growth.

FLYING COVER SLIPS (Fig. 35). Set out eight narrow cover slips on a sterile block such as the back of a 2- × 4-inch deep-well hollow-ground slide, placing a drop of sterile water under each to prevent them from slipping during handling. Coat these with a thin layer of plasma. Now, with a cataract knife, pick up and arrange six squares of skin on each of four slips, being careful that the edges of the pieces do not curl. Similarly, place an equal number of bits of muscle on the remaining covers. Add thrombin or embryo extract to the plasma and mix thoroughly. After the plasma is well clotted, place the covers back to back in pairs and insert them in roller tubes.

CARREL FLASKS. Set out 24 Carrel flasks. To 8 of these add 0.5 ml. of plasma. Eight more should be charged with cellophane (p. 86). Inoculate each flask with three bits of tissue—heart, lung, muscle, or frontal bone—placing the bits *under* the cellophane and orienting all bits in a triangular pattern. To the flasks containing plasma, add enough thrombin or embryo extract to ensure clotting, mixing with a spatula without disturbing the tissue fragments. Now stopper all flasks and place them in the incubator for about four hours. Then add to the plasma flasks 0.5 ml. of 20 : 40 : 40 nutrient. Add the same nutrient, 1 ml. in quantity, to half the other sets, both with and without cellophane, and add MB 752/1 to the other half; finally, return the cultures to the incubator.

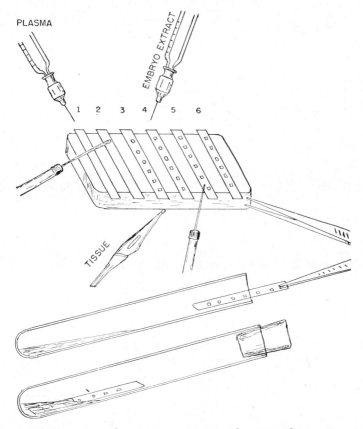

FIGURE 35. Preparing cultures on narrow cover-glass strips for insertion in roller tubes or Leighton tubes: Six strips are laid out on a large, sterile culture slide with a drop of water under each slip to attach them firmly and prevent slippage. Plasma is added to each from a pipette or syringe (1) and is then spread evenly with a cataract knife or platinum spatula (2). A series of bits of tissue—skin, for example—are then added in a single row (3), and embryo extract is added to each fragment from a second syringe (4). The embryo extract and plasma are quickly mixed with a needle or knife (5) and allowed to clot. The strips are then taken up (6) and slipped into tubes or flasks where they will be bathed in nutrient. They can be inserted singly, or they can be placed back to back in pairs, which prevents growth of cells on the backed faces. Cells will quickly grow out over the exposed surfaces of such strips, which can be removed at will for fixation, staining, and mounting. Such mounts are suitable for study at much higher magnifications than can be used with cultures grown directly on the walls of roller tubes.

WATCH GLASSES. Prepare six Petri dishes, each containing 7 micro-Syracuse watch glasses. Provide 14 watch glasses with stainless-steel mesh tables (Shaffer, 1956; Trowell, 1959) (Fig. 26[6]). These glasses will be charged with liquid nutrient, half with 20 : 40 : 40 and half with synthetic nutrient. To a second series of 14 add 0.5 ml. of Wolff's agar nutrient, and to a third add 0.5 ml. of freshly prepared plasma : embryo extract, 1 : 1. Allow the agar and plasma to gel. On top of half of the dishes place disks of sterile rayon-acetate voile. Now transfer to each dish one of the limb bones prepared from the dissected embryos. Place a 22-ml.-round cover glass on each watch glass, and add enough water to each Petri dish to provide a humid atmosphere. Cover the dishes and place them in the incubator.

SPONGE MATRICES. These are best prepared in Leighton tubes, and the sponge should be prepared ahead of time. Take a piece of fine cellulose sponge, and, with a razor, cut it in strips about 15 mm. wide by about 5 mm. thick. Then compress a single strip between two glass slides, allowing about 0.5 mm. to project, and slice again. Repeat, removing strips 0.5 mm. thick. Discard any which are thicker than this and any which are imperfect. You now have a series of pieces $15 \times 5 \times 0.5$ mm. These should be washed in half-hourly repeated changes of ether, alcohol, and distilled water; boiled in water; autoclaved; and, finally, placed in 20 : 40 : 40 nutrient or a synthetic nutrient until thoroughly saturated. Insert one such piece into each of eight Leighton tubes. Now place a bit of muscle on one end of each strip of sponge and a bit of lung on the other end. Half of these should be attached with drops of freshly pre-pared plasma–embryo extract mixture. Allow the tubes to stand for four hours, then add 1 ml. of nutrient to each, using 20 : 40 : 40 or synthetic nutrient to correspond to that in which the sponges were initially soaked. Place in the incubator.

It will be of interest to try the effects of dissociating all of these tissues into discrete cells by digestion with trypsin or Versene as we have already described. Cultures from such preparations will usually be in monolayers and will be made directly on the glass, without underlay, although a plasma or agar layer may be used in preparing clones (Chapter 7). Such cultures will be made in tubes, flasks, or Petri dishes.

RENEWAL OF NUTRIENT. Any culture which grows rapidly will quickly alter the nutrient by withdrawing nutritive constituents such as dextrose, iron, phosphorus, etc., and by excreting waste products—lactic acid, CO_2, and other toxic materials. To maintain a high and continuous level of growth, the nutrient must be renewed at frequent intervals, usually two or three times a week. These periods can be lengthened by lowering the incubation tmperature (Fischer, 1926), as Hanks has done in his studies of leprosy (1947, 1948), or by using nutrients of low energy value such as pure serum or agar dilutions, as in some of Wolff's studies. For most work, however, renewal is a routine necessity. Carrel flasks with a plasma clot overlaid with a fluid medium, Carrel flasks without clot, and roller tubes may all be treated much alike. The usual practice has been to aspirate the nutrient by pipette; replace it with a wash solution, usually Hanks solution, using a second pipette; allow the solution to stand for ten minutes or more; remove this by aspiration with a third pipette; and charge with fresh nutrient with a fourth. This procedure runs grave risks of contamination. We have devised a method which we believe to be more satisfactory. Let us take as an example Carrel flasks with "L"-strain cells growing directly on glass in an MB 752/1 nutrient.

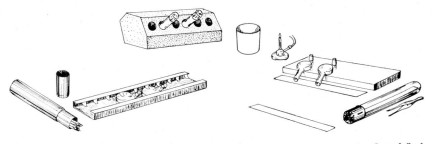

Figure 36. Arrangement of equipment for renewing nutrient in Carrel-flask cultures (see text).

A rack carrying ten flasks is placed at the operator's left (Fig. 36), a low support (an empty rack inverted makes an excellent one) at the right, a waste beaker between the two, and a micro-Bunsen burner within reach, next to the beaker. A strip of sterile blotting paper is placed immediately in front of the right hand rack and a second strip in front of the operator. Then a flask is taken up (Fig. 37[1]); the stopper is lightly flamed, removed (Fig. 37[2]), dried by a quick touch to the blotter in front of the operator, and placed, small end up, on the rear of the rack. The mouth of the flask is flamed quite thoroughly (Fig. 37[3]); the flask is then inverted over the beaker to pour off the old nutrient (Fig. 37[4]). Keeping the flask in the inverted position, touch its mouth to the blotter (Fig. 37[5]), tapping lightly to shake down any fluid in the mouth, and place the flask on the support, with its mouth resting on the blotter in such a way that any drops accumulating will be absorbed (Fig. 37[6]). Repeat this until all ten flasks are resting mouth down, draining onto the blotter. Then run the flame quickly over the stoppers. Now take up the flasks; tap their mouths on the blotter again; and return them to the original rack, this time in the upright position. Run the flame over their mouths thoroughly. Pipette fresh nutrient (or wash fluid) into the flasks; a single pipette will serve for all ten (Fig. 38). Again flame the mouths and stoppers lightly, and return the stoppers to their proper flasks.

By this method no pipette is inserted beyond the mouth of any flask and only a single pipette, that containing the fresh nutrient, is approached

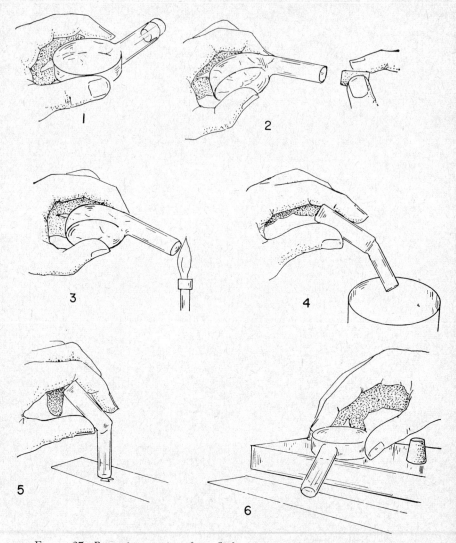

FIGURE 37. Removing nutrient from flasks. See text for explanation of numbers.

to the mouth; the manipulations are performed in series for an entire rack at a time. The method is rapid, and we have never encountered any difficulty from contaminations traceable to faults at this point. The method must be modified slightly for roller tubes by providing special racks to hold the tubes in an almost vertical position for draining. Special racks for Leighton tubes suitable for this purpose are on the market.

This method is of course not applicable to cover-glass cultures or to watch glasses. Plasma cultures on Maximov cover slips can be washed by

FIGURE 38. Pipetting in fresh nutrient and flaming flasks before reinserting the stoppers.

adding sufficient sterile water under the cover to float it free; the cover can then be lifted with cover-glass forceps and transferred to a dish or a Coplin jar of Hanks solution. When the culture has been washed long enough it is picked up, dried by touching one corner to a sterile blotter, placed on a fresh supporting cover with its attaching drop of water, charged with fresh nutrient with a pipette, and returned to its slide. Here contact with a pipette cannot be avoided.

Organ cultures such as bone or ovary, on plasma clots or on agar in watch glasses, must be lifted with a spatula, any excess halo of fibroblasts being trimmed off and the culture being transferred to a fresh clot. If the culture has been grown on voile, the bit of voile can be lifted and either transferred directly or washed as one does with Maximov cover slips. Cultures grown on steel or tantalum mesh tables have an advantage over these; here the old nutrient can be aspirated with a pipette and replaced without disturbing the culture, or the entire table can be picked up and transferred to a freshly charged container.

MAMMALIAN EMBRYOS. With slight modifications these procedures can be adapted for any tissue. In preparing mouse embryos we choose a gravid female of about 18–20 days gestation. The mouse is killed by pinching the neck with the thumb and forefinger (Fig. 39[A]), which separates the vertebrae (an anesthetic is not desirable in such cases), and is pinned out on a piece of cork or pine board covered with white paper and wet with alcohol. These operations are all carried out under the

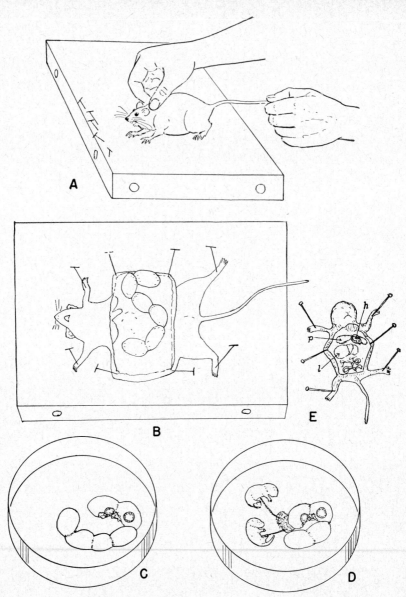

FIGURE 39. Preparing embryonic material from a mouse: A pregnant female is killed by pinching the neck (A). It is then pinned out on a board and opened by a median and two transverse incisions, and the body wall is pinned back, exposing the uterus (B). In the case shown there were four embryos in the left-hand horn, two in the right. The uterus is lifted out, cutting away the supporting mesenteries, and is transferred to a sterile Petri dish (C). Here the membrane is opened, and the embryos are removed (D) and transferred to a second dish for further dissection. In E one of these embryos has been pinned down and opened, exposing the heart (h), lung (p), liver (l), and other organs from which tissue can be taken for cultivation.

dissecting hood. The belly is swabbed with alcohol and opened with sharp scissors, and the skin, underlying muscle, and peritoneum are pinned back (Fig. 39[B]). The lower end of the uterus is grasped with forceps and raised, snipping the attached membranes until the entire uterus can be severed and lifted out into a Petri dish (Fig. 39[C]). The carcass is discarded. The uterus is then snipped with scissors between the embryos, and these are lifted out, pulled away from the placentas, and transferred to a second Petri dish. They are then removed one by one to a Columbia watch glass containing 0.5 ml. of salt-dextrose solution or nutrient, and their thoraxes are opened to remove the hearts or other organs (Fig. 39[D]). Skin taken from the back of such an embryo in sheets 3–15 mm. on a side makes excellent material for epithelial cultures. The tissues, once isolated, can be treated exactly like those of the chick. Newborn or day-old mice also make good material. They can be killed by pinching the neck with a forceps. The surface is sterilized by dipping the entire body in 70 per cent alcohol for about a minute, and the carcass is then pinned out on a board, opened without further sterilization, and dissected (Fig. 39[E]). Thoracic muscle and diaphragm from such mice also make good cultures.

SPECIAL PROBLEMS. One particular tissue, the ovary, may serve to exemplify certain special problems. Ovaries and ovarian tissues have been successfully grown by Gaillard (1948) and his students, but they succeed only when capsular epithelium is present; pure oogenous tissue without capsule rapidly degenerates. The ovaries of a mouse embryo or of a newborn mouse are removed to a depression slide containing nutrient, and the outer capsule is peeled off under the dissecting microscope. Organs as small as a mouse-embryo ovary should be cultured whole or divided into at most four pieces. Human or rat embryonic ovaries are large enough to be divided more drastically. After the capsule has been removed, the ovary is laid on a slide moistened with Hanks solution and, with a sharp knife, is sliced transversely into a series of layers about 1 mm. thick (Fig. 40[3]). These are then divided by a series of radial cuts into wedges about 1 mm. wide at the outer end (Fig. 40[4]), and any excess core tissue is cut away (Fig. 40[5]) to provide blocks of tissue having intact cortex for one face and oogenous core for the opposite (Fig. 40[6]). These blocks are used as inocula into watch glasses. In practice the epithelium grows out around the parenchyma (Fig. 40[7]), most of which breaks down (Fig. 40[8]). Once a new epithelial capsule is established, however, the persistent oogenous cells on the inner face will regenerate to form a new functional core (Fig. 40[9]). It is possible to replace this epithelium by corresponding cells from quite distant body parts: pericardium, perichondrium, or kidney

1.

2.

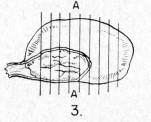

A

A

A

3.

4.

5.

6.

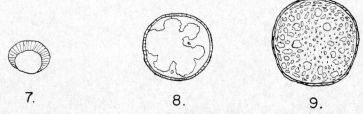

7.

8.

9.

FIGURE 40. Preparation of ovary material for cultivation (after Gaillard): (1) An ovary (rat, human, etc.). The muscles are at the top, left, the efferent duct below. (2) These are removed. (3) The ovary is sliced transversely into pieces about 1 mm. thick (A–A). (4) Each slice consists of a marginal layer of germinal epithelium, within this the cortical tissues containing follicles in various stages of development and regression, and at the center a mass of mostly degenerating materials and fluid. This slice is now cut by a series of radial incisions into wedges with the germinal epithelium at the wider margin. (5) These wedges are further reduced by a cut parallel to the surface of the ovary, the central portion being discarded. (6) The resulting blocks of tissue, consisting of equal parts of germinal epithelium (above) and cortex (below), are ready for use as inocula in watch-glass cultures (Fig. 26, Fig. 28[O], [P], [Q], [R]). (7) In culture the epithelium extends out around the cortex. Cultures succeed only when this closure becomes complete. (8) Once a spherical "organule" is reconstituted, the cortical layer breaks down. It is replaced by chords of tissue growing inward from the face of the epithelium; this new-formed tissue produces new follicles. (9) The interior is finally completely filled with follicle-bearing tissue, and approximately normal ovarian function is re-established.

capsule can supply epithelium for ovary cultures quite successfully (Wolff, 1957), but oogenous parenchyma without some sort of epithelial capsule does not, apparently, succeed in coping with the nutritional problems involved in its survival and normal function. The same principle seems to apply to other glands and even to bone; pure glandular epithelium or pure stroma does not function organotypically in isolation, atlhough it may grow as non-functional sheets; only when an intact radially symmetrical organ is reconstituted can the explant function successfully.

ADULT TISSUES. Adult tissues and pathological specimens require somewhat more complex treatment. They must be removed with the utmost sterile precautions, which is not always possible, or else, as is the case with most malignant or diseased tissues, they must be rendered sterile by suitable treatment, usually with antibiotics. Two examples may be chosen. If it is desired to make cultures of skin taken from a living animal, from a person's arm, or from a cadaver, the area in question should first be washed and shaved. It is then swabbed with 70 per cent alcohol, then with ether, and again with alcohol, and the area is allowed to dry. The skin is then removed by pinching it into a fold with broad forceps and cutting tangentially as close to the surface as possible with a sharp razor moistened with balanced salt solution. The bits are immediately transferred to a Petri dish or watch glass of nutrient, after which they can be treated as described for chick-embryo skin. Such tissue should be quite sterile unless actually diseased.

A bit of an internal organ or of a tumor removed surgically cannot be relied on to be sterile. Such a specimen should first be washed in normal saline, then in balanced salt solution containing 1,000 units of penicillin G and 0.5 mg. of streptomycin per milliliter (Metzger *et al.*, 1954). Damaged parts and all excess tissue should be dissected off and discarded, and the tissue, while still in the solution, should be cut into bits not more than 2 mm. thick. The solution is then removed and replaced with a fresh balanced salt-antibiotic solution, and the whole is placed in the refrigerator at 4° C. overnight. The antibiotic is then replaced by a nutrient without antibiotic; the tissue is now ready to be prepared for culturing. This treatment will eliminate most surface contaminants and will destroy all but the most intimately permeating and stubborn infections. If, however, the cultures still prove to be contaminated, and are so valuable as to justify further precautions, they may be grown for one or more passages in nutrient containing 20–50 units of penicillin G per milliliter, followed, if necessary with 50 μg. of streptomycin and 50 μg. of mycostatin per milliliter. Such treatment can also be used to eliminate contaminations which, even in the best of laboratories, may occasionally get into valuable cultures. This subject is treated at length by Coriell (1962).

It should be remembered, however, that all antibiotics are by their nature toxic substances, their toxicity being merely somewhat greater for most bacteria than for most tissue cells. There are also strains of organisms which are resistant to antibiotics. It has been the experience of some investigators that *all* strains of cells which have been treated for long periods with antibiotics are eventually found to harbor chronic infections with symbiotic pleuropneumonia-like (PPLO) organisms. Antibiotics are therefore always to be used only as a last resort and to be avoided wherever possible. Asepsis is far more important than antisepsis.

One other special method should be considered briefly here. Sometimes it is desirable, for any of several reasons, to break up the pattern of a tissue *before* cultures are established, rather than to wait for this to result from growth. For this purpose tissues may be digested with trypsin under such conditions that the cells are not killed. A sterile specimen taken by biopsy or from surgery, or a previously established culture, is cut into small pieces and washed thoroughly in a Hanks solution from which calcium and magnesium salts have been omitted. The wash fluid is then replaced by a similar one containing 0.05 per cent of trypsin, and the flask is set in the incubator. It should be agitated gently, either mechanically or manually. When the tissue mass breaks up, the digestion is stopped by decanting most of the fluid and replacing it with complete nutrient without trypsin. The suspended cells can then be spun down briefly in the centrifuge and used to inoculate flasks, tubes, or an agar substratum. Spread out, the different types of cells will develop as discrete colonies of epithelium, muscle, connective tissue, or other types and can be examined as such or used in the making of pure-line subcultures (Chapter 7). This sort of culture has proved useful for many special purposes, especially in the cultivation of viruses, both for production and for diagnostic purposes.

Human Materials

There are no special methods for human tissues. What has been said above applies equally to human materials. We need only to remark that, of course, certain limitations are placed on their treatment by our social mores. Embryonic materials can be obtained from abortions or stillbirths. Gaillard has used cells so obtained in his studies on the cultivation of glandular tissues and on their transplantation to patients. Adult materials must come from biopsies, from members removed during surgical operations, or from cadavers. These are all likely to be taken from diseased or moribund sites and are therefore likely to require treatment with antibiotics. Cultures of healthy human skin are sometimes grown for examination of the chromosome complements, in the diagnosis of hereditary defects. Similarly, cultures from biopsies of complex tumors may serve to clarify their origin, particularly in the case of metastases. The methods used, however, will be no more than adaptations of those developed for the handling of animal tissues, organs, and cells.

BLOOD CELLS. Blood cells were among the first to be studied in tissue culture (Lewis and Lewis, 1926; Carrel, 1934). Their use in short-term cultures has become of particular importance for analysis of genetic defects. They are also important in the study of such physiological problems as the effects of radiation and the development of treatments for radiation damage. Two methods of preparing such cultures will be described.

Fawcett and Vallee (1952) have prepared pure cultures of monocytes by the following method: A 10-ml. syringe is filled to 8.4 ml. with a 35 per cent solution of bovine albumin (Armour's crystalline albumin in sterile distilled water) and 1.6 ml. of salt-dextrose solution (Earle, Hanks, or other) are added. Five milliliters are then injected into each of two 15-ml. centrifuge tubes. Ten milliliters of fresh heparinized blood (chick, human) are taken up in a second syringe, and 5 ml. are carefully layered onto the albumin. The tubes are stoppered and centrifuged at 600 G for ten minutes. The leucocytes should now be floating at the serum-albumin interface, well above the red cells. A narrow pipette is introduced through the supernatant fluid, and the leucocyte layer is aspirated with about 1 ml. of fluid, being careful not to draw up erythrocytes. The material from two tubes is combined and resuspended in 10 ml. of 10 per cent chicken serum in salt-dextrose solution. This is centrifuged at low speed for five minutes to wash out any remaining plasma or albumin. The supernatant containing the leucocytes is removed and 10 ml. of nutrient medium added. This is then pipetted into flasks, 0.5 ml. per flask. The monocytes will be attached to the glass within 24 hours. A sharp shake of the flask will then dislodge all other cell types. The nutrient containing these loose cells can then be removed and fresh nutrient added. Such a culture should cover the bottom of the flask in about 72 hours. It may require the addition of one or two drops of 1.4 per cent bicarbonate solution each day to maintain the proper pH (Fig. 41).

Moorehead et al. (1960, 1962) prepare cultures of peripheral blood for genetic analysis as follows: Ten millilters of venous blood are drawn into a sterile chilled syringe wet with heparin solution and are transferred to a siliconed conical centrifuge tube containing 0.2 ml. bactophytohemagglutinin solution (Difco); these are mixed and allowed to stand 30–60 minutes in an ice bath, then centrifuged at 25 G for 5–10 minutes at 5° C. to remove the erythrocytes. The supernatant plasma containing the leucocytes is decanted and the cells counted. These are then planted in small screw-capped pharmaceutical bottles or similar

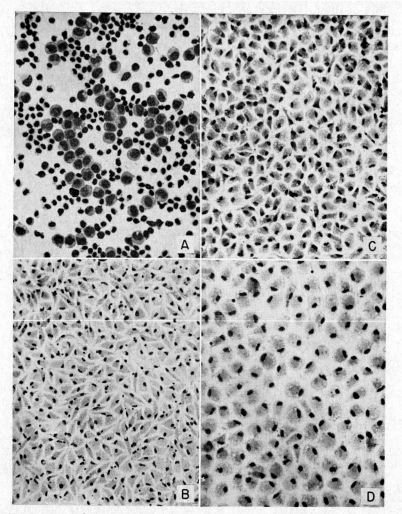

FIGURE 41. Cultures of chick leucocytes isolated by Fawcett's albumin flotation method and grown in Carrel flasks without plasma: (A) A fresh smear consisting of monocytes, lymphocytes, and thrombocytes. (B) A four-day culture of almost pure monocytes with a few small degenerating thrombocytes (small pycnotic nuclei). (C) A culture of the same age, but with larger cells, resembling both monocytes and macrophages. (D) Another four-day culture, in this case consisting entirely of macrophage-like cells. (A) × 150 (Weiss and Fawcett, 1953); (B), (C), (D) × 90 (Don W. Fawcett).

containers, in a medium consisting of 30 per cent of autologous or homologous plasma and 70 per cent of a defined nutrient such as Difco 199 or Waymouth's MB 752/1 to which penicillin and streptomycin have been added. Each bottle should contain 8–10 ml. of nutrient and an inoculum sufficient to provide 1.0–1.2×10^6 cells per milliliter. Adjust the pH to

7.0–7.2 and maintain this with CO_2 gas or $N/10$ HCl as required daily. Incubate at 37° C. After three days, add colchicine to a final concentration of 0.5–1.0×10^{-6}M. Let stand for six hours (not longer), then loosen the cells by repeated pipetting with a siliconed pipette and centrifuge at 800 rpm for 5 minutes. Remove most of the supernatant medium, and resuspend the cells in 5–6 ml. of warm BSS at pH 7.0. Recentrifuge, then remove all but 0.5 ml. of the supernatant. Carefully resuspend the cells in this small volume, and add, with constant mixing, 1.5 ml. of warm distilled water. Let stand in the incubator at 37° C. for 3–5 minutes, then centrifuge at 600 rpm for 5 minutes. Now remove all supernatant, and replace with freshly prepared fixative (1 : 3 glacial acetic acid : absolute methyl alcohol) without disturbing the cells. Let stand for 30 minutes, then break up the clump of cells by repeated pipetting. Centrifuge at 600 rpm for 5 minutes, decant, and add 0.5 ml. of fresh fixative so as to provide a dense cell suspension. Dip a clean slide in chilled distilled water, shake off the excess, and pipette two or three drops of the cell suspension onto the wet slide; tilt the slide carefully and draw off the excess fluid with a blotter, leaving the cells on the glass. Let the preparation dry; fanning or gentle warming should complete this in 30–60 seconds. The quality of the slide can be checked immediately by means of phase optics. The slide can now be stained in freshly prepared aceto-orcein (60 ml. glacial acetic acid, 40 ml. H_2O, 1 g. orcein), dehydrated, and mounted in diaphane.

Methods for handling such materials are currently under active study, and many modifications have been proposed. The above examples will suffice to introduce the student to the field.

Plant Materials

Let us now turn to the setting up of cultures of plant materials. The general arrangement of the operating room will be the same as for animal cultures. We will need the same dissecting shield, instrument sterilizer, Bunsen burner, and instrument rack. Only the details and, especially, the instruments will be new. We should have available

1 pair Heymann nose-and-throat scissors
2 pairs dissecting scissors, 3-inch straight blades
2 cataract knives or other small cutting instruments
2 Bard-Parker knives, No. 7 handle, No. 10 blade
2 carton knives, Stanley
2 pairs large forceps, 10 inch
2 pairs round-end forceps, 5 inch
2 pairs mosquito forceps, straight
2 pairs mosquito forceps, curved
2 section lifters

2 bacteriological loops, 3 mm.
1 ear curette, 1 mm.
1 cork borer, 5 mm.
1 chisel, ¾ inch
1 carpenter's hammer
1 saw
1 wire paint-cleaning brush
6 pairs Columbia watch glasses
6 Petri dishes, 60 mm.
6 Petri dishes, 100 mm.
1 beaker, 50 ml.
1 box 10-ml. pipettes
70 per cent and 95 per cent alcohol
Cotton, absorbent
Tubes, bottles, and flasks of nutrient

Again, not all of these will be used for any one type of culture.

The first plant "tissue" (organ) to be grown successfully (White, 1934a) and still one of the most versatile materials is the root tip. Such tips are made available in two ways: from seedlings and from cuttings. First, one must have aseptic roots. With many plants having fleshy fruits or membranous capsules (tomato, squash, tobacco, pea, etc.), it is possible to obtain aseptic seeds without special treatment of any sort by merely washing the fruit thoroughly and then tearing it open in such a way that the seeds do not touch any surface which might be contaminated (White, 1943a). In all cases such tearing, without disinfection, will be the preferred method, since it involves no chemical treatment. In other cases, for example, with the grains and small-podded legumes such as alfalfa, this cannot be done and it is necessary to treat the seeds with chemical disinfectants. Bromine water is excellent because of its high volatility, but it is rather difficult to prepare and use. Sodium or calcium hypochlorite, "Dakin solution," mercuric chloride, and the like are more commonly employed. Commercial Clorox (sodium hypochlorite) diluted 1 : 6 with water makes an excellent substitute for Dakin solution, or it can be prepared by one of the methods outlined by Parker (1961). Antibiotics such as penicillin have shown no advantage over synthetic disinfectants and are not now used for plant materials.

One of the most satisfactory methods has been as follows: First, the seeds are treated briefly with a wetting agent such as 95 per cent alcohol. They are then placed, without rinsing, in a 1 per cent hypochlorite solution such as Clorox for periods of 5–30 minutes, depending on the species. During this treatment they should be shaken frequently or, better still, treated in a bottle which is rotated slowly on a wheel. The disinfectant is poured off and the seeds rinsed thoroughly with sterile water. They are then distributed to Petri dishes either on moist, sterile filter paper or on a layer of 3 per cent agar and allowed to germinate in the dark. When the roots are 2–3 cm. long, all infected seedlings are discarded and a selection is made among the rest for vigor and uniformity. The selected tips are severed with a sharp scalpel and inoculated into flasks for cultivation. Seeds may also be placed for germination directly in the culture flasks of nutrient, but contaminated or non-viable seeds then require discarding of the entire flask.

The above procedure is quite satisfactory for most purposes. Occasionally, however, it is for some reason impossible to use seedling roots. An example is the case where it is desired to cultivate roots carrying a series of related virus infections (White, 1934b). The inoculation of viruses into roots after their establishment in vitro has proved to be extremely difficult. For such studies it is therefore more satisfactory, where possible, to obtain roots which are already infected. For this purpose adventitious roots developed from infected plants may be used. This can be done in two ways, which will be described below.

Freshly isolated stem tissues of many plants such as sunflower, tobacco, tomato, and carrot will produce occasional roots during the first few weeks when cultured on a nutrient containing traces of one of the growth hormones such as indoleacetic acid (10^{-6}). With these plants one may isolate tissues as if for the preparation of cambial cultures (p. 117), and when roots appear they can be severed and transferred to fresh flasks. Indeed, they must be so transferred, for roots, although initiated freely in a solution containing a growth substance, will not continue to grow in such a solution for even very brief periods after excision (Nobécourt, 1940). These growth substances are extremely toxic to unattached roots.

This method involves little risk of secondary infection. It is, however, uncertain of results. In many cases it is better to use cuttings. Tomato stems, for example, will grow adventive roots quite easily. Pieces of stem about 20 cm. long are washed thoroughly with a detergent, then with a disinfectant such as hypochlorite, and finally with sterile water. They are then rigidly attached to a suitable sterilized cover and suspended in a jar whose atmosphere is kept saturated by a layer of filter paper resting in the sterile water at the bottom and bent around the inside of the jar. Roots will emerge from such cuttings after a week or ten days and will in many cases be quite aseptic. They can then be removed for cultivation. The chief hazard here is the possibility of occasional infections being spread in the film of water on the stems. Nevertheless, the experimenter may be surprised at how free such stems generally are of infections (White, 1934b; 1943a).

The principles for the isolation of stem growing points are essentially the same as those for root tips, only complicated somewhat by the presence of enclosing leaves or bud scales. These serve as a protection against contamination and, if removed carefully, will leave an aseptic core (White, 1933a). Ball (1946), Sussex and Steeves (1953), and others have used such stem growing points. When it becomes a question of isolating cultures from more massive stems and roots, however, somewhat different procedures must be applied. Such tissues will consist of (1) procambium, (2) lateral primary cambium, (3) secondary cambium, and (4) parenchymatous or other tissues which have retained a meristematic character.

PROCAMBIUM. There are three general procedures for isolating tissues from young stem tips, all specially applicable to fleshy stems such as tomato, tobacco, and sunflower. The stem should be cut to a length of 15–20 cm., and the leaf petioles should be severed close to the stem. Then, beginning 3–5 cm. from the tip, lift the epidermis and underlying cortical parenchyma with a scalpel and tear them forward so as to strip off the entire surface (Fig. 42[A]). When these surface tissues, which may be contaminated with epiphytic molds or bacteria, have been eliminated, cut the now aseptic core transversely into slices 0.5–1.5 mm. thick, using a scalpel. Transfer these slices to the nutrient medium. A second method, which is often equally successful, is to break the stem cleanly, where it is sufficiently lacking in fibrous materials to permit one to do so (Fig. 42[B]). This exposes two sterile areas, distal and proximal, from which two cones of meristematic tissue can be removed with a sharp scalpel, taking care not to touch the possibly non-sterile epidermis in the process. A third method (Fig. 42[C]) is to remove the epidermal layers from only one side of the tip. When an aseptic area has been exposed, a well-sharpened surgeon's ear curette of 1.0-mm. diameter is pushed into the soft meristematic tissue and a sharp turn will remove a 1-mm. "melon ball" of tissue. This last method is especially useful when dealing with young galls or tumors or with plants whose epidermis does not strip well. In such cases the stem may be split some distance back of the tumor or growing tip and torn forward. If the tear passes through the desired tissue, the curette can be used to remove the specimen. This is essentially equivalent to "punch biopsies" with animals.

CAMBIUM. There are likewise two methods of securing specimens of lateral cambiums from older plants such as trees. The first, developed especially by Gautheret (1934, 1935, 1959), is useful principally for isolation during the growing season—April to August in northern climates—while the second, introduced by Gioelli (1938) but also much used by Gautheret (1942b, 1959), serves equally well at all seasons. If one is

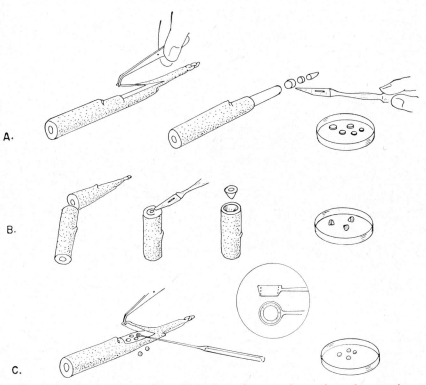

FIGURE 42. Preparing sterile explants from the tips of succulent plants such as tobacco, geranium, etc.: (A) by stripping the bark around the entire tip, exposing a cylinder of sterile tissues from which disks can be cut; (B) by breaking the stem to expose two sterile surfaces from which two cones (proximal and distal) can be removed; (C) by stripping the bark along one sector only, from which spheres of tissue can be removed with a sharp surgeon's ear curette (shown in insert).

dealing with woody stems only a few centimeters in diameter, the entire branch should be cut and brought into the laboratory. If it is during the growing season while the cambium is soft, an incision can be made around the stem at two points—above and below the region of interest and 2–4 cm. apart, depending on the size of the branch—then a longitudinal connecting incision can be made and the bark can be peeled off (Fig. 43[A]). These incisions need not be aseptic. Next, care being taken to touch only the edges of the exposed areas, the bark is flattened on a block of wood so as to expose the inner surface. A series of shallow incisions are then made in such a manner that they intersect in a checkerboard pattern but do not extend to the edges of the piece (Fig. 43[B]). The incisions should not pass more than halfway through the bark. The exposed inner surface is, of course, aseptic; and, if the incisions have extended neither deep enough to reach the contaminated outer bark nor

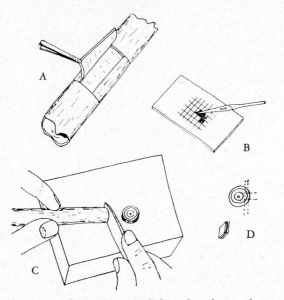

FIGURE 43. Preparing cultures from small branches during the growing season: Above, the bark is peeled back (A) and laid out on a block (B); a series of crossed incisions are made from the cambium side, being careful *not* to pass through the bark to the possibly contaminated outer surface; and a series of rectangular blocks containing cambium and phloem are removed for cultivation (Gautheret's method). Below, a stem is thoroughly surface sterilized; then it is cut into transverse slices; (C) and, finally, blocks containing cambium, phloem, and some xylem are dissected out (D) for cultivation (Gioelli's method).

far enough laterally to intersect the possibly contaminated marginal primary incisions, a series of similar aseptic explants can be lifted out. These are placed in culture flasks, on nutrient agar, with the cambium face up, or they may be set on edge and pushed into the agar to a depth of about half their width. They should then be oriented in a position opposite to that in the plant so as to take advantage of the normal polar movement of auxin.

The same method can be used for larger stems of trees and other plants. Here an area of bark is cleaned with a sharp chisel or drawknife. Then four intersecting incisions are made with chisel or saw, 10–15 cm. apart and passing through the cambium. By means of a broad chisel inserted tangentially 5–10 mm. within the wood, the enclosed block is lifted out, care being taken that it does not split at the cambium, and brought into the laboratory. These operations do not require aseptic precautions. In the laboratory, under sterile conditions, the cambium is now exposed and the same procedures followed as above. Cultures from such blocks are more likely to succeed from the phloem side than from the wood.

The method described above is that introduced by Gautheret. It is most easily applied when the cambium can be exposed, but during the dormant season this is not possible. Small branches or excised blocks may then be brought into the laboratory as before. In the case of branches, the surface must be sterilized. An effective method is first to clear away adherent debris by scrubbing with a stiff brush. The branch is then dipped in, or swabbed with, 95 per cent alcohol, which is burned off several times. This will usually provide reasonable asepsis without injuring the underlying living tissues. The stem is then laid on a sterile block, and a series of transverse cuts are made, about 1 mm. apart. If the stem is small (2–5 mm. in diameter), the entire transverse disk may be used as explant (Fig. 43[C]). If it is more than 5 mm. in diameter, it may be best to divide the initial disk into sectors and dissect off and discard the outer cortical tissues (bark) and much of the wood (Fig. 43[D]). This provides a rectangular block with its long axis tangential to the original surface and traversed by the cambium. If this block is pushed into the agar perpendicular to the surface and to such a depth as to leave about half the block exposed, growth will occur from the cambium above the agar surface and will ultimately spread out onto the agar, at which time it can be dissected away from the original block and subcultured.

The same principle can be applied to the preparation of cultures from the trunks of large trees, for example, from the massive tumors found on certain species of spruce (White and Millington, 1954a, 1954b; Reinert and White, 1956). With a saw, two cuts are made in the bark, about 10 cm. apart and 10–15 cm. long, penetrating well into the wood (Fig. 44[1]). These are intersected at the ends by two perpendicular cuts, laying out a rectangular block. With a chisel, the bark and wood are cut away along one side of this block to a depth of about 1 cm. into the wood. The chisel is then carefully driven in at this level, parallel to the tree's surface so as to split out the block as a slab (Fig. 44[2]). This is brought into the laboratory. The bark is scrubbed with a stiff wire brush to free it of lichen and loose bark. The corky layers are then removed with a chisel or drawknife down to the living phloem (Fig. 44[3]. The surface is now washed with 95 per cent alcohol, and the alcohol is burned off (be careful not to burn yourself in doing this!). Then, being careful not to touch the phloem surface with the hands and using a sharp, sterile chisel, the phloem is further cut away down to within 1 mm. of the cambium. A series of incisions are made about 2–3 mm. apart, parallel to the side of the block, and a similar series of perpendicular incisions are made at 10- to 15-mm. intervals (Fig. 44[4]). By means of a scalpel inserted about 1 mm. below the level of the cambium, the first row of blocks is now removed and discarded, since they may have been contaminated in the unavoidable preliminary handling of the original piece.

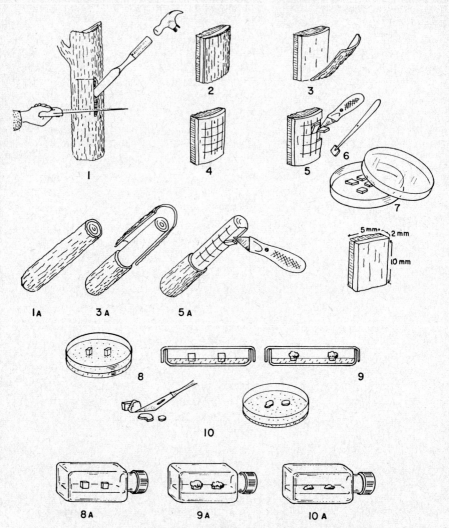

FIGURE 44. Preparation of cultures from large trees (1)–(5) or from moderately large, woody branches (1A), (3A), (5A): This method (modified after Gioelli) is applicable at all seasons of the year but especially during the dormant seasons. A block of tissue penetrating well into the wood is removed (1), or a branch an inch or more in diameter is severed (1A), and brought into the laboratory. There the bark is thoroughly cleaned in such a way as to expose under aseptic conditions about 1 mm. of phloem and cortical tissues (2)–(4), (3A). On this surface a series of intersecting incisions are made, an edge penetrating into the wood exposed (4)–(5), (5A), and a series of blocks about 5 × 10 × 2 mm. are removed, each containing cambium sandwiched between phloem and wood (6), (7). These are pushed on end into agar, leaving about half their length exposed (8), (8A). Growth occurs only above the agar (9), (9A). When the new-formed callus is about 2 mm. thick, it can be excised (10) and transferred to fresh nutrient, the old original tissue being discarded. Here it will grow (10A) as cultures consisting entirely of new-formed cells.

Blocks at the ends of the rows and any blocks traversed by branch traces or other imperfections are also avoided. All other sound blocks are removed one by one (Fig. 44[5], [6]) and immediately placed in a series of small (60-mm.) Petri dishes containing 10 ml. of liquid nutrient, not more than a dozen blocks being placed in each dish (Fig. 44[7]). When the excision has been completed, the explants are taken up with sterile forceps and inoculated into Petri dishes (Fig. 44[8]), bottles (Fig. 44[8A]), or tubes charged with nutrient agar, one end being pushed into the agar far enough so that the block will stand upright.

Growth from the explant will become visible in about ten days (Fig. 44[9], [9A]), first from the cambium, later from the phloem, and sometimes finally from medullary rays in the xylem. In about a month, the new callus should be large enough to be removed and placed directly on nutrient (Fig. 44[10], [10A]). Exactly the same schedule can be used for normal tissues from trees. This method has been successful with wood of elm, oak, beech, willow, pine, spruce, and many other trees, as well as with shrubby plants such as lilac, rose, and raspberry, and with vines such as grape and Virginia creeper.

SECONDARY CAMBIUMS AND PARENCHYMA. The same general principles apply to the isolation of secondary cambiums or of parenchyma from fleshy organs such as tubers. An aseptic surface is exposed by breaking (carrot, Fig. 45); tearing; or, when necessary, first disinfecting a surface

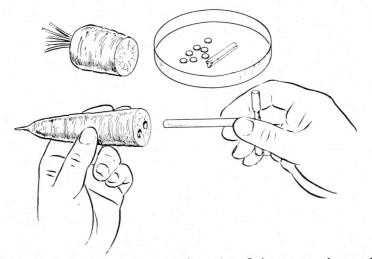

FIGURE 45. A method for preparing cultures from fleshy organs, tubers, and the like: In this case a carrot is represented. The carrot is washed but is not chemically disinfected. It is then broken. With a sterile cork borer, a series of cores which contain the cambium layer are removed. These cores are cut transversely into disks of uniform diameter and thickness, which are used as primary inocula.

area and then cutting it away (potato, for example). Then, with a sterile cork borer of 2- to 3-mm. diameter, a series of cores are removed and laid in a moistened Petri dish. With a scalpel or a specially designed cutter (Steward and Caplin, 1954), a series of transverse cuts are made in these cores, providing a series of comparable disks.

The most rapid and reliable growth will be obtained if these cores are extracted in such a manner that they contain the cambium. In the carrot, for example, they should be taken from a region at the boundary between the often dark orange core and the lighter-colored outer layers. Steward, however, prefers to prepare his cores from phloem tissues at some distance outside the cambium. These are very uniform and are nutritionally somewhat like "depleted" explants, requiring special nutrients to permit their immediate growth; this may be a distinct advantage in studies of growth stimulation (Steward and Caplin, 1954). Skoog has found the same advantage to a marked degree in tobacco pith (1951; Das, Patau, and Skoog, 1956).

There remain a number of special tissues. The intercalary meristems of grasses, rushes, and certain vines offer theoretical advantages in being easily isolated with relatively little trauma but have been little studied. The fleshy axillary (stipular) gemmae of *Marattia* and *Lycopodium* should be ideal cryptogamic material comparable in structure to the tubers of phanerogams; they have not yet been studied, so far as this author knows. The most important of these materials is the embryo proper, which has gained great significance in studies of the genetics of certain usually "sterile" hybrids and in shortening of the dormant period of grasses. Very young embryos have not been successfully grown by direct isolation, but, by the time the cotyledons have been fully initiated, in the early "torpedo" stage, they can usually be excised and grown quite readily. Once this stage has been identified in terms of days after fertilization, the young ovules can be removed. An incision at the micropylar end, if not too deep, will expose the embryo uninjured, and sharp pressure at the opposite end of the seed will eject the embryo (Fig. 46). In the case of monocotyledons, the scutellum can be dissected off and the embryo removed. In all these cases it is important that the embryo or tissue fragment shall not be allowed to become desiccated, and, when it is implanted, that it shall have adequate surface contact with the agar but shall not be covered by too deep a film of liquid.

Anthers and ovaries of flowers for cultivation as carried out by Maheshwari's group can usually be obtained in an aseptic condition without special sterilization, if they are removed before anthesis. For later stages it may be necessary to dip the flowers briefly into 95 per cent alcohol, just long enough to wet all surfaces, then to transfer them to a 10 per cent solution of Clorox (about 1 per cent final chlorine concen-

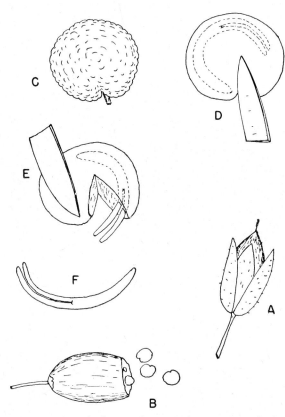

FIGURE 46. Preparation of plant embryos: The common chickweed (*Stellaria media*) is represented. The fruit (A) is about 6 mm. long. This is surface-sterilized and is then opened by a transverse cut and the seeds pressed out (B) onto a sterile glass plate moistened with nutrient solution. The seeds (C), which are about 1 mm. in diameter when ripe, are cut so as to remove a wedge, so placed that it does not intersect the enclosed embryo (D). Then, with the flat of the knife, pressure is applied at the micropylar end so that the embryo is forced out (E). These embryos (F) can be used as inocula, or the root can be removed for cultivation. The same general method applies to the removal of still younger embryos. (Compare Fig. 9[K].)

tration) for five minutes, then to wash them in sterile water. After this, further dissections can be carried out, or the members can be transferred direct to the culture medium.

These, then, are the methods of isolating animal and plant materials for cultivation. The methods outlined for animals apply equally to human materials.

Chapter 7

CLONING

A Special and Important Case

The original objective of tissue culture, as set forth in 1902 by Haberlandt, was to isolate, grow, and study *single cells*. For many years this proved an illusive ideal. It was not until half a century later that Sanford *et al.* (1948), by isolating single animal cells in capillaries and introducing the capillaries into preconditioned media, succeeded in obtaining clones. The principle that even the best of our nutrients are not fully satisfactory and must somehow be "conditioned" seems to be of universal applicability. Single cells can alter or "condition" the nutrient, provided their metabolic products can accumulate around each cell without being removed too rapidly by diffusion. Restriction of rate of diffusion seems to be necessary. In a compact tissue this is accomplished by the juxtaposition of many cells within a small space. Cells in isolation lack this cooperative factor and it must be provided in other ways. Sanford accomplished this in two ways: first, by placing each initial cell in a capillary, thus strictly limiting the amount of fluid in which diffusion occurred, and, second, by placing the capillaries in a nutrient preconditioned by growing massive cultures briefly therein and then removing the original cells by filtration. Puck *et al.* (1955, 1956) have accomplished the same objective, again in two ways: first, by providing a nurse layer which has been inactivated by treatment with X-rays, on which growing cells are then seeded, and, later, by growing isolated cells in dilute agar nutrient which served to slow the rate of diffusion. Dulbecco (Lwoff *et al.*, 1955) and Jones *et al.* (1960) accomplish the same objective by cultivation in microdrops under mineral oil, a method originated by Marchal and Mazurier (1944). Muir *et al.* (1954, 1958) have separated the nurse layer and the culture by a permeable membrane or filter paper. These methods will be outlined in more detail later.

The concept of "clones" is an old one in agriculture but is so little known in general biology that it may be best to define the term. Webster defines a *clone* as "the aggregate of individual organisms descended by

124

asexual reproduction from a single sexually produced individual." The best-known examples are among the vegetable crops: strawberries propagated by runners, potatoes multiplied from cuttings, or apple trees established by grafts. Less familiar are the colonies of wasps or aphids derived by parthenogenetic division of a single fertilized egg. A pair of monozygotic twins constitute a "clone." In terms of tissue culture, the descendants of a single cell, uncontaminated by other progenies, constitute a special sort of clone. In strict terms, any organism is a clone in the sense that all its cells are derived from a single fertilized egg, but this is true only when the individual cells rather than the whole are thought of as the "organism"; we should encounter no confusion from using the narrowed definition. The importance of the concept resides in the fact that, at least initially, all members of a clone have identical genetic constitutions and can be expected to behave in identical fashion in a given complex of environmental conditions. Although this quality is somewhat weakened by the tendency of cells in large numbers to undergo somatic mutations, the principle is nevertheless sound and important.

Sanford's method of isolating clones (Fig. 47) is irreproachable and has served to give important results. It is nevertheless too cumbersome

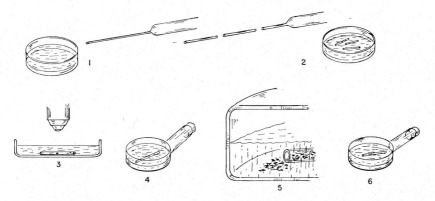

FIGURE 47. Cloning cells—Sanford's method: A healthy culture at the peak of its growth is agitated to form a suspension and is then taken up in fine capillary tubes which are broken into segments (1), (2). Under the microscope, these are sorted out and rebroken until only segments containing single cells are retained (3). A second culture in its logarithmic phase of growth is centrifuged at high speed, the fluid is placed in fresh flasks, and bits of the capillary containing single cells are inoculated therein, one cell per flask (4). As the cell multiplies within the capillary, it develops into a many-celled colony which finally spills out into the external, preconditioned nutrient (5), (6). The colony, derived from a single cell, can now be treated like any other mass culture. Although, when successful, this method is irreproachable, there are, in practice, many failures. The method has given important results but, because of its technical difficulty, has not come into common use. (Sanford *et al.*, 1948.) A modification of this method has been used with plant cells by deRopp (1955) with only moderate success.

and too dependent on individual skill and patience to become widely used. There are other methods which are more flexible. Two important methods both derive from studies by Dulbecco (Dulbecco and Vogt, 1954; Lwoff *et al.*, 1955) and are themselves applications of methods long current in bacteriology.

The first method has been perfected by Puck. A flask containing the desired strain of cells in its logarithmic phase of growth is selected; the nutrient is removed and replaced with a balanced salt solution lacking calcium and magnesium; and the culture is washed until as free as possible of loose ions of these substances. The wash fluid is then replaced with an 0.05 per cent solution of trypsin in the same calcium-magnesium-free solution and is placed in the incubator at 37° C. for five to ten minutes. Meanwhile a series of 60-mm. Petri dishes are charged each with 5 ml. of a growth medium, either a complete synthetic nutrient or, more commonly, such a medium fortified with 10–20 per cent of serum. A corresponding series of test tubes are similarly charged with 4.5 ml. of the same medium. When the original flask has incubated sufficiently to free the cells, it is agitated gently, the suspension is mixed by repeated pipetting, and, finally, an equal volume of nutrient is added to stop the action of the trypsin. The concentration of this suspension is then determined by counting in a hemacytometer (Fig. 48). A half milliliter is transferred to the first tube and mixed thoroughly; 0.5 ml. is taken from this and transferred to the second; and so on until a dilution of 1,000–2,000 cells per milliliter is reached, as calculated from the original count. This dilute suspension is then used in 0.1 ml. aliquots to inoculate the series of Petri dishes. If a salt solution with a high bicarbonate concentration has been used in preparing the nutrient, it will be necessary to place the Petri dishes in some form of CO_2 incubator to maintain their *p*H. If a special incubator is not available, an ordinary desiccator can be charged with CO_2 or with a reaction mixture of sodium bicarbonate–citric acid calculated to free the required amount of CO_2 and can then serve as a container for small numbers of cultures. If a nutrient of the Fell-Gaillard type is used, this should not be necessary. The dishes now contain 100 to 200 cells spread more or less evenly over the surface. They should be incubated undisturbed for a week or ten days. By this time each cell will, in theory, have given rise to a discrete colony. Clonal subcultures can be made by selecting an appropriate colony, placing over it a glass or metal ring the bottom of which has been coated with silicone, removing the nutrient occluded in the ring, and replacing it with a trypsin solution. When the cells are free, they are pipetted off and inoculated into fresh flasks.

This method is simple enough to be used routinely. It is reasonably effective, sufficiently so for most purposes, but it is not entirely reliable

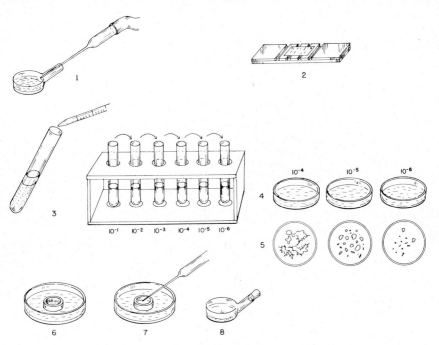

FIGURE 48. Cloning animal cells—Puck's method: A healthy culture is reduced to a fine suspension by moderate trypsinization (1), and the cells are counted in a hema-cytometer to determine their density (2). A series of dilutions are then prepared (3), and those having a calculated density of no more than about 100 cells per ml. are inoculated (4) onto plates containing either living cells inactivated by X-rays (nurse method) or a dilute agar which retards diffusion of metabolic products away from the cells and prevents mixing. These plates are incubated in a CO_2 incubator until visible, discrete colonies are formed (5). Under the microscope, an isolated colony is chosen, a steel or glass ring is placed over it (6), and the old nutrient is withdrawn and replaced by a trypsin solution (7). This will reduce the new, now clonal colony to a suspension which can now be taken up and inoculated into fresh flasks (8). (Puck and Marcus, 1955.) Modifications of this method have been used with plant cells by Muir *et al.* (1954, 1958), by Torrey (1957), and by Bergmann (1959, 1960).

as a method of cloning, since trypsinization may sometimes result in small clumps rather than single cells. Clonal origin can be established with certainty only when single cells have been selected under the microscope.

A second relatively simple method (Fig. 49), likewise due to Dulbecco, provides this guaranty. A series of fine Pasteur pipettes should first be prepared. These are initially drawn from 4-mm. tubing, using an ordinary Bunsen flame. Then, using a #18 hypodermic needle as a micro-burner, they are redrawn to provide tips of about 50 μ diameter. To 200 ml. of sterile liquid paraffin (light mineral oil) are added 20 ml. of nutrient and the whole is shaken thoroughly and placed in the incubator at 37° C. until clear. This may require several days. The lower half of

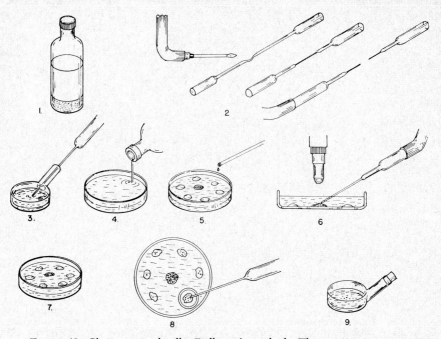

FIGURE 49. Cloning animal cells—Dulbecco's method: This requires two preparatory steps. A supply of sterile mineral oil is saturated with nutrient solution by shaking with a layer of nutrient and allowing to stand for a week at 40° C. (1). A series of very fine capillary pipettes are prepared, using a hypodermic needle as a gas burner (2). A healthy culture is reduced to a suspension by trypsinization as in the methods of Sanford and of Puck. A layer of sterile, nutrient-saturated mineral oil is poured into a Petri dish (4). A ring of drops of nutrient is placed around this dish (5), the nutrient sinking through the oil to the bottom. A drop of a cell suspension is placed at the center, also under the oil (3), (5). Then, under the microscope (6), single cells are taken up in a capillary pipette and transferred to the peripheral drops or to similar drops in other dishes. After incubation these will grow into clonal colonies (7). A suitable colony is chosen, surrounded by a glass or metal ring as in the Puck method (8), trypsinized, and taken up for use in inoculating new cultures (9) (Dulbecco and Vogt, 1954). A modification of this method has been used with plant cells by Jones *et al.* (1960).

a clean, sterile 60-mm. Petri dish is rinsed with ether; the ether is decanted; and, when dry, the dish is flamed briefly on the outside to make sure that no ether remains. The dish is filled to about half its depth with the nutrient-saturated mineral oil. Then, by means of a pipette, a series of drops of nutrient are placed on the surface of the oil, about 1 cm. apart and at the same distance from the edge of the dish. These drops will fall through the oil and come to rest on the bottom of the dish as discrete drops. Their volume should be adjusted so that they spread to about a 5-mm. diameter.

In the center of the dish is then placed a drop of dilute suspension of cells prepared by trypsinization. Under the binocular microscope and by means of the capillary pipette, single cells can be selected from the suspension, taken up in the pipette, and transferred one by one to the surrounding drops. When all drops have been charged, the dish is closed and placed in the incubator. A CO_2 incubator is not required, since the oil layer prevents loss of CO_2 from the drops. Colonies will develop within the drops of nutrient, from which they can be recovered by individual trypsinization. Such colonies are, of course, true clones and are not subject to the doubt always present after the earlier method.

Plant cells can also be cloned, although not as yet with the same ease and precision as animal cells. Trypsinization does not separate plant cells as it does animal cells, and, although some pectinases should theoretically serve this purpose, they have, in practice, so far proved to be too toxic (Tanaoki *et al.*, 1960). Versenes have recently been tried on animal cells with some success (Melnick *et al.*, 1955) and might succeed with plant materials. Many colonies will break up into single cells or small clumps if grown on a reciprocal shaker. Single cells can then be selected from such suspensions and transferred to suitable substrata. Bergmann (1959, 1960) has distributed them on dilute agar nutrient in Petri dishes, corresponding to Puck's plating method. Muir, Hildebrandt, and Riker (1954, 1958) have placed single cells on bits of filter paper which were in turn placed on top of established "nurse" cultures of the same or other sorts of cells. Torrey (1957) places single cells in a ring around a larger nurse culture. Jones *et al.* (1960) have placed cultures in drops under mineral oil, in this following the lead of Marchal and Mazurier (1944). Only by the last method have plant cells been grown in the absence of a nurse culture, and even in this case they have multiplied only when provided with a preconditioned nutrient, that is, with a once-removed nurse culture. In the hands of Steward, Mapes, and Smith (1958a, 1958b) and of Nickell (1956), propagations of multiple cultures in flasks or tubes have been obtained which are interpreted as having come from single cells. Single cells have indeed been shown to divide in such preparations, and all stages in the formation of colonies and of mature plants have been observed in selected examples, but, since, by the nature of the method, no individual can be followed through all its stages, the origins of such colonies and plants from single cells which had divided in isolation are still subject to the same uncertainty as are those of Puck. This question has recently been discussed by Torrey *et al.* (1962).

Chapter 8

MEASUREMENTS

The Assembling of Information

As we have said before, the chief aims of "tissue culture" are, first, the setting up of a group of conditions which shall adequately duplicate in simplified fashion all the *essential* features of the environment in which the organ, tissue, or cell lives within the body, in such manner that its behavior therein is quantitatively and qualitatively "normal," that is, similar to what it would have been in its natural environment, and, second, the study of the quantitative and qualitative changes which take place in the behavior of the cell, tissue, or organ when single elements of these conditions are altered or when cells or tissues are recombined in new ways. This gives us a measure of the importance and function of each characteristic of the environment in the economy of the material under investigation, permits us to sort out the significant from the purely fortuitous elements of behavior, thus simplifying our picture of the real organism, and should lead to a better understanding of behavior itself.

While a qualitative evaluation of resultant changes is an essential part of any set of observations, such evaluations, being largely descriptive, are of necessity subjective in character. They must inevitably fall short of the ideal requirements of scientific precision. Science rests on quantitative representation, even of changes in quality, and quantitation is essentially synonymous with measurement. It is thus natural that measurement should play a dominant role in cell-culture studies and that the accuracy, reliability, and significance of measurements should be major concerns of the student of the subject. What, however, are we to measure?

Living organisms, particularly those which, like most plants, are incapable of autonomous movement or which, like massive tissues and many tissue cells, are restricted in their movements, react visibly to changes in environment chiefly by changes in the character, velocity, and extent of growth. Growth consists of increase in either mass or complexity of one or more parts of the living material or its products. Which of these is to be measured will depend on available techniques. Increase in mass may be estimated in terms of linear dimensions; wet or dry weight; cell number or volume; rate of increase in cell number (mitotic index); increase of some vital constituent such as phosphorus, amino nitrogen, sugar, or nucleic acid; removal of some specific constituent such as phosphorus or sugar from the environment; or some metabolic measure such as respiratory rate. Increase in complexity may be measured by decrease in cell size or change in ratio between total mass and cell number. These are only examples.

Perhaps the simplest of all such methods is that applicable to root cultures. When in culture, roots do not undergo secondary thickening. As a result they ordinarily take up within a few millimeters of the growing point a diameter characteristic of the species and of the particular culture medium, and retain this diameter throughout the length of even very old cultures. The cross-sectional area is thus a constant and can be ignored in comparing measurements, so that length alone becomes an accurate measure of volume. Fiedler (1936), by parallel measurements and weighings of a series of cultures of different lengths, verified that length and weight bear a constant relation to one another. This, of course, takes no account of any branches which may form, but study has shown that within the one-week passage generally used for such cultures the error introduced is never more than 10 per cent and seldom more than 3 per cent, and this error is always negative in value (White, 1943a). Daily measurements can be made on a single culture without disturbing the culture and with an experimental error of less than 10 per cent. Growth curves can thus be established, and the environmental effects can be studied with a satisfactory degree of both precision and flexibility (Fig. 50). Growth is usually measured with a flexible plastic rule, either by bending the rule to approximate the curvature of the root or by washing the root up onto the side of the flask, where it can be laid out straight. Roots can, of course, be removed from the culture medium and laid out directly on a sterile rule, but the risk of contamination is great and the degree of accuracy obtainable without such removal is sufficient that the more precise method is seldom justified.

Unfortunately, no animal tissue is adapted to such simple methods except perhaps bone primordia. The nearest approach is that developed by Ebeling (1921) which is now seldom used. When animal-cell cultures such as fibroblasts are grown in plasma clots, either as hanging drops or in flasks, there is a regular increase in colony diameter, with a fairly sharp visible margin. If the image of such a culture is projected and traced at hourly, daily, or weekly intervals (Fig. 51) and the area of the consecutive images is measured with a planimeter, fairly regular and duplicable growth curves can be plotted (Ebeling, 1921; Parker, 1932). It is recognized that this method may err in making no distinction between cell

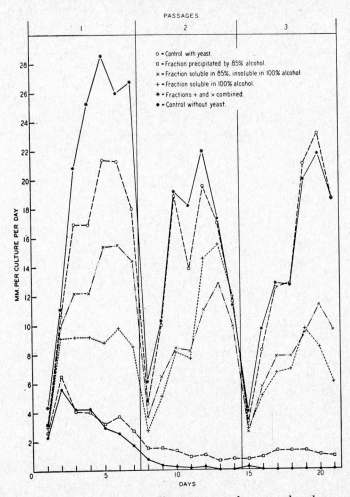

FIGURE 50. Graph showing in millimeters per culture per day the average day-to-day increments over three consecutive passages of seven days each of groups of ten clonally derived tomato roots grown in six nutrient solutions consisting of a standard salt-sucrose solution to which have been added six different fractions or groups of fractions of an extract of dried brewer's yeast. This shows the degree of precision obtainable in using excised roots in the study of nutritional problems. (White, 1937a, Fig. 8.)

increase and cell migration and in taking no account of changes in the thickness of the cultures. In cultures of fibroblasts these errors may be unimportant so long as the physical and chemical properties of two nutrients under comparison are not notably dissimilar, but these differences may, in fact, be so great as to completely vitiate the results. Even in cultures grown under standard conditions, the individual variations be-

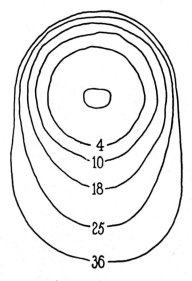

FIGURE 51. Projection tracing showing the increase in area of a strain of skeletal fibroblasts grown in a plasma clot for 36 days. (Parker, 1932, Fig. 4.)

tween different strains of cells may be fairly great (Parker, 1932). This method is, therefore, not a valid one for physiological studies (Cunningham and Kirk, 1942).

For plant-callus cultures and for many types of animal cultures, resort must be had to alternative methods. That most used for plant cultures has involved weight. Hildebrandt, Riker, and Duggar (1946) and Hildebrandt and Riker (1953) have taken the average initial weight of a group of explants and then sacrificed all cultures at the end of the experiment. This gives a measure of total increase but provides no growth curves. Caplin and Steward (1948, 1949) refined this by taking carefully standardized initial explants, setting up large numbers of cultures, and then sacrificing a standard small number of cultures (four, for example) at daily or biweekly intervals to obtain growth curves. Because of the small numbers represented by each point on such a curve, individual variations among cultures may play an important disturbing role. White (1953) and Heller (1953; Gautheret, 1959) have shown that it is quite possible to weigh such cultures at daily or biweekly intervals without destroying them. The culture is lifted out on a spatula or platinum loop, placed on a sheet of sterile filter paper to remove excess moisture, then transferred to a 2- × 2-cm. square of sterile paper (White, 1953) or to a special paper container (Heller, 1953) on the pan of a precision balance, weighed, and returned to its vessel. Under a dissecting shield this can be done aseptically, and growth curves can be established for single cultures. A similar method can be used for animal-organ cultures such as those of Fell (1931) and Gaillard (1948, 1953); it is not, however, applicable to the more minute animal-cell cultures except by pooling many cultures for each weighing (Meier, 1931).

Sanford *et al.* (1951) have long measured "growth" by preparing suspensions of known dilution from trypsinized cultures and counting these cells in a hemacytometer. This is usually done by treating the cells with citrate to dissolve the cytoplasm and isolate the nuclei, then staining these preparatory to counting. This method is reasonably accurate but tedious. Waymouth (1956a) introduced an equally accurate and much more rapid method. The flasks to be measured (usually Carrel 3.5-cm. flasks) are treated with trypsin or Versene until the cells separate easily. The suspended cells are then taken up *in toto* in Van Allen microhematocrit tubes, one tube for each flask. Centrifugation at a standard speed for a standard time, usually 30 minutes, causes the cells to settle with uniform packing into the stems of the hematocrits, where their volumes can be read directly. This method has proved reasonably accurate (Fig. 52), and the number of cultures which can be prepared and read simultane-

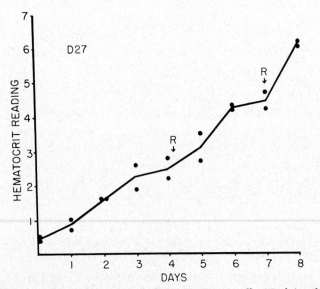

FIGURE 52. Increments of Strain L, Clone 929 mouse cells (Earle) cultivated in a defined nutrient, as measured by Waymouth's (1956a) microhematocrit method. Two flasks were measured on each of nine successive days. The closeness of the pairs indicates the reliability of the general methods of establishing cultures, the uniformity of growth, and the accuracy of the method of measurement. An increase from 0.5 to 6.5 units (13-fold) is recorded. "R" indicates renewal of nutrient; the acceleration of growth following each renewal is evident. A reading of 10 is the maximum recognizable by this method. Densities below 0.5 must be estimated either by direct count or by one of the electronic counters.

ously by a single observer is limited only by the capacity of the centrifuge. The method is not useable, however, for small numbers of cells. Below the effective range of the hematocrit, cells must be counted either by hemacytometer or in an electronic counter. The Coulter B counter will record individual cells above a previously chosen threshold (10,000 cells per milliliter, for example) and will also provide a measure of cell sizes. It is precise (Fig. 53), rapid, and not difficult to use (Harris, 1959).

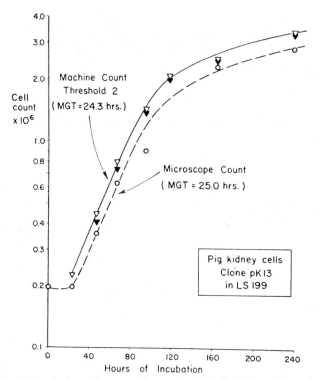

FIGURE 53. Comparison of counts of a series of flask cultures of pig-kidney cells made by means of a hemacytometer (dotted line) and by means of a Coulter B electronic counter (solid line). (Harris, 1959.)

Unfortunately the counter itself is expensive and, hence, beyond the reach of many laboratories.

None of these direct measurements distinguish between living material and its non-living products (cellulose, collagen, etc.) or between growth by increase in mass and growth by increase in complexity, which may involve an actual diminution in mass as it does in the first blastomere divisions of the mammalian egg. Indirect methods must be used to obviate these difficulties. One of these methods involves the determination of rates of cell division. If the thin areas of a culture are either fixed and stained or examined by phase contrast, cells in mitosis can be recognized. If the number of cells in a given mitotic stage, in metaphase, for example, is compared with the total number of living cells in a given area, a figure is obtained which, when compared with a corresponding figure for another culture, gives a measure of the relative rates of increase of cell number in the two cultures. While this can be done with fair precision, the method must be used with caution. Marginal areas, which are the only ones in plasma cultures in which such cells can be observed in the living state, are supposedly in a more active mitotic state than are those in the core of a massive culture, so a rapidly migrating, hence widely spread culture, may falsely seem to be growing more actively than a more compact one. Moreover, cell divisions tend to occur in cycles, so indexes obtained at different times of day on different cultures cannot safely be compared.

While the above methods are excellent for unorganized cultures such as the monolayers, suspensions, or loose aggregates which we find in cultures of fibroblasts, lymphocytes, epithelium, sarcomas, etc., they give little valuable information on the activity of organized cultures such as bone, nerve, or glands. For these some form of metabolic measure is likely to prove more important. Most such methods, although not all, require the destruction of the culture, hence the use of large numbers of cultures, to obtain significant results. This is true for determinations of amino nitrogen, nucleic acids, and sugars and for indirect measurements of respiration. Direct-method respiration studies can be made continuous (Barcroft method), and methods of this sort have been refined by Danes and Leinfelder (1951) (Cartesian diver method) so that studies can be made on single cultures. Interestingly enough these workers as well as Kirk *et al.* have shown that a high respiratory rate may be negatively correlated with both mitotic index and migration rate (Cunningham and Kirk, 1942).

Finally, as an extension of this last method, Brues, using animal cells (Wilson, Jackson, and Brues, 1942), has made use of the rate at which certain substances such as radioactive phosphorus and glucose disappear from the nutrient (Fig. 54). This gives excellent measures of metabolic activity and can be carried out without disturbing or destroying the cultures. Methods of metabolic study are more extensively treated in Paul's (1960) text than can be done here. The use of radioisotopes, either for emission counts or in the preparation of autoradiographs, has taken on great importance in the last few years; the methods employed are so specialized, however, that it does not seem wise to attempt to describe them in a work of this sort, and the author knows of no general review of the subject to which the reader might be referred.

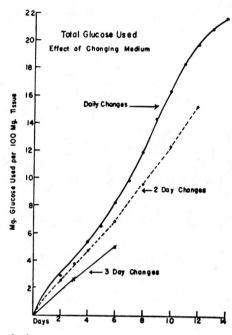

FIGURE 54. Graph showing amounts of glucose utilized, expressed as milligrams of glucose per 100 mg. of tissue per day, by three sets of chick-fibroblast cultures under three different experimental conditions. (Wilson, Jackson, and Brues, 1942, Fig. 1.)

Replications

Biological materials are, at best, variable. This is true even of clonal strains such as our 30-year-old strain of tomato roots or Carrel's old strain of fibroblasts. Recognizing the reality of such variability, even under well-controlled conditions, it is evident that such materials can seldom be treated as individuals but must in general be treated statistically. It is important, therefore, to decide, first, how many replications are needed to obtain significant results and, second, how wide a difference in result a given experimental variable must produce in a series of a chosen number of cultures before that difference can be considered to be due to this variable and not to chance. Decision on the first point involves a compromise between, on the one hand, the ideal of a very large number on which to base averages and, on the other hand, the number which can be practicably handled in a laboratory with restricted space and facilities and limited time. This whole problem is extensively treated in an Appendix to Gautheret's monumental *La Culture des Tissus Végétaux* (1959), to which the reader is referred. In dealing with root and callus cultures, this laboratory has chosen 20 as the standard number to be used in establishing averages, and each experiment is repeated at least three times. The testing of only two concentrations of three different substances in all possible combinations would involve 27 experimental combinations, hence 540 simultaneous cultures. To handle animal materials in such numbers is still more difficult. Even with these numbers a wide spread between experiment and control is usually necessary before results are statistically significant. One example, involving 400 root cultures, is given in the accompanying table.

In this group of experiments, each set of 20 root cultures grown under one set of conditions on a particular date is compared with 20 cultures grown either under a different set of conditions on the same date or else under the same conditions but on different dates. Here differences of up to 12 per cent between series (Nos. 1, 2, 3, 4, and 10) are without statistical significance and differences of 24 and 25 per cent (Nos. 5 and 8) are of doubtful significance (odds of less than 20 : 1 against the results being due to chance), while differences of 31 per cent or more (Nos. 6, 7, and 9) are highly significant (odds of more than 20 : 1 against the results being due to chance). This analysis indicates that, in experiments carried out in this way and using 20 replications in each experiment, differences of 30 per cent and over can, in general, be relied on to indicate the true difference in behavior and not merely fortuitous differences due to the variability of the material. Data on animal-cell cultures have usually not been presented in numerical terms, and it is doubtful if we are yet ready for their treatment with mathematical and statistical precision except by the nuclear-count method of Sanford et al. (1951), Waymouth's hematocrit method (1956a), or, best of all, the electronic-counter method (Harris, 1959). Under exceptional conditions, area measurements such as those carried out by Ehrmann and Gey (1953) may be effective.

Presentation of Results

The numerical data of an experiment should seldom be given in toto. Results are usually better presented in the form of graphs. Where average final results for total passages are desired, histograms will be most useful, while curves will be required where temporal trends are important. Where a number of simultaneous experiments are to be compared, the results may be presented in absolute units, for example, millimeters (Fig. 55[A]), milligrams, percentage of nitrogen, or Q_{0_2}. Where experiments are carried out on different tissues, or under conditions where uncontrolled variables in the environment may have as great or greater effects on growth rates as do the intentionally manipulated experimental variables, expression in absolute units may be meaningless. Since all cultures of one cell type react on the average in approximately the same way and to the same extent to most variables in the environment, uncon-

GROWTH OF EXCISED TOMATO ROOTS CULTIVATED EITHER SIMULTANEOUSLY OR CONSECUTIVELY IN DIFFERENT NUTRIENT SOLUTIONS, WITH A STATISTICAL ANALYSIS OF THE SIGNIFICANCE OF THE RESULTS †

No.	Series I	Series II	Mean total increments in mm. I	Mean total increments in mm. II	Difference I minus II	Diff. = % of I	t*	Odds in favor of difference being significant
1	Yeast June 7–14, 1938	Yeast June 9–16, 1938	77.7 ± 6.1	71.4 ± 6.1	6.4 ± 8.7	8	0.74	nil
2	Yeast June 9–16, 1938	Yeast June 19–26, 1939	71.4 ± 6.1	68.2 ± 6.6	3.2 ± 9.1	4	0.35	"
3	Yeast June 7–14, 1938	Glycine + 10^{-7} B$_1$ June 9–16, 1938	77.7 ± 6.1	79.7 ± 8.8	− 2.0 ± 10.7	3	0.19	"
4	Yeast June 7–14, 1938	Glycine + 10^{-7} B$_1$ June 9–16, 1938	71.4 ± 6.1	79.7 ± 8.8	− 8.3 ± 10.7	12	0.78	"
5	Yeast Jan. 19–26, 1939	Glycine + 10^{-9} B$_1$ Jan. 19–26, 1939	68.2 ± 6.6	51.6 ± 6.0	16.6 ± 3.6	24	1.93	< 20:1
6	Yeast Jan. 19–26, 1939	Glycine + 10^{-10} B$_1$ Jan. 19–26, 1939	68.2 ± 6.6	47.2 ± 4.2	21.0 ± 7.8	31	2.69	> 20:1
7	Yeast June 9–16, 1938	10^{-7} B$_1$ June 9–16, 1938	71.4 ± 6.1	34.0 ± 2.5	37.4 ± 6.7	52	5.58	> 100:1
8	10^{-7} thiamin (B$_1$) June 9–16, 1938	10^{-7} B$_1$ Jan. 19–26, 1939	34.0 ± 2.5	44.8 ± 3.7	− 10.8 ± 4.5	25	2.40	< 20:1
9	Glycine + 10^{-7} B$_1$ June 9–16, 1938	10^{-7} B$_1$ June 9–16, 1938	79.7 ± 8.8	34.0 ± 2.5	45.7 ± 9.2	58	4.97	> 100:1
10	Glycine + 10^{-7} B$_1$ June 9–16, 1938	Glycine + 10^{-7} B$_1$ Jan. 19–26, 1939	79.7 ± 8.8	82.3 ± 7.7	− 2.6 ± 11.2	3	0.23	nil

* t = ratio of mean differences to the standard deviation of the mean difference.

† Table 3, White, 1943a.

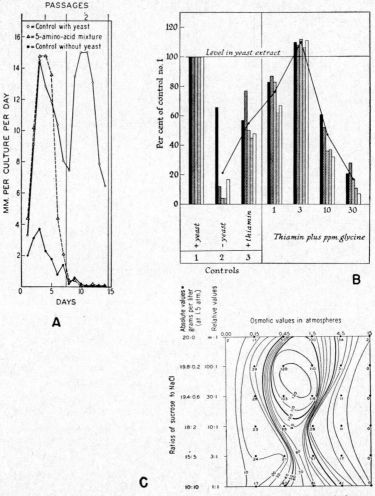

FIGURE 55. Three methods of presenting in graphic form numerical data on the increments of excised tomato roots: (A) Line graph representing increments in millimeters per culture per day over two seven-day passages under three sets of experimental conditions. (B) Histogram representing increments in terms of percentage of a control over five passages under six sets of experimental conditions. (C) Isopleth diagram showing total increments in millimeters of a series of cultures grown in 36 solutions representing the simultaneous variation of two sets of nutrient variables—osmotic value and ratio of sucrose to NaCl concentration. ([A] from White, 1943a, Fig. 45; [B] from White, 1939c, Fig. 4; [C] from White, 1942, Fig. 5.)

trolled as well as controlled, this difficulty can often be obviated by setting up a control in each series, treating this control always as the norm and comparing all other cultures within a series with the control. The percentage results can then be compared from one experiment to another, which could not be done with absolute values (Fig. 55[B]). Thus, in two series on the effects of vitamin B_6 (pyridoxine) on two different strains of roots using 1.0 ppm. pyridoxine as the only accessory organic substance (in addition to salts and carbohydrate) but carried out on two different dates, the series completed July 13, 1939, gave a numerical index of 58.6 mm. while that completed December 7, 1939, gave an index of only 21.8 mm., but the percentage values for the two were 60 and 62, respectively. While the use of percentages may be objected to on the grounds that it involves a subjective choice of standard, it is the only way in which non-simultaneous experiments can be compared and has proved very satisfactory as a method of presenting results. Three examples of graphic representation will serve to show the types found most useful (Fig. 55).

Interpretation

Results should, wherever possible, be presented in numerical form with a definite indication of the degree of accuracy and significance which can be attached to them. The interpretation of these results is the duty of the observer. It is necessary for him to take into account not merely the numerical data but also many qualitative features of the results which cannot be set down in numerical form. Interpretation involves the integration of many sorts of information which only the person who handles the cultures can have available. This is a subjective matter. How it is to be done is entirely personal and cannot be set down in any handbook. Yet it is in this, just as much as in the planning of an experiment and the recording of data, that a scientist shows his true caliber. It does not seem amiss, therefore, to emphasize its importance as well as its difficulty. And its importance makes it imperative that observation should *not* be left entirely to assistants.

Chapter 9

THE RESULTS

Applications of the Cultivation of Cells

The history of any biological method covers three phases which may or may not be concurrent. These are the development and perfection of basic techniques, the application of these techniques to already recognized problems, and the formulation of new and unforeseen applications. Harrison (1907) began with the second phase in this series, having before him a definite problem, the elucidation of the origin of nerve fibrils. Having solved that problem by relatively simple methods, he found no further incentive to perfect or expand the technique and turned to other problems amenable to other methods. Carrel, on the other hand, without a specific problem but with a less formulated concept of a vast field of problems, took this technique and perfected it to a very high degree (1912a, 1924). The application to new but specific problems passed to a third set of workers. Fell used it in studying bone-phosphatase activity (Fell and Robison, 1929, 1930, 1934) and local hypervitaminosis (Fell and Mallanby, 1952, 1953); Warburg, in studying tumor metabolism (1923; Warburg and Kubowitz, 1927; Lipmann and Fischer, 1932), Rivers, Haagen, and Muckenfuss (1929), Li and Rivers (1930), and, most recently, Enders (1952), Salk (1953), and others, in preparing vaccines; Murray and Stout (1942, 1947a, 1947b, 1954), in the diagnosis of tumors; Gey and Gaillard, in studies of endocrine function (Gey et al., 1938; Gaillard (1948, 1955); and many others. Since 1950 its use has expanded enormously. While it is not the function of this book to review these aspects of the field in detail, it may be well to indicate some of the directions which research has already taken and may be expected to take in the future.

Applications of the cell-culture technique to date have fallen for the most part into six categories: (1) cell nutrition—the degree and manner of dependence of a single cell, type of cell, or tissue on the chemical properties of the external medium; (2) cellular metabolism—those aspects of cellular behavior which have an internal origin and control; (3) hormone relations—the behavior of cells toward the specific products, other than nutrients, of other cells, and the function of cells in producing such products; (4) morphogenesis—the production of integrated patterns of development by the interaction of cells or groups of cells; (5) pathology—the response of cells and tissues to agents of extracellular origin which, being neither nutrients, hormones, nor normal self-metabolites, are injurious to the cells in question; and (6) genetics—the behavior of individual cells as bearers of specific inherent characteristics. All of these aspects of cellular activity may be, and many have been, studied in tissue cultures of both plants and animals.

Nutrition

Nutrition can mean many things. There is a basic nutrition necessary for survival. This requires a relatively simple set of formulas. The elements which a plant cell *requires* for survival are 15: oxygen, hydrogen, nitrogen, phosphorus, sulfur, calcium, potassium, magnesium, iron, zinc, copper, molybdenum, boron, and perhaps cobalt and iodine. Some investigators would add sodium and chlorine. Most of these elements must be supplied as inorganic salts. Certain ones—oxygen, hydrogen, nitrogen, carbon, and phosphorus—must, for some tissues, be combined in the forms of sugar and of certain vitamins. Oxygen must be available as a gas, and oxygen and hydrogen must be combined as water. The basic requirements for animal cells will be essentially the same, except that here the needs for sodium and chlorine are definite, and those for molybdenum and boron are less well established. Only through tissue-culture studies have all of these been firmly defined, although all could be inferred from earlier work. With plant tissues the first of such studies were done with roots (Fig. 56). Callus cultures were later shown to have essentially identical requirements. The studies of Lewis et al. (1911 *et seq.*) constitute an attempt to establish similar basic formulas for animal tissues, although even today it can scarcely be said that these formulas have been established with equal certainty and precision; in fact they could not be so established until the advent, within the past few years, of fully defined synthetic nutrients.

Once these basic lists are established, it becomes possible to pass to a second level—nutrition for growth. The lists will be the same as for survival but they must be elaborated. We must establish minimum and optimum levels, and ranges of suitable concentrations. This, likewise, was first done for roots, especially by White (1934a, 1943a), then for callus cultures by Riker (Hildebrandt *et al.*, 1946 to date) and by Heller (1953), and most recently for certain animal cells, especially by Waymouth (1956b, 1959), Eagle (1955a, 1955b), Evans *et al.* (1956a, 1956b), and others. The absolute concentrations vary enormously, for example, from about $10^{-2} M$ for calcium and magnesium to less than $10^{-11} M$ for molybdenum and cobalt, yet the acceptable range is about the same for all—from about 0.5–5.0 times the optimum.

For plant tissues the organic requirements are, with few exceptions, quite simple. This is not true, or at least we do not believe it to be true, for animal tissues. The synthetic capacities of animal cells do not seem to be so great, and with these cells it is necessary to enter the metabolic

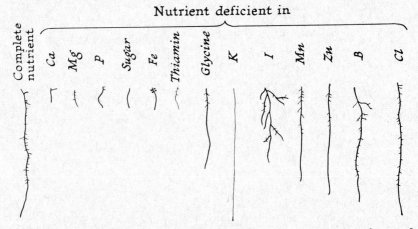

FIGURE 56. Effects on growth of excised tomato roots of omitting single ingredients from an otherwise complete nutrient. (White, 1943b.)

pathways at levels of greater complexity. Where plant cells will, in the presence of sugar, thiamine, and pyridoxine, transform inorganic nitrate into amino acids and thence into protein, animal cells apparently cannot make this first synthesis and must be fed ready-made amino acids and perhaps purines, nucleotides, fatty acids, and more complex molecules. This question is at present under study and cannot be said to be by any means fully resolved. Parker, Morgan, Evans, Eagle, Swim, Waymouth, and others are currently active contributors to these studies.

Once the basic requirements, the optimum levels, and the alternate pathways for survival and growth are established, it becomes possible to proceed to a third level, that of differentiated *function*. Thyroid cells can survive and grow with a minimum of iodine; in fact no clear *requirement* for iodine has been established for thyroid cells, yet the normal function of thyroid tissue includes the synthesis of thyroxine, which in turn requires the assimilation of large quantities of iodine. This sort of question has as yet been scarcely touched; it was indeed inaccessible in the absence of defined nutrients. That such questions can be approached, even by older methods, is clear from the brilliant work of Fell and Mellanby with vitamin A, which will be discussed in some detail under the heading of morphogenesis. Suffice it to say that here is probably still one of the most fertile fields for future research.

Metabolism

Tissue metabolism has been intensively studied in the past 30 years in many laboratories, through the use of tissue slices. In this respect Warburg, Keilin, Krebs, Lipmann, and Potter are among the outstanding names associated with animal tissues; Blackman, Kostytchev, Priestley, Steward, Goddard, and Thimann have been similarly noteworthy with plant tissues. These studies have, of course, dealt almost entirely with tissues which had been subjected to massive trauma and were surviving under conditions of incipient death; they can scarcely be considered to have represented "normal" tissues in any precise sense. Valuable though these contributions have been, it seems probable that their value might be still further enhanced by repetition with tissue cultures which are stabilized in relation to their environment and are either growing and functioning or at least capable of growth and function under suitable modification of the environment. In the study of respiration in tissue cultures, a beginning was made long ago by, for example, Warburg and Kubowitz (1927) and Lipmann (1932, 1933) with animal cells and by Plantefol (1938; Plantefol and Gautheret, 1939) and White (1945) with plant cells. One of the outstanding examples is Fell and Robison's studies of phosphate metabolism in isolated bones in watch-glass culture (1929, 1930, 1934), an approach matched by Street's work (1950) on phosphorylation in excised plant roots grown in culture. An interesting example is Dawson's demonstration (1942) of the site of synthesis of nicotine, not in the leaf where it accumulates in large quantities but in the root where it does not accumulate. This was followed by other studies with roots (West and Mika, 1957; Solt et al., 1960) and on the metabolism of callus cells (Weinstein et al., 1959). These possibilities have been exploited even less than have those of studies of cell nutrition. They represent an open field.

Hormone Relations

The role of plant hormones in tissue culture is so closely bound with the problems of morphogenesis that—except for discussion of the demonstration of hormone synthesis in excised tissues, in roots by van Overbeek (1939), and in callus tissues, especially tumor tissues, indirectly by White and Braun (1942) and deRopp (1947, 1948) and directly by Kulescha and Gautheret (1948)—little need be said here. The problems with animal tissues are both more complex and more important. Attempts have been made to demonstrate the production of hormones by glandular tissues grown in vitro. Thyroid tissues apparently do not synthesize thyroxine in vitro; at least thyroid tissues grown in vitro and implanted into thyroidectomized amphibian larvae do not induce metamorphosis (Carpenter, 1942), yet this conclusion is of doubtful validity since the tissues were grown in nutrients of admittedly low iodine content. Of greater reliability are the positive results obtained by Gaillard (1948, 1953, 1955) and by Martinovitch (1955) with ovarian, adrenal, and parathyroid tissues.

Tetany is a well-known symptom of parathyroid deficiency which may arise from damage to the glands by disease, or from their removal either intentionally in cases of malignancy or accidentally in operations on the thyroid. In any of these cases the deficiency generally requires continued replacement therapy. On the other hand, parathyroid hyperfunction due to benign or malignant hypertrophy is often accompanied by general destruction of bone throughout the body, with accompanying accumulation of calcium in the blood. It had long been presumed that both sorts of symptoms were due to indirect effects of excess or deficiency of parathyroid hormone in the blood. Gaillard showed (1955, 1957) that, if parathyroid cells are grown in tissue culture and then placed in contact with fragments of bone, either in culture or in vivo, as can be done by placing cultures on the exposed frontal bone of chick embryos *in ovo*, there is a *direct* attack of bone by migratory parathyroid cells, without hormonal intervention. If, on the other hand, parathyroid is grown in tissue culture to produce considerable masses of glandular tissue and the cultures are preadapted by cultivation in serum drawn from a particular victim of parathyroid tetany and then are grafted into the axillae of the patient, they may, if the patient is young (under twenty-five), establish active grafts which secrete parathyroid hormone and have often produced permanent remission of symptoms. Ovarian insufficiency has been treated in similar fashion with some success. And the method has been used in analysis of the metabolism of the adrenal cortex (Schaberg, 1955; Schaberg and de Groot, 1958). These studies open up great possibilities not only for the analysis of theoretical problems but for clinical therapy as well. The exploration of these possibilities has been scarcely more than touched to date.

Morphogenesis

At the beginning of this volume, it was suggested that the technique of cultivating excised tissues had its chief *raison d'être* and gave its greatest promise in the study of the origins of form and function, that is, in the problems of morphogenesis. Harrison's original problem, which led to the first in vitro cultivation of animal cells—whether the nerve fibrils originate *in situ* from the inervated cells or their products, or whether they originate *ab extra,* by growth from the distant ganglia—was a morphogenetic problem. So was Robbins' original problem—whether the root was dependent on the leafy portion of the plant for anything more than its basic carbohydrate nutrition. So likewise was the problem—what is the nature of the stimulus by which crown-gall organisms or their products induce abnormal proliferation of the host cells and ultimately autonomy and malignancy—which led the author of this volume to undertake the development of a plant-tissue-culture technique. The number of problems which it should be possible to attack by this means is legion. And it is in this field and in pathology that the cultivation of excised tissues has made its most spectacular contributions in the past two decades, in both the animal and the plant fields.

The developmental and behavioral patterns in higher animals are greatly influenced by metabolic products known as "hormones." But how do these effects come about? A defect in the pituitary causes abnormal development of the long bones of the body. Is this a direct effect on the bone cells? That can be tested only in cell cultures. The nearest approach was in the experiments of Fell and Mellanby (1952) in which ossification was reversed and the cartilage matrix finally left naked when mouse or chick tibias were cultivated in hyper-A-vitaminotic media (Fig. 57). Certain of the adrenal hormones and their relatives, such as cortisone, have marked effects in relieving arthritis. Is this a change in degrees or patterns of ossification or in the texture of interosteal tissues? If the latter, is its origin neurogenic (antihypertensive), osmotic, or something else? Again, if the effect is a direct one, only cell-culture methods will elucidate its nature.

Plant morphogenesis presents a similar picture. The generalized plant hormone, "auxin," originally studied for its orientation effects (photo- and geotropism) has subsequently come to be looked upon as an important morphogenetic factor. It seems to induce the differentiation of roots from tissues which rarely if ever produce roots, to control the formation and development of buds, to influence the abcission of leaves and of fruits, to initiate the activity of cambium, to regulate the specific branching habit of plants, to mediate between genes and growing tissues in controlling the erect versus procumbent habit and in producing dwarfness, and to take part in the formation of root nodules. It has been shown to be one of several factors involved in the induction of plant tumors; and it has been shown to control the differentiation of vascular strands induced by in-grafted buds. The mechanism of some of these effects can certainly best be studied by use of tissue-culture methods. If auxin is truly a specific root-forming hormone, it should be possible to set up conditions under which its local application to an unorganized callus culture would regularly induce the local formation of roots. The cell-

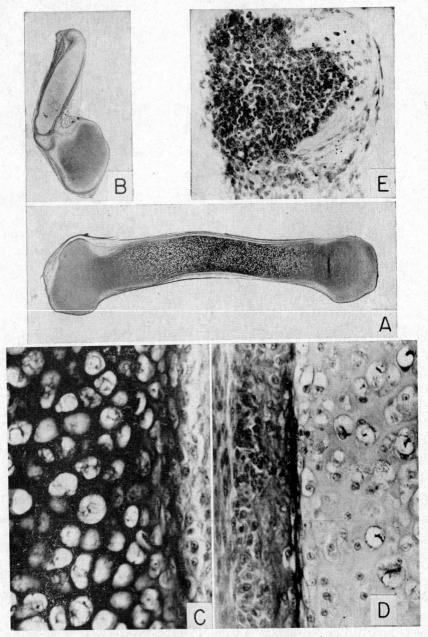

FIGURE 57. (*Explanation on opposite page.*)

culture technique seems to offer possibilities for the analysis of these relations under conditions relatively free of uncontrollable variables. The nearest approach to date is the work of Skoog (1951) and his group on the interrelations of auxin, kinetin, phosphate, adenine, and carbohydrate (Fig. 58).

This theory of specific inducing substances, however, is countered by a considerable amount of evidence that the formation of organs may also be controlled, to some extent at least, by concentration gradients of non-specific substances, hence by polar (physical) as well as chemical relationships. The cell-culture technique thus offers a means of approach to the phenomenon of polarity mentioned at the beginning of this book in connection with the work of Vöchting, Goebel, and others, which was not previously available. Priestley attributed the formation of cambium in radial plant bodies to a radially distributed hydrogen-ion gradient (1928). Rosene and Lund (1937) have shown that there is a corresponding electrostatic-potential gradient which can be modified by imposing artificial oxygen-hydrogen gradients. White has shown that an oxygen gradient may be correlated with the response by which undifferentiated callus cultures are induced to form stems and leaves (1939b). White (1938b) and Rosene (1941) have shown that there is a hydrostatic flow correlated with the electrostatic gradient along excised and intact roots. But it is as yet quite undecided which of these gradients—of pH, of redox-potential, of electrostatic potential, of hydrostatic potential, and of tendency to differentiate—is primary and which secondary. It should be possible in cell or tissue cultures artificially to impose or modify any or all of these gradients, except the last, along controlled spatial axes and thus to determine with which other gradients they bear a causal relationship. Brachet (1937) has applied this method in animal embryology to study the effects of imposed oxygen gradients. Huxley (1926), Gilchrist (1928), and Vogt (1932) have applied it to the study of temperature gradients. Weiss (1929) has studied the orientation of animal-cell cultures in response to lines of tension in the medium. Fife and Frampton (1936) applied it in plant pathology to the study of the causal factors

←————————————————————————————

FIGURE 57. Effects of Vitamin A nutrition on the differentiation of bone: (A)–(D) Femurs of six-day chick embryos. (A) Control femur grown for nine days in a standard plasma–embryo extract medium. (B) The opposite femur from the same chick, grown in an experimental medium fortified with vitamin A. Note the complete degeneration of the shaft. (C) A section through the diaphysial region of (A). (D) The corresponding region of (B). (E) Terminal cartilage of a fetal mouse radius grown for four days in a hyper-A-vitaminotic medium. A crescent of cartilage at the right was damaged (killed?) in excision and has remained unchanged. In the remainder of the culture, however, the matrix has completely disappeared and the liberated chondroblasts, which appear healthy, are lying free on the surface of the nutrient substratum. (A) and (B) × 19; (C) and (D) × 400; (E) × 220. (Fell and Mellanby, 1952, Figs. 2–4, 22.)

involved in the orientation of a parasitic insect's proboscis in the tissues of the host, with brilliant results.

Pomerat has demonstrated the importance of this matter of organization in a striking way. Taking a culture of cat brain and growing it in a dilute plasma clot on a cover slip in a roller tube it is possible to establish

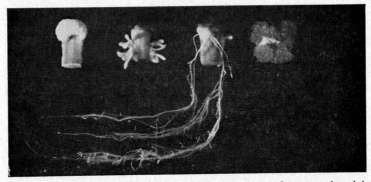

FIGURE 58. Effects of varying the concentrations of adenine and indoleacetic acid on the growth in vitro of bits of tobacco pith. From left to right: control showing moderately compact callusing; adenine, 40 mg. per l., showing production of buds but no roots; indoleacetic acid, 0.08 mg. per l., showing production of roots only without buds; and a combination of both adenine and indoleacetic acid, in which neither roots nor buds have formed but are replaced by a massive, loose hyperhydric callus. (Skoog, 1951, Fig. 3A, captions corrected.)

a culture which, when it reaches a diameter of 3–4 mm., becomes "stabilized." It takes on a definite pattern, with large "protective" cells oriented in radial fashion but with a crenelated margin at the outside. Next to these is a ring of smaller glial cells which are generally oriented tangentially, forming a fairly compact ring of cells. The center is traversed by

———→

FIGURE 59A. Structural organization in culture—a culture isolated from the cerebellar folia of a newborn kitten: At the upper left is a picture of a 41-day-old culture grown on a cover-glass strip inserted in a roller tube, × 5. The figure below represents the area blocked out in this picture and is reproduced × 40. The four figures at the right are representative of the regions lettered and are × 200. At the margin (a) there are large epithelioid cells which anchor the colony to the plasma clot. These are believed to be pial in origin. The darkly stained cell is probably a neuron of the stellate type. The submarginal zone (b) contains many closely packed astrocytes and occasional neural strands. The dark-stained cell at the center is a granule cell. Below this (c) is a region in which the clot is markedly liquefied, characterized by a loose glial organization with argentophilic cells believed to be Golgi Type II neurons. The center of the culture (d) is made up of crisscrossed fibers, Purkinje cells, and glial cells. The over-all pattern is relatively stabile, the epithelioid marginal cells and the neural fibers showing little change from day to day, yet cinematographs show that the glial cells are constantly moving about like pedestrians in a busy city. The regular development of this pattern suggests the possibility of analyzing complex patterns in vitro in terms of "societal cytology." (Bodian technique. Published by permission of C. M. Pomerat from unpublished data.)

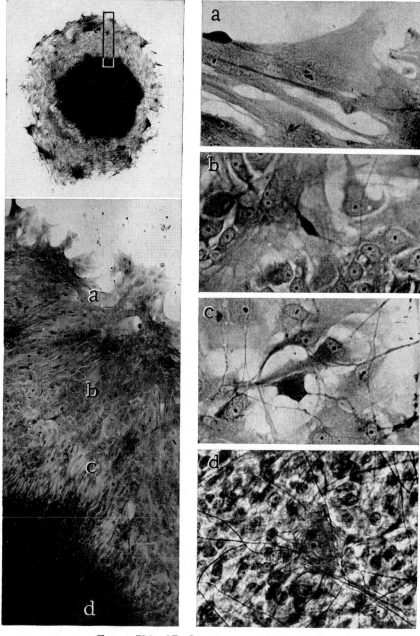

FIGURE 59A. (*Explanation on opposite page.*)

radial or randomly anastomosing long strands of nerves, and interspersed with these there is a constantly moving, circulating mass of fibroblasts, lymphocytes, and glial cells (Fig. 59A). Motion pictures show that all of these, with the exception of the nerves, are in a constant state of flux and that there is a constant traffic across this central area, an exchange between center and margin and around the margin. Yet the general pattern is stable for weeks on end. The pattern appears to be a matter of organization, and the culture is itself a complex, well-integrated organism. Plant-callus cultures, though lacking the possibility of internal movement, sometimes show a surprisingly similar over-all pattern of organization (Fig. 59B).

The method of transplantation, developed to a high degree by Harrison and Spemann, has proved especially fruitful in the study of problems of organization. The technique of transplanting *Avena* coleoptile tips or agar blocks containing extracts from such tips, developed consecutively by Boysen-Jensen (1910), Paál (1914), and Went 1928), is essentially a comparable method, the coleoptile or agar block acting in the same way as did Spemann's organizers. The method of cultivating tissues of endocrine glands in the serum of an anticipated recipient, and then implanting the cultures into the source of the serum, developed by Stone *et al.* (1934a, 1934b) and by Gaillard (1948) is an extension of this approach, as is the transplanting of excised buds into plant-tissue cultures by Camus (1949) and Wetmore and Sorokin (1955).

These approaches have been given a new level of precision in two studies which are worth mentioning. The nature of the stimulus by which certain organs such as the kidney are induced to form at specific sites has long interested investigators. Grobstein (1955, 1956) has shown that, if a culture of unorganized mesoderm is prepared on one side of an ultrafine filter and bits of apparently indifferent ectoderm from the regions which would later give rise to nephros or to salivary gland are planted on the other side, the mesoderm can be induced to organize into the appropriate organ at will (Fig. 60). This establishes the fact that

→

FIGURE 59B. Structural organization in culture—A culture isolated from the procambial region of an individual of the hybrid tobacco *Nicotiana glauca* × *N. Langsdorffii:* At the upper right is a horizontal section through an eight-week-old culture, × 10. The two pictures below are from the area blocked out in this picture and are reproduced × 70. The four figures at the left are representative of the regions lettered and are × 435. At the margin are many large cells (a) which arise by hyperhydric enlargement of parenchyma cells and are apparently moribund. At (b) large cells have divided, and at (c) division has become still more active, forming nests of dense, meristematic cells. In the center of the culture, on the other hand, the cells are stabilized and in some cases (d) have differentiated into incipient conducting strands of scalariform cells. Such a pattern is repeated in each culture and shows the tendency to organize into societies of cells with some segregation of function. (Saffanin-Delafield's haematoxylin. From White, 1939a.)

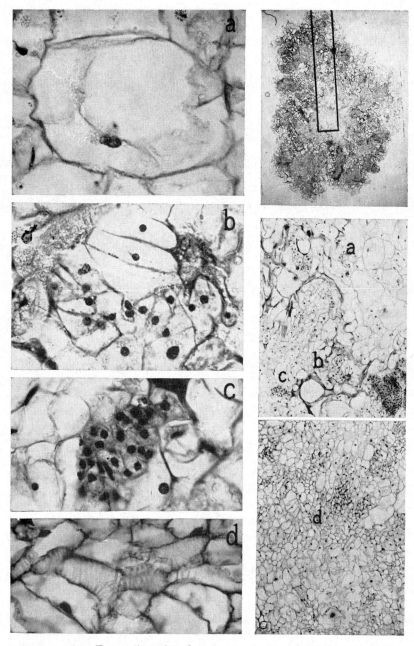

FIGURE 59B. (*Explanation on opposite page.*)

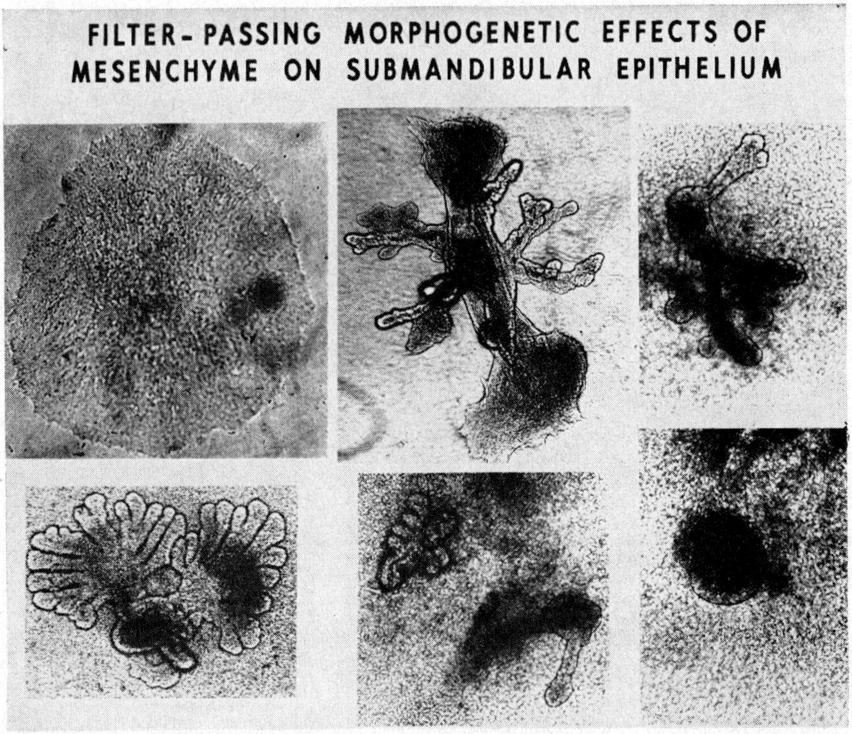

FILTER-PASSING MORPHOGENETIC EFFECTS OF MESENCHYME ON SUBMANDIBULAR EPITHELIUM

FIGURE 60. Controlled morphogenesis in isolated mouse tissues: Upper row, left—submandibular epithelium placed on a nutrient substratum without other tissue. It has developed as an undifferentiated sheet. Center—the same tissue, in the presence of a bit of spinal cord, has developed into a group of recognizable kidney tubules. Right—the same tissue, when separated from the spinal cord material by a millipore filter, has likewise organized into kidney tubules, but the organization is less well defined. Lower row—the same tissue when placed in contact with a bit of submandibular mesenchyme has developed into a well-organized salivary gland. Center—when epithelium and submandibular mesenchyme are separated by a millipore filter, the gland induction is less clearly defined but is not obliterated. Right—if epithelium and mesenchyme are separated by a perforated cellophane membrane which is impermeable to diffusable metabolic products except at the pores, induction is limited to the region above the pore; the surrounding epithelium is without organization. (Clifford Grobstein.)

protoplasmic continuity is not necessary for induction, and places an upper limit on the size of the diffusible molecules responsible for induction. It does not yet identify these substances, but it does narrow the possibilities.

In quite a different direction the organization of the complex known as a "nerve," especially the role of the auxiliary "Schwann cells," presents intriguing problems. Electron micrographs have shown that the nerve fiber is surrounded by a sheath made up of multiple layers which form a continuous spiral as if wrapped or spun around the nerve (Ben Guren, 1956). The nucleus of the Schwann cell is imbedded in the outer-most layer of this sheath. Murray and Peterson, using hanging-drop cultures of nerves and following them by serial photographs over several days, showed that the Schwann-cell nucleus does indeed circle the nerve slowly as it spins its web (Fig. 61). More recently, Pomerat (1959),

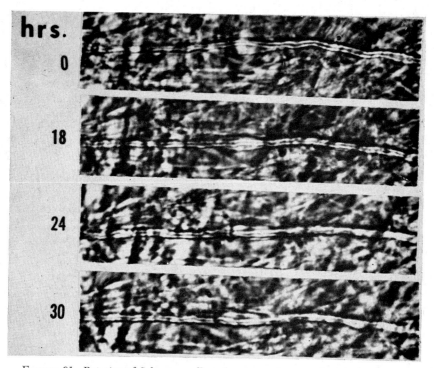

FIGURE. 61. Rotation of Schwann-cell nucleus around a neural axon—four consecu-tive photographs of a single preparation: At 0 hours the nucleus at the center is behind and slightly below the center of the axon; at 18 hours it is directly behind; at 24 hours it has moved to a position slightly above center; at 30 hours it is resting on top of the axon. It has thus rotated through about 90° in 30 hours. × 800. (Edith Peterson.)

using a more refined perfusion technique (Rose *et al.*, 1958) and cine-micrographs, has been able to demonstrate the discontinuous, pulsatile nature of this spinning movement.

Another interesting approach to the problem of organization has come from the recently developed methods of tissue dissociation by treatment with trypsin (Rous and Jones, 1916; Moscona, 1952). If kidney tissue is dissociated and the cells are allowed to grow in flask cultures, they will reorganize into simple tubules. If kidney cells of two unrelated species such as mouse and duck are mixed, they will come together to form chimerical tubules, species differences offering no barrier to successful coordination (Wolff, 1954, 1957). If, on the other hand, heart cells and kidney cells are mixed, they will sort themselves out to form separate organization centers, the one exception so far noted being that epithelium of pericardial origin can serve equally well in establishing the capsule around kidney, ovary, or other organs. Unfortunately, we do not as yet have satisfactory methods of disaggregating and reaggregating plant cells for comparable studies.

Another field is the transplantation or explantation of eggs and young embryos. In animals this has involved the transplantation of an ovum (fertilized or unfertilized) from one female to another (mouse, rabbit). This has been done either to overcome physiological problems in the donor, such as tendency to early abortion, or to study the relative importance of hereditary versus maternal environmental factors in subsequent development. This second matter has not been studied in plants, but a great deal of important work involving cell-culture methods has been done on the first.

It has in general not proved possible to grow plant embryos outside the ovary at the early stages desired. Nevertheless an extension backward in terms of developmental stages has been attained with both plants and animals by excising not the embryo or egg but the embryo sac, ovule, or ovary. With plants, Nitsch (1951) early developed methods of growing fruits in vitro. Adapting his methods, Maheshwari and his school have grown in vitro a considerable variety of fruits, ovaries, and seed primordia, have followed the development of embryos divorced from the grosser controls of the plant as a whole, and in many cases have obtained viable progeny, thus opening up a whole new field of early morphogenesis (Anantaswamy Rau, 1956; Chopra, 1958; Maheshwari, 1958; Maheshwari and Lal, 1958; Sachar and Baldev, 1958; Ranga Swamy, 1958). Similar methods have been applied to the study of male sporogenesis by cultivation either of pollen mother cells or of whole anthers (Vasil, 1957).

Correspondingly Gaillard, while unable as yet to carry animal eggs to complete embryogenesis in vitro, has been able to cultivate bits of excised ovaries and to follow the stages of oogenesis imbedded in these simplified tissue systems. Stevens (1960) has made a significant contribution by placing not normal eggs but disaggregated teratomatous tissues of the mouse in culture or in the peritoneal cavity and following their development into embryoid bodies simulating embryos of about the five-day stage (Fig. 62). These are significant beginnings and only require further perfection of techniques to attain much more precise and more varied goals.

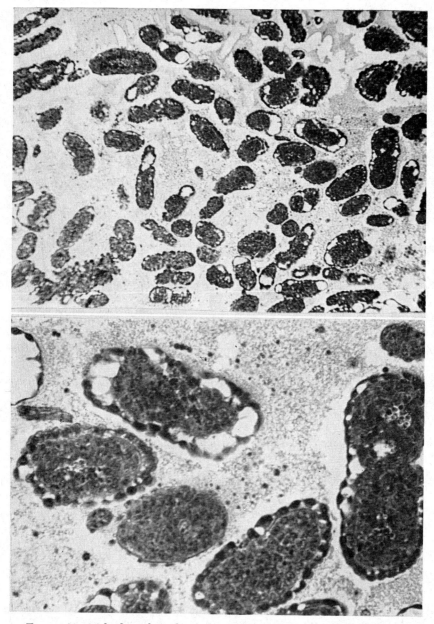

FIGURE 62. Multiple embryoids of the mouse: Tissues of a testicular teratoma (a hereditary abnormality) were disaggregated by treatment with trypsin. The cell suspension was then injected into the peritoneal cavity of a healthy mouse of the same genetic strain. Each cell has formed an embryoid body that develops by stages which are relatively normal up to the equivalent of about the fifth day of gestation; after this point, development becomes abnormal and teratoid. (Leroy C. Stevens.)

Pathology

A great many problems in both gross and cellular pathology, but especially in the latter, can best be approached at the cellular level. One of these problems of great current importance in the use of either true cell cultures or surviving tissues is that of the production and evaluation of vaccines. Li and Rivers produced a vaccine of vaccinia virus in vitro in 1930. White (1934b) used excised root cultures for propagating tobacco mosaic virus in vitro, titrating its progressive migration in growing tissues (Fig. 63), and with Stanley (1938) demonstrated that the

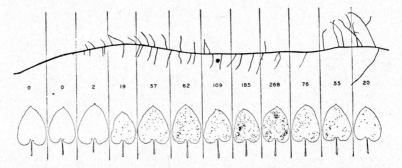

FIGURE 63. Titration of aucuba mosaic virus propagated in excised tomato roots grown in vitro: A root was isolated from a systemically infected plant so that it carried the virus permanently in all parts. After being cultivated for 25 passages, a typical root about 120 mm. long was divided into 10-mm. segments and each segment was crushed and rubbed into a leaf of *Nicotiana glutinosa*. The number of local lesions produced at the end of 36 hours (numbers) gives a measure of the number of free virus particles per segment. The virus concentration is very low in the rapidly growing apex, high in the maturing regions 8–10 cm. back of the tip, and apparently low in the oldest basal region. Since, however, this last is the region in which massive "striate bodies" make their appearance, this apparent drop is probably no more than a result of aggregation of many units into single masses. (White, 1943a, Fig. 59.)

process of virus multiplication in a polyvalent virus is independent of host species and of the photosynthetic mechanisms. A corresponding technique has recently become very important indeed in the propagation and study of a great many animal and human viruses (Enders, 1952) and in the preparation of vaccines against them. Since 1950 this approach has begun to fan out into a vast array of applications. The details of the effects of viruses as cytotoxic agents are gradually becoming clear by such methods. The mode of attack of viruses, their intracellular multiplication, and their release from infected cells, first studied in bacteria and their phages, are now being elucidated by a combination of the methods of cell culture and electron microscopy, applied to human and other animal cells grown in vitro.

An illuminating example is that of the viral agent, the so-called milk factor, responsible for the pseudogenetic transmission of breast cancer in certain strains of mice. This case is particularly instructive, since it exemplifies a wide range of problems to be overcome. The cultivation of mammary-gland tissue had long proved unrewarding because of the presence both of fatty tissue which diluted the small quantities of accompanying functional secretory epithelium and of fibrous tissues whose exuberant growth as fibroblasts tended to further swamp any epithelial growth which might escape the fatty dilution. Lasfargues overcame the first by selective predigestion with lipase (1957a, 1957b). The second he overcame by preliminary digestion with collagenase, followed by disaggregation with trypsin. The cells could then be spread out so that each cell, whether fibroblast or epithelium, established its own discrete colony, unhindered by colonies of the other sorts. From these it was a simple matter to select pure strains of glandular epithelium for further study. These pure epithelium cultures could be inoculated with the milk-factor virus separated by filtration from carrier mammary cells. The titer of virus obtained from such cultures, undiluted by functionally inert (so far as virus was concerned) fatty and fibrous tissues, proved to be much higher than in any normal body tissues. These cultures have proved to be excellent material in which to study virus-host relations. The origin and the dual nature of the virus particle—a central core of about 30 mμ diameter (the virus proper) enclosed in a 100 mμ vesicle consisting of material pinched off from the host cell membrane—have been elucidated in considerable detail by means of electron micrographs of such cultures (Fig. 64).

On the plant side Morel (1944, 1948) has used tissue cultures of grape as a substratum on which to cultivate the fungus causing grape mildew (*Plasmopara viticola*) (Fig. 65). Hotson has made similar cultures of *Gymnosporangium* (1953; Hotson and Cutter, 1951).

Many processes of parasitism should be studied in this way. Another aspect of the value of such cultures is in the extensive programs of screening both organic and inorganic toxic agents, carcinogens, steroids, carcinostatic agents, and the like (Pomerat and Severinghaus, 1954). One of the most promising approaches is the use of perfusion-chamber cultures in the study of antihistaminics and similar pharmacologically active agents (Painter, Pomerat, and Ezell, 1949).

Similar approaches have recently been developed with plant materials. An interesting one is that of Melchers and Bergmann (1957, 1959). Certain chemical agents had been introduced into agricultural practice as means of combating viral infections, especially tobacco mosaic disease, in tobacco and tomato plants. Using excised tomato roots and introducing controlled concentrations of these agents directly into the nutrient,

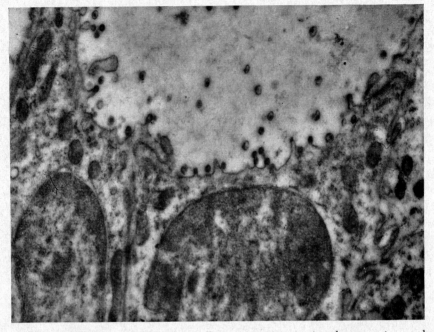

FIGURE 64. Virus production in cells grown in vitro: An eletcron micrograph showing parts of four cells of mouse mammary tissue infected with the "milk factor" virus which produces carcinoma in this host. The clear area at the top is the culture fluid; the cells are at the bottom and sides, with two nuclei and a number of mitochondria shown. At the cell-fluid boundary, virus particles are in various stages of extrusion through the cell membrane. The typical complete particle, shown best at the upper right, consists of a dark core (the virus proper), an outer sheath which is a bit of host cell membrane, and between these a clear portion of host cytoplasm which has been included in the pinching-off process. ×35,600. (Etienne V. Lasfargues.)

these authors showed that, although the virus was indeed destroyed and eventually eliminated, the toxicity of the agent for the roots themselves was such that no level could be chosen which would attack the virus but not the root; the tissue yield was drastically lowered at all concentrations which had any effect on the virus. The agents were therefore useless as a means of protecting the crop. Gautheret and Longchamps reached somewhat similar conclusions as regards the value of certain hormonal weed killers, from experiments first carried out on plant calluses grown in vitro and later verified by field studies.

An interesting approach in quite a different direction was initiated by Hamburger and Levi-Montalcini. In some cases of cancer, pain of obscure origin and ultimate malfunction have been traced to the penetration of nerve endings into the lumina of blood vessels, forming local and developmentally benign neuromas which are not metastases and are in no way

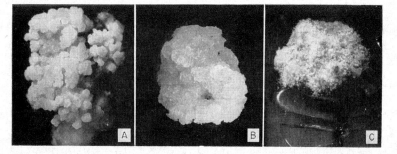

FIGURE 65. Cultures of grape (*Vitis vinifera*): (A) Normal tissue, requiring auxin in the nutrient in order to continue growth. (B) "Habituated" tissue derived from (A) but which has spontaneously altered its metabolism so that it now requires no external source of auxin and in fact now manufactures a measurable excess of auxin. (C) A culture of normal tissue inoculated with grape mildew (*Plasmopara viticola*) an obligate parasite. This thus provides the first successful continuous laboratory culture of the fungus. (Morel, 1948, Pls. XIIIA, B; XXA.)

directly related to the primary tumor. Their presence suggests the existence of a nerve-stimulating substance in the bloodstream. Levi-Montalcini showed that, if ganglia of healthy animals are explanted into a nutrient prepared with serum taken from animals bearing sarcoma 180, they will often grow much more exuberantly than in normal serum (Fig. 66) and that, if healthy ganglion tissue and sarcoma tissue are grown side by side but some distance apart in the same clot, the nerve fibers will grow by preference toward the tumor fragment (Levi-Montalcini *et al.*, 1954). This seems to be limited to sarcoma, but, if it proves to be a general phenomenon, it would seem to offer a possible method of diagnosing tumors.

One field in which tissue culture has given particular promise is the study of the processes of carcinogenesis itself. This has been attacked by Earle (1943b), applying known carcinogens to healthy cells in vitro. Chemical carcinogenesis was demonstrated in this way, but, since it also appears to have occurred spontaneously and repeatedly in tissue cultures in the laboratories of Earle (1943b) and of Gey (Firor and Gey, 1945) and elsewhere, the significance of this result is still uncertain. A somewhat similar result has occurred with plant tissues in the laboratories of Gautheret, where tissues of carrot (Gautheret, 1942a), grape (Morel, 1947), *Scorzonera* (Camus and Gautheret, 1948), tobacco (Limasset and Gautheret, 1950), and other plants have undergone a spontaneous and permanent change, acquiring the capacity to synthesize excess quantities of auxin, which is one of the distinguishing features of most tumorous as opposed to normal plant tissues. The tissue-culture method has been used by White and Braun (1942) for the propagation of plant-tumor tissues and the demonstration of their malignancy. Similarly, cell culture

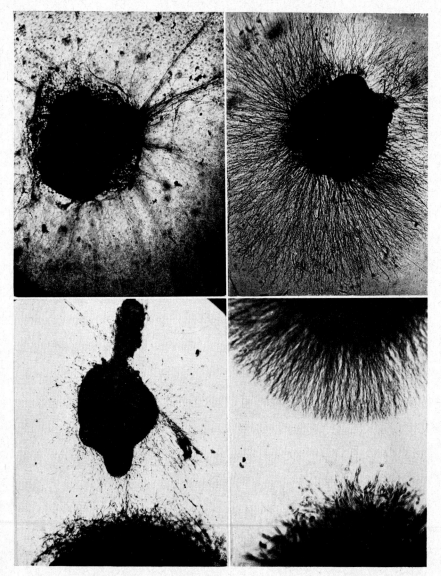

FIGURE 66. Effects of pathological metabolic products on development of sympathetic ganglia of the chick: Upper left—ganglion from a chick embryo grown in a nutrient prepared with serum of a healthy mouse; 24 hours; there has been very little growth. Upper right—a similar culture in serum from a mouse carrying a transplant tumor of sarcoma 180; 24 hours; profuse development of neurofibrils. Lower left—ganglion (above) grown together with a fragment of chick embryonic heart (below); 36 hours; there has been very little growth. Lower right—a similar ganglion culture grown in the presence of a piece of sarcoma 37 tissue taken from a mouse; 48 hours; profuse neurofibril formation. ×65. (Rita Levi-Montalcini.)

is a major tool in the propagation of animal tumors and, in the hands of Murray and Stout (1947b, 1954) and others, has served as an important tool in the diagnosis of certain obscure neuromas and other diseases. One of the most beautiful examples is the study of demyelination and re-myelination in cultures of cerebellar nerves subjected to serum of animals affected with experimental "allergic" encephalomyelitis (Bornstein, Appel, and Murray, 1962) (Fig. 67).

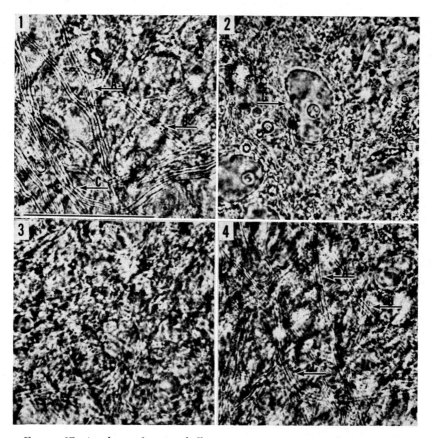

FIGURE 67. A culture of rat cerebellum grown on a Maximov double cover slip: (1) Sixteen days in culture, with well-developed, healthy myelinated axons. (2) The same area after 4½ hours' exposure to a 20 per cent concentration of serum from a rabbit affected with experimental "allergic" encephalomyelitis. The myelin sheaths have blistered and sloughed off and are breaking down. (3) The same, after 24 hours in toxic serum followed by 24 hours in normal serum. The axons are indistinguishable against the background of debris and of neuroglial cells. (4) The same area after 12 days in normal serum. The axons are again visible and have developed new myelin sheaths. Individual axons can be traced at "A," "B," and "C." ×800. (Bornstein et al., 1962.)

Genetics

In both plants and animals the problem of sterillity is a major one. Particularly in hybridization studies, a considerable proportion of theoretical progenies may fail to develop owing to abortion. In plants this is often the result of failure of the nutritive tissues to develop properly. In animals it may be due to inadequate implantation and vascularization or to hormonal imbalances in the mother. In either case, potentially valuable progeny may be lost. And in both cases the embryos themselves are often perfectly viable, the fault lying in their physical relationships with the maternal organism. Theoretically it should be possible, by the use of refined cell-culture techniques, to remove the egg cell after fertilization and cultivate it in vitro, bringing it to maturity and adulthood. To date this has been only partially successful. The dividing egg can be removed from an animal, at any stage up to the blastocyst, and placed in culture (for a general review, see Austin, 1961). The eight-cell stage has proved most satisfactory. At the blastocyst stage, the cultures are reimplanted into castrated mothers of a suitable receptor strain, in whose bodies they can be brought to maturity (McLaren and Biggers, 1958). The same end is sometimes accomplished by transplanting parts of ovaries of a "physiologically sterile" race, either with or without intermediate cultivation, into hosts capable of raising the young produced from such parts of ovaries. This method is important in the propagation of obese strains of mice, strains carrying a genetically determined muscular dystrophy (Stevens et al., 1957), etc.

Plant cultures cannot as yet be established from embryos before the torpedo stage. Thereafter, however, they have been grown successfully to maturity (Tukey, 1933; Nickell, 1951). As it has with animals, this method has been pushed back to earlier stages in development by the excision and cultivation of ovaries and the production of viable seeds therein (Mahashwari and Lal, 1961; and others). These methods, with both plants and animals, are contributing to the conduct of breeding programs and to our understanding of the nature of sterility.

One of the most interesting and important applications of the cell-culture technique to genetics is that developed from somewhat different points of view by Hsu (1959; Hsu and Pomerat, 1953 et seq.) and by Puck (Puck and Marcus, 1955 et seq.). The chromosomes of man and of other animals have long been studied by the classic methods of fixation and sectioning. With a diploid number as high as 46 and with small cells this is a difficult and imprecise method. Using a technique originally devised by Hughes (1952) of treating cells with a hypotonic solution to cause swelling, and applying this method to monolayers obtained in tissue culture, Hsu was able to spread the chromosomes and thus to obtain much more brilliant images. Cells for this purpose were first taken from skin biopsies (Hsu and Moorhead, 1957), later from cultures of peripheral blood (Moorhead *et al.*, 1960; Moorhead and Nowell, 1962). Three facts soon became apparent. First, the earlier count of 48 for man was incorrect; the fundamental number is 46 (Fig. 68). Second, the

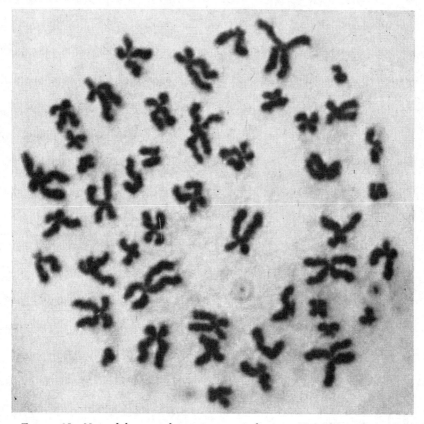

FIGURE 68. Normal human chromosome complement: Metaphase plate from a short-term tissue culture of bone marrow, taken by sternal puncture from a normal person. ×3,000. (Ford *et al.*, 1958, Fig. 1.)

number is not always constant and changes in number may be associated with specific disease syndromes as in the case of hydrocephalus associated with the number 45 (Hsu and Moorhead, 1957). And third, the sex chromosomes become clearly identifiable in somatic cells so that, for example, true hermaphroditism can be distinguished from developmental pseudohermaphroditism. The method thus becomes an important tool in diagnosis. These are specific clinical applications; they have been extended, especially by Ford *et al.* (1958), to the study of tumors, many of which have been shown to represent stabilized aneuploid races of cells (Ford and Mole, 1958). More recently the whole field of human constitutional disease has begun to be examined from this point of view.

Combining this method with his own method of plating single cells of dissociated tissues (cloning), Puck (1958) has developed means of isolating multiple strains of cells and identifying them genetically. This was done initially with tumor strains such as the HeLa strain (Puck and Fisher, 1956) but also in the form of fresh isolations from a variety of mammalian sources. From this there has already emerged important evidence of the existence, which was suspected but needed overt demonstration, of metabolically distinct races of cells within a given strain. Similar differences exist in plant neoplasms (deTorok and White, 1959). Torrey has suggested (1959) that, in plant materials at least, these strains may become segregated in vitro because of the particular nutrients and environments used. These observations open up the possibility of a true genetics of somatic cells.

The fields of biological research in which the methods of tissue or cell culture can continue to make important contributions are daily widening.

Appendix I

SELECTED BASIC EXPERIMENTS [1]

The intention of this book, as set forth in the Preface, has been to make the techniques of cell culture available to as wide an audience as possible. The methods are not intrinsically difficult. It has therefore seemed not amiss to append a few brief "exercises for class use." I have tried to choose examples which are as simple as possible, so that they will not be beyond the facilities of small institutions. At the same time I have tried to formulate exercises which are typical of large groups of problems and are representative of most of those which the student is likely to encounter. They should be sufficient to serve as a foundation upon which wider, more varied and imaginative, and more specialized studies can be based.

Plant Cultures

Let us consider the cultivation of roots, of embryos, of callus from fleshy vegetables, of callus from tree cambium, and of crown-gall tumors of sunflower. Cultures of all of these can be initiated on a standard nutrient which is available commercially or can be made up in any laboratory with reasonably complete facilities.

Prepare or purchase the following stock solutions:

1. A salt solution, White's or Heller's formula (pp. 60–61)
2. An organic accessory solution (pp. 60–62)
   (Solutions 1 and 2 are combined, together with a carbohydrate and a source of iron, in Difco's No. TC 0784.)
3. An indicator solution (pp. 60–63) (Do not make the mistake of using phenol red instead of chlorophenol red!)

[1] In the following pages I have listed commercial sources of a number of products by name and number as an aid to purchasers, and in doing so I have chosen two houses in particular—Difco in Detroit and A. H. Thomas in Philadelphia—not because they are superior to other sources, but because they are among the oldest sources and are the most likely to be familiar to the reader. Where the products named are available from other sources, this choice is not intended to imply any preference; it is made for convenience only.

4. Solutions of 2,4-D, biotin, calcium pantothenate, and other vitamins as desired (p. 62)

Have ready twenty 125-ml. Erlenmeyer flasks, sixty 1-ounce French square bottles (AHT No. 2207-K), twenty 25- × 150-mm. Pyrex test tubes, six 100-mm. Petri dishes, fourteen U.S. Bureau of Plant Industry watch glasses (AHT No. 9850), and two battery jars, all scrupulously clean. The watch glasses and Petri dishes should be sterile.

Dissolve 10 mg. of ferric sulfate ($Fe_2[SO_4]_3$) in 200 ml. of water. Dissolve 40 g. of sucrose in 500 ml. of water. To the 500 ml. of sucrose solution, add 100 ml. of the ferric sulfate solution, 200 ml. of salt solution 1, 2 ml. of accessory solution 2, and 10 ml. of indicator solution 3, and make up to 1 l. with water. If Difco's No. TC 0784 is made up to half the concentration indicated on the label and indicator is added, it will be equivalent to the above.

Divide this into two parts, of 600 and 400 ml. each. Dilute the larger portion 1 : 1 to make 1,200 ml. This is our standard *liquid* nutrient. Distribute 1,000 ml. in 50-ml. portions to twenty of the 125-ml. flasks, plug with cotton wrapped in gauze, cap with 50-ml. beakers, and sterilize at 18 pounds pressure for 20 minutes in an autoclave or household pressure cooker. The remaining 200 ml. should be distributed in 20-ml. portions to ten 25- × 150-mm. Pyrex test tubes, plugged and autoclaved.

Dissolve 4 g. of thoroughly washed and purified agar such as Difco "Noble" agar in 400 ml. of water, and add to the 400 ml. portion of nutrient to make 800 ml. Heat until thoroughly melted. Then distribute 300 ml. in 8-ml. portions to thirty of the French square bottles, and 100 ml. in 20 ml. portions to five test tubes. To the remaining 400 ml., add 4 ml. each of the 2,4-D and biotin. Distribute as before, 300 ml. to French squares and 100 ml. to test tubes. These should then be autoclaved. While they are still hot, add 1 ml. of calcium pantothenate solution, aseptically, for each 10 ml. of nutrient in the individual containers. Then "slant" the bottles to cool.

We now have

20, 125-ml. flasks of standard liquid nutrient
10 tubes of standard liquid nutrient
30 French squares of standard agar nutrient
30 French squares of agar nutrient supplemented with 2,4-D, biotin, and pantothenate
5 test tubes of standard agar nutrient
5 test tubes of supplemented nutrient

These will suffice for cultures of all the plant materials with which we will wish to deal in this section.

TOMATO ROOTS. *First Method*. Purchase in the market a sound, ripe tomato. Be sure that it was not produced by hormone treatment to induce fruit set, since such tomatoes have no seeds. Wash carefully with water, then with 70 per cent alcohol, and set aside in a sterile container until dry. Now, with sterile instruments cut the skin, penetrating into but not through the flesh, along four sectors, beginning about a centimeter from the stem and running around to the flower end, dividing the fruit into quarters. Break it open, laying the sectors back so as to expose the seeds, being careful that the latter are not touched in the process and that they do not come in contact with possibly non-sterile surfaces. With sterile forceps, remove twenty-five sound-appearing seeds and place in five Petri dishes lined with sterile No. 1 Whatman filter paper. Set aside for several days until the seeds are thoroughly dry. Then moisten the paper with sterile water and place in the dark. The seeds should germinate within a few days. When the roots are 2–3 cm. long, select ten of the best, sever them with a sharp scalpel, and transfer them individually to as many flasks of liquid nutrient. Some of these roots should grow well, and, at the end of a week, 2-cm. tips, either of the main root or of well-established branches, can be severed and transferred to fresh nutrient. If such clones of roots are cut back and subcultured each week, they should grow indefinitely. Our strain is now in its twenty-ninth year. They can be used for many kinds of nutritional and morphogenetic studies.

Second Method. Make six straight cuttings from a healthy tomato plant, and remove the leaves. Wash thoroughly with a 1 : 10 solution of Clorox, rinse with sterile water, and shake off the surplus. Insert these cuttings firmly, stem end up, in holes in two sheets of heavy, paraffined cardboard a little larger than the battery jars so that about 25 cm. of stem protrude downward. Line the jars with sterile blotting paper, add about 3 cm. of sterile water in the bottom, and cover with the cardboards so that the tomato stems hang in the moist interior. Set aside in the dark at room temperature. Adventitious roots should appear in about ten days. When they are 3–5 cm. long, select ten sound-appearing roots, cut them carefully with sterile scissors to a length of about 1 cm., and drop the severed tips into as many flasks of standard nutrient. Some of them may be contaminated with epiphytic molds or bacteria, but some will be sterile and should grow well. These can be used as starting material for clones capable of unlimited survival and growth.

CHICKWEED EMBRYOS. Melt a tube (20 ml.) of standard nutrient agar without supplement, and distribute 1-ml. portions to the fourteen miniature Syracuse watch glasses in two Petri dishes.

The common chickweed (*Stellaria media*) survives freezing with only temporary cessation of activity and can usually be found blooming at any season of the year except midwinter, in any community—in lawns, at the edges of gardens, around shrubs, and in similar places. Bring in a healthy plant, and, with tweezers, pick off a dozen sound seed pods, choosing those which are young enough to have the remains of the corolla still present and not completely shriveled. Wash briefly in 1 : 10 Clorox, and transfer to sterile water. Keep covered. Place a sterile glass plate on the stage of the dissecting microscope, and add a large drop of sterile water. Transfer a seed pod to this drop; then, holding it lightly with mosquito forceps in the left hand, with a cataract knife or other small knife (excellent ones can be made by grinding flat blades on the ends of large sewing needles), cut off the end of the pod. Then, with a fine needle, pull out the seeds. These should be transferred to a hollow-ground slide or small watch glass containing sterile nutrient (use a few drops of nutrient from one of the tubes). When a sufficient number have been isolated, prepare a fresh plate with a drop of nutrient (just enough to keep the seeds moist). Transfer a seed to this drop—the seeds will be about 1 mm. in diameter—and, again with fine forceps and a small knife, remove a narrow sector adjacent to the micropyle and toward the chalazal end. Then, pressing with the flat of the knife over the micropyle, force the embryo around and out through the cut surface. As each embryo is removed, it is transferred to a watch glass of standard agar and covered with a 1-inch round No. 2 cover glass. Use a fresh drop of sterile nutrient for the dissection of each seed, and be sure that all instruments are dipped in boiling water and cooled after each dissection. Two sets of instruments will facilitate this. When fourteen embryos have been transferred, put a little sterile water around the watch glasses in each Petri dish to maintain a high humidity, cover, and set aside in the dark at room temperature. These embryos, if uninjured and aseptic, should grow. They can be transferred to larger watch glasses or to flasks, or they can be cut up and used to start further cultures.

Embryos of purslane (*Portulaca oleracea*), another common weed, can be used. The embryos of the larger grasses and sedges and of many garden plants are also satisfactory material for the beginner.

CARROT TISSUE. Select a sound, crisp carrot about 6 inches long, wash thoroughly, dry, and break in the middle. This exposes an aseptic broken surface. With a sharp, sterile cork borer 3–5 mm. in diameter, remove a series of cylinders of tissue so placed that the cambium (the line forming the boundary between the orange core and the lighter colored outer region) passes through their centers. As these are removed, transfer them to a sterile Petri dish. Then, with a sharp, sterile scalpel, make a series of transverse slices across these cylinders, 1 mm. apart, forming disks of tissue. Transfer one of these to each of ten of the French square bottles of standard nutrient agar, and set aside in the dark. Callus should begin to form from the cambium in about a week. At the end of two weeks to a month, this callus can be cut away and transferred to fresh nutrient, the older tissue being discarded. Some isolations may not continue to grow on the standard nutrient, but, if transferred to that containing 2,4-D, they should establish clones capable of unlimited survival and growth. We have such a clone currently in its twenty-fifth year.

Tissues of sweet potato, dahlia, or other tubers can be substituted for carrot, and explants can be prepared by first slicing and then cutting out blocks of tissue; in these cases, however, greater care must be exercised in making certain that *all* outer surfaces are sterile, precautions which are unnecessary if a *broken* surface can be exposed and explants taken from cores.

TREE CAMBIUM. Bring into the laboratory a piece of willow, poplar, birch, or other softwood, a foot or more long and 2–3 inches in diameter, being sure that it is sound and free of dead branchlets. If the bark is rough, scrub with a dry brush and peel away any corky tissues until the white or yellow inner bark is exposed. Wipe with 95 per cent alcohol, and burn this off (be *careful* that you do not burn yourself!). Peel off further cortical tissues down to within 1 mm. of the cambium. Now, with a stiff-bladed knife or scalpel sterilized in boiling water (the knives sold for opening cartons are excellent for this purpose), make a series of longitudinal incisions about 3 mm. apart, and a perpendicular series 6–10 mm. apart, cutting out thirty clean blocks, carrying the incisions to about 1 mm. into the wood. Remove one row, and discard, thus exposing the side of the second row. Now, with a second scalpel, cut into the wood, parallel to the cambium and remove the second row of blocks. Be careful that they do not fly out at the last moment and thus be lost. Transfer them one by one either direct to bottles of agar nutrient or first to Petri dishes containing a few milliliters of liquid nutrient. In being planted in the bottles, they should be grasped with strong forceps and pushed on end into the agar so that about half their length is exposed. Set aside in the dark.

Callus will begin to appear from the cambium in about a week, from the phloem somewhat later, and somewhat later still from xylem medullary rays. This callus should be 2–3 mm. thick at the end of a month. The blocks can then be removed, the new-formed callus carefully cut away and transferred to fresh nutrient, and the original pieces discarded.

Such blocks may not form callus on standard nutrient, depending on the species of tree, but will almost always do so on the supplemented formula. Whether they will subsequently establish permanent clones will depend on the particular species and even individual chosen. Many such clones exist today, but there have also been many failures. This is an excellent field for individual student experiment, and the chances of success or failure may add zest to the attempt.

SUNFLOWER SECONDARY TUMORS. (This exercise is added for those who may care to attempt an experiment which requires somewhat more time but is of considerable interest.) Purchase from Carolina Biological Supply House a culture of *Agrobacterium* (*Phytomonas*) *tumefaciens*, the crown-gall bacterium (CBSH No. LBa 150). Plant six seeds of "giant Russian" sunflower (*Helianthus annuus*) in each of ten 6-inch pots of good soil. When they are well established, thin them to one good plant per pot. When the seedlings are 4-inches high above the cotyledons, inoculate each plant just above the cotyledons with a single needle puncture of a 48-hour broth culture of the bacteria. Primary tumors will develop at the point of inoculation. After about six weeks, some plants, varying from 10 to 60 per cent, should develop secondary tumors at the bases of the petioles of leaves one or more nodes above the site of inoculation. These will be bacteria free. Choose one or more plants with well-developed, smooth secondary tumors, and cut off 6 inches above and below the secondary, not including the primary. Bring these into the laboratory. Split the stems at the basal end in a plane which will pass through or behind the tumor so as to expose the tumor's interior. This exposed torn surface should be sterile. With a sharp-pointed sterile scalpel, remove from this exposed interior bits of tissue a millimeter or more on a side and transfer them to tubes or bottles of unsupplemented agar nutrient. Some of these are likely to be contaminated with casual epiphytic fungi and bacteria, but a considerable proportion should grow into massive cultures of disorganized tissue. These grow rapidly on standard nutrients and should be subcultured at one-month intervals. They are highly malignant (to other sunflowers, *not* to man!) and will produce massive sterile tumors if bits of cultured tissue are implanted under flaps of bark of healthy sunflower or Jerusalem artichoke plants.

Animal Cultures

Prepare (pp. 63–74) or purchase (see Appendix III) the following:

1. Fowl plasma, fresh (Difco No. TC 0483)
2. Horse, fowl, or human serum, fresh (Difco No. TC 0569, 0518, or 0610)
3. Chick-embryo extract, fresh (Difco No. TC 0470)
4. Hanks balanced salt solution, fresh (Difco No. TC 0775)
5. $1/10\%$ trypsin in BSS lacking calcium and magnesium (Difco No. 0153 diluted 1 : 50 with Difco No. 0662)

6. Waymouth's complete nutrient solution, fresh (Difco No. TC 0043)
7. Wolff's agar nutrient (pp. 74–76)
8. Classic embryo-extract–salt-solution–serum nutrient, 20 : 60 : 20

Set aside

Depression slides, Rockefeller Institute type (AHT No. 7047)
Maximov slides (AHT No. 7048C)
Test tubes, 16 × 150 mm., Pyrex, lipless
Leighton tubes, short type (Bellco No. 14–1951)
Carrel flasks (Kontes No. K88200) or Falcon plastic flasks (Falcon No. 3008) or ½-oz. screw-cap pharmaceutical bottles
Petri dishes, 100 mm. and 60 mm., glass or disposable plastic
Columbia watch glasses (AHT No. 9851) in pairs
Syracuse watch glasses (AHT No. 9850)
Cover glasses,

> 35 × 40 mm., No. 2, Maximov
> 22 × 22 mm., No. 1, square
> 16 mm., No. 0, round
> 10 × 50 mm., No. 0, rectangular strips

Syringes, 1 ml., tuberculin
　　　 5 ml.
Needles, No. 26, 2 cm. long
An egg incubator and a 37° incubator will also be required.
If a tube rotor is available it may also be used.
Candle two dozen fertile eggs (they may have to be purchased from specialized poultry raiser's sources, since most eggs from the grocery will *not* be fertile), and set them to incubate, large end up.

We will prepare

1. Hanging-drop cultures, heart muscle
2. Roller-tube cultures, skeletal muscle
3. Flask or bottle cultures, lung
4. Leighton-tube cultures, skin
5. Watch-glass cultures, bone
6. Petri-dish cultures, disaggregated whole embryos

HANGING-DROP CULTURES. *Heart Muscle.* Open six 6-day embryonated eggs, and remove the embryos to sterile 60-mm. Petri dishes. Remove the hearts and legs, and transfer them to separate Columbia watch glasses containing Hanks solution. Transfer the hearts through two changes of solution, leaving for five minutes in each change, then transfer to dry watch glasses. Cut up with sharp scissors or scalpels into bits 1 mm. or less in diameter, and cover with a few drops of Hanks solution. They will cut better if the solution is added *after*, not before, cutting.

Lay out twelve 22- × 22-mm. clean, sterile square cover glasses. With a pipette or 1-ml. tuberculin syringe provided with a No. 26 needle, apply to each of six of the cover slips a drop of fowl plasma, and apply a drop of double the volume of Waymouth's MB 752/1 nutrient to the others, spreading the drops to a circle about 10 mm. in diameter. Place a bit of heart tissue in each drop. To the plasma cultures add a small drop of 1 : 1 embryo extract, and stir quickly with a sterile needle. This will ensure a firm clot. When these cultures are well clotted, add a drop of serum–embryo extract–salt solution to each, to provide a total volume equal to that of the synthetic nutrient used for the others.

Apply two drops of Vaseline at opposite sides of the cavities of twelve deep-depression 1- × 3-inch slides (Rockefeller type), and invert the slides over the twelve cultures, pressing down firmly so that the covers are attached to the slides. Invert by a quick centrifugal motion, and seal with hot 1 : 3 paraffin : Vaseline mixture. Best results will be obtained if the slides are re-inverted for a few hours in the incubator; this will allow the cultures in liquid drops to settle to the glass and to attach themselves rather than to settle away from the glass to the liquid : air interface. Once they are firmly attached, that is, after 3–4 hours, they can be re-inverted for microscopic study or more prolonged incubation. They should be observed daily. They will serve for class observation and study for several days without attention other than incubation. If they are to be kept for longer study, the nutrient must be renewed twice a week and cultures must be cut up and transferred whenever they attain diameters of 5 mm. or more.

Maximov Slides. Lay out twelve clean, sterile 35- × 40-mm. No. 2 cover glasses, and place on each a small drop of sterile water. Cover each of these drops with a 16-mm. round cover glass. Prepare cultures on these glasses as described above. Place two drops of Vaseline on opposite sides of the cavities of twelve Maximov slides, and invert over the cultures. These can then be re-inverted and sealed as before.

The heart muscle will spread over the glass and will continue to beat, at first in scattered points and with varying rhythms which will finally fuse and become synchronized into powerful, widespread, and rhythmic beats. Such cultures make especially dramatic demonstrations for class use.

ROLLER-TUBE CULTURES. *Skeletal Muscle.* Open four 10-day embryonated eggs, remove the embryos, dissect off the skin of the legs, cut them at "heel" and "hip," and transfer to a watch glass of Hanks solution.

Remove and discard the bones. Wash the muscle, drain, and cut up as fine as possible. The resulting mass will be soft and semiliquid, and it may be rather difficult to tell whether the cutting has been effective or not.

Lay out in a sloped rack twenty 16- $\times$ 150-mm. Pyrex lipless test tubes. With a bulb-pipette, streak plasma in a broad band along one side of the interior of ten tubes, to a distance about halfway from tip toward mouth, this streak being placed downward. Now, with a second pipette, take up the chopped muscle and spread it over the plasma streaks and over corresponding areas in the tubes without plasma. Stopper the tubes, and let them stand at room temperature for one hour, to permit clotting of the plasma and attachment of the other cultures. Now turn the tubes with the tissue streaks up, and charge each tube with nutrient, using a 20 : 60 : 20 nutrient for half and Waymouth's MB 752/1 nutrient for the other half of both types. Place in the rotor in the incubator. If a rotor is not available, they may be set at a slight slope, tissue down, in any incubator, but, in that case, only those bits of tissue toward the mouth of the tube and under a shallow layer of nutrient can be expected to grow. These cultures should likewise be examined daily and the nutrient renewed, if so desired, once or twice a week.

These provide an excellent demonstration of random muscular contraction and fibrillation. Note also the much more luxuriant development of fibroblasts in the plasma–serum–embryo-extract cultures, which will overrun and replace the muscle. Muscle retains its function better in a less "rich" nutrient.

FLASK OR BOTTLE CULTURES. *Lung.* Lung is best taken from older embryos. Open six 12-day eggs, remove the embryos, dissect out the lungs, cut these up as fine as possible with scissors, and wash them through several changes of Hanks solution *after* they are cut up.

Set out twenty Carrel 3.5 flasks, Falcon plastic flasks, or ½-ounce medicine bottles. Coat the interior of the bottoms of half of them with a thin layer of plasma. With a pipette, inoculate lung material into all flasks, spreading well, and allow to stand for an hour. Now add 1 ml. of nutrient to each flask or bottle, using 20 : 60 : 20 for half and synthetic nutrient for the remainder. Stopper and place in the incubator. Flasks or bottles can be inverted for inspection, but be careful that the microscope is sufficiently sloped that nutrient does not come in contact with the stoppers. Nutrient should be renewed at two- to three-day intervals.

Lung cultures make especially valuable demonstrations of peristalsis, which will usually be active during the first two or three days after excision, and of ciliary activity, which generally does not become evident before the eighth day.

LEIGHTON-TUBE CULTURES. *Skin.* Prepare twenty clean, sterile Leighton tubes. Lay out twenty sterile 5- × 40-mm. cover slips. Coat ten of them with plasma, spreading it over the entire upper surface.

Remove sheets of skin from the ventral surface of a number of 8-day embryos, spread them on a sterile moist surface, and, with scalpels, cut a series of rectangular or square pieces 2–3 mm. on a side and transfer them to a watch glass of Hanks solution. When a sufficient number are ready, transfer them with a scalpel to the cover glasses, four–six pieces per cover, being sure that they lie flat, without rolled edges. Add a drop of embryo extract to each bit of tissue on plasma. Insert the cover slips into the Leighton tubes with just enough nutrient to prevent their drying out, and let stand for one hour. Then add 1 ml. of nutrient, using 20 : 60 : 20 and MB 752/1 for half of each group.

These should grow as solid sheets which can be cut up for transfer. They are especially valuable as demonstrations of the epithelial type of growth, at a more complex level of differentiation than that shown by lung.

Similar preparations can be set up from skin of 18-day mouse embryos. Human or rabbit skin can be prepared by shaving a suitable area, sterilizing with alcohol and ether, washing with alcohol, and, when it is dry, removing skin with a sharp scalpel. For such cultures it will be advisable to add penicillin-streptomycin to the initial nutrient (p. 109).

WATCH-GLASS CULTURES. *Bone.* Prepare sixteen clean, sterile miniature watch glasses in two 100-mm. Petri dishes. Charge half of them with Wolff's nutrient agar (p. 75), and provide all the others with "tables" of stainless-steel or tantalum wire mesh topped with disks of acetate voile. Charge these last with MB 752/1 synthetic nutrient.

Open eight 6-day eggs and transfer the embryos to a Petri dish. Dissect off the skin of the legs, sever these at the hip, and transfer to Hanks solution. Now, under a dissecting binocular microscope, carefully remove the flesh from the bones, separate these at the joint, and transfer one to each watch glass. Cover the glasses with round cover slips, add a little water in the bottom of the Petri dishes, measure the length of the bones, and set in the incubator. Nutrient should be renewed or cultures transferred to fresh dishes twice a week.

These provide an excellent demonstration of the organotypic growth of animal members.

PETRI-DISH OR BOTTLE PRIMARY MONOLAYERS. Set out six 60-mm. Petri dishes and six small pharmaceutical bottles. Cut up a whole 6-day chick embryo into small bits in balanced salt solution, in a watch glass. Transfer to a test tube or small flask, remove the solution, and replace it with an 0.1 per cent solution of trypsin in a salt solution prepared without calcium or magnesium (Difco No. 0153 diluted 1 : 50 with Difco No. 0662). Place in the incubator, agitating or stirring at intervals until the cells separate. When separation is reasonably complete, draw off the suspension in a pipette, leaving behind any unbroken masses, transfer to a fresh tube, allow the cells to settle, decant, and add an equal volume of fresh Hanks solution. Resuspend by shaking, and transfer 1 ml. of the suspension to each of the Petri dishes and bottles. Add 9 ml. of fresh nutrient, with or without 2 per cent serum, to each vessel and set in the incubator.

The cells will settle to the floors of the receptacles and grow there as monolayers. Different types of cells will form discrete colonies, giving an interesting demonstration of the diversity of body tissues. Nutrient should be renewed at 2- to 3-day intervals.

Virus Cultures

Like the exercise involving preparation of cultures from crown-gall tumors of plants, this exercise is introduced for the benefit of those whose particular interests may induce them to attempt a more specialized problem which is concerned, in this case, not with a true cell or tissue culture but rather with the use of surviving cells for the propagation of a disease agent. For this purpose, any of the common viruses—vaccinia, mumps, polio, etc.—will be suitable. For a class exercise, vaccinia is probably the most easily available and least dangerous. Two methods should be tried:

1. FLASK METHOD (MAITLAND). Charge ten 125-ml. Erlenmeyer flasks or 4-ounce medicine bottles with nutrient, half with Hanks solution and half with MB 752/1, 10 ml. per flask. To each, add a 1-ml. suspension of sterile chopped rabbit kidney and 1 ml. of an active culture of vaccinia virus such as is represented by a suspension of dried (lyophilized) skin from an active lesion. Set the flasks in the incubator at 37° C. At the end of a week, 1 ml. of fluid drawn from such a flask can be used as inoculum for a second series. Titration in susceptible animals should show that the virus has multiplied during the interval, although the number of viable host cells may have decreased even to the point of complete absence. Large test tubes can be used in place of flasks or bottles but provide less satisfactory conditions for cell survival.

2. ROLLER-TUBE METHOD. Prepare a series of cultures of embryo rabbit or mouse skin on plasma clots, either in roller tubes or on strips of cover glass in Leighton tubes. Charge the tubes with ML 752/1, with or without 5 per cent rabbit serum. When growth is well established,

add 0.1 ml. of a suspension of lyophilized vaccinia-infected tissue to each tube. The virus will quickly establish itself in the growing epithelium and can be propagated for long periods by serial transfer to similar cultures.

All of these exercises can be elaborated at the wish of the instructor and the students.

Appendix II

STORAGE, PRESERVATION, AND
SHIPPING OF CULTURES

The maintenance of large numbers of cultures under optimum conditions of growth is a time-consuming and costly task: nutrients must be renewed at 48- to 72-hour intervals; cultures must be subcultured about once a week, and they require a large turnover of glassware and consume large quantities of nutrient. It is also common experience that many, though not all, cultures maintained for long periods at or near the logarithmic phase undergo frequent mutations so that they are not constant in character. For all these reasons it is desirable to be able to retard growth or to maintain cultures for prolonged periods in a quiescent state.

This has long been done with plant-tissue cultures. White (1937e) showed that, if tomato-root cultures were maintained at 15° C. instead of the usual 25° to 27°, the period between subcultures could be increased from the routine one week to eight weeks without impairing their viability. Cultures could be kept at temperatures as low as 5°, at which level they made no growth, but recovery after such temperature was somewhat uncertain.

Parker (1936) restricted the growth of animal fibroblasts by providing a nutrient of dilute serum only, without embryo extract. In such a medium, cultures grew slowly and required a minimum of attention. Hanks, for somewhat different reasons, chose to slow down growth by use of lower-than-usual temperatures. Cultures grown at 30° instead of 37° grew slowly and required much less frequent feeding and subculturing (1947, 1948). Fischer (1926) had earlier tried lowered temperatures.

The observation that embryo extracts prepared by freezing and thawing sometimes gave rise to spontaneous viable cultures, together with Luyet's general studies on survival of tissues and organisms after freezing, led ultimately to an intensive examination of the behavior of animal-tissue cultures at low temperatures. Out of these studies have grown important practical applications.

Cultures in their logarithmic phase of growth which are chilled gradually with temperature drops of about 1° per minute and which after freezing are thawed *rapidly* can be brought to temperatures of −70° C. and will survive for many years at this temperature (Hanks and Wallace, 1949, 1958; Scherer and Hoogasian, 1954; Swim and Parker, 1955; Swim *et al.*, 1958; Stulberg *et al.*, 1958; Hauschka *et al.*, 1959). They will *not* survive if the storage temperature is higher than −30° C. Survival is apparently improved if cultures are first placed in 15 per cent glycerol. The explanation is supposed to be that glycerol osmotically extracts water from the cells, producing a physiological dehydration; slow freezing further permits ice to form *outside* the cells, further extracting water from the protoplast so that crystals do not form within the living substance. Metabolic processes will continue at −20° to the extent of producing denaturation of proteins, which does not occur at −70°. And rapid thawing does not permit crystallization within cells, following reabsorption of water from the previously thawed circumambiant fluid.

The method is generally as follows: A culture in the logarithmic phase is freed from the glass of the flask by scraping or by trypsinization, washed in fresh nutrient, and centrifuged; 20 per cent glycerol is added in a fresh charge of nutrient; the cells are resuspended; and the culture is placed in a thin-walled test tube or ampule which is then placed in a salt-ice bath to reduce the temperature somewhat below zero, left for 30 minutes, then transferred to an alcohol–dry ice bath for a further 30 minutes, and finally placed in the deepfreeze at −70°. This will generally provide a sufficiently gradual temperature drop. When the culture is to be revived it is thawed by plunging the ampule directly into a circulating water bath at 38° C. with frequent agitation. As soon as thawed it is centrifuged, the glycerol nutrient is decanted, fresh nutrient is added, and the culture is placed in a shallow culture flask, allowed to settle, and incubated. The percentage of recovery from such treatment is usually quite high. Morgan *et al.* (1956) report that cultures so treated lose their immunological species specificity.

This method permits prolonged storage of strains under conditions where they do not undergo mutations or other massive changes characteristic of continuously cultured strains. They thus provide not only a source of stocks but a basis of comparison, a standard with which to compare current strains.

It is often desirable to send cultures from one laboratory to another. The HeLa strain of human cells is used all over the world. White's root-culture and plant-tumor strains and Gautheret's and Morel's strains of normal plant tissues have likewise been widely distributed. Plant tissues are best shipped in plastic tubes almost filled with nutrient which have tight slip-on caps. Roots are shipped when about 5 cm. long.

BIBLIOGRAPHY

This list contains only publications to which specific reference is made in the text. It is by no means exhaustive. For more complete citations, the reader is referred to Murray and Kopech's monumental *A Bibliography of the Research in Tissue Culture* (1953), which covers the period up to 1950. A revision of that list up to 1960 is in preparation.

ANANTASWAMY RAU, M. 1956. Studies in growth in vitro of excised ovaries. I. Influence of colchicine on the embryo and endosperm in *Phlox drummondii* Hook. *Phytomorphology* **6**: 90–96.

ARCHIBALD, R. M. 1945. Chemical characteristics and physiological rôles of glutamine. *Chem. Rev.* **37**: 161–208.

ARISTOTLE OF STEGIRA. Ca. 340 B.C. *Historia animalium.* Translated by D'ARCY W. THOMPSON, 1910. Oxford: Oxford University Press.

ARNOLD, J. 1887. Über Theilungsvorgänge an den Wanderzellen, ihre progressiven und retrogressiven Metamorphosen. *Arch. Mikr. Anat.* **30**: 205–326.

AUSTIN, C. R. 1961. *The mammalian egg.* Springfield, Ill.: Charles C Thomas, Publishers.

BAKER, J. R. 1952. The cell theory: A restatement, history and critique. III. The cell as a morphological unit. *J. microscop. Sci.* **93**: 157–190.

BAKER, L. E. 1936. Artificial media for the cultivation of fibroblasts, epithelial cells and monocytes. *Sci.* **83**: 605–606.

BAKER, L. E., and A. CARREL. 1926. Effect of the amino acids and hydrolyzable constituents of embryonic tissue juice on the growth of fibroblasts. *J. exp. Med.* **44**: 397–407.

BAKER, L. E., and A. CARREL. 1928. Effect of liver and pituitary digests on the proliferation of sarcomatous fibroblasts of the rat. *J. exp. Med.* **47**: 371–378.

BAKER, L. E., and A. H. EBELING. 1939. Artificial maintenance media for cell and organ cultivation. I. The cultivation of fibroblasts in artificial and serumless media. *J. exp. Med.* **69**: 365–378.

BALL, E. 1946. Development in sterile culture of stem tips and subjacent regions of *Tropaeolum majus* L. and *Lupinus albus* L. *Am. J. Bot.* **33**: 301–318.

BARKER, W. C. 1953. Proliferative capacity of the medullary sheath region in the stem of *Tilia americana. Am. J. Bot.* **40**: 773–778.

BARSKI, G., J. MAURIN, C. WIELGOSZ, and P. LÉPINE. 1951. Conditions de nutrition cellulaire in vitro en culture sans support plasmatique: Rôle des fractions micro-et macro-moléculaires. *Ann. Inst. Pasteur.* **81**: 9–24.

BEN GEREN, B. 1956. Structural studies of the formation of the myelin sheath in peripheral nerve fibers. In *Cellular mechanisms in differentiation and growth.* (DOROTHEA RUDNICK, ed.) 14th Growth Symposium. Princeton, N.J.: Princeton University Press. Pp. 213–220.

BERGMANN, L. 1959. A new technique for isolating and cloning single cells of higher plants. *Nature* **184**: 648.

BERGMANN, L. 1960. Growth and division of single cells of higher plants in vitro. *J. gen. Physiol.* **43**: 841–851.

BERNARD, C. 1878–79. *Leçons sur les phénomènes de la vie communs aux animaux et aux végétaux.* (2 vols.) Paris: Baillière.

185

BONNER, J. 1938. Thiamin (vitamin B₁) and the growth of roots: The relation of chemical structure to physiological activity. *Am. J. Bot.* **25**: 543–549.

BONNER, J., and F. ADDICOTT. 1937. Cultivation in vitro of excised pea roots. *Bot. Gaz.* **99**: 144–170.

BONNER, J., and D. BONNER. 1938. Ascorbic acid and the growth of plant embryos. *Proc. Nat. Acad. Sci.* (Wash.) **24**: 70–75.

BONNER, J., and P. S. DEVIRIAN. 1939. Growth factor requirements of four species of isolated roots. *Am. J. Bot.* **26**: 661–665.

BORNSTEIN, M. B., S. H. APPEL, and MARGARET R. MURRAY. 1962. The application of tissue culture to the study of experimental "allergic" encephalomyelitis: Demyelination and remyelination. *Proc. 4th Internat. Congr. Neuropathology* **2**: 279–282.

BORODIN, J. 1878. Über die physiologische Rolle und die Verbreitung des Asparagins im Pflanzenreiche. *Bot. Zeitng* **36**: 801–832.

BOYSEN-JENSEN, P. 1910. Über die Leitung des phototropischen Reizes in *Avena-keimpflanzen. Ber. Deut. bot. Ges.* **28**: 118–120.

BRACHET, J. 1937. Some oxidative properties of isolated amphibian germinal vesicles. *Sci.* **86**: 225.

BROWN, R. 1833. Observations on the organs and mode of fecundation in Orchideae and Asclepiadae. *Trans. Linnean Soc.* **16**: 685–745.

BUCHSBAUM, R., and C. LOOSLI. 1936. *Methods of tissue culture in vitro.* Chicago: University of Chicago Press.

BURROWS, M. T. 1910. The cultivation of tissues of the chick embryo outside the body. *J. Am. Med. Assoc.* **55**: 2057–2058.

BURROWS, M. T. 1911. The growth of tissues of the chick embryo outside the animal body, with special reference to the nervous system. *J. exp. Zool.* **10**: 63–83.

BURROWS, M. T. 1912. Rhythmic activity of isolated heart muscle cells in vitro. *Sci.* **36**: 90–92.

CAMERON, GLADYS. 1950. *Tissue culture technique.* New York: Academic Press, Inc.

CAMUS, G. 1949. Recherches sur le rôle des bourgeons dans les phénomènes de morphogénèse. *Rev. Cytol. Biol. végét.* **11**: 1–199.

CAMUS, G., and R. GAUTHERET. 1948. Sur le caractère tumoral des tissus de Scorsonère ayant subi le phénomène d'accoutumance aux hétéro-auxines. *C. r. Acad. Sci.* (Paris) **226**: 744–745.

CAPLIN, S. M., and F. C. STEWARD. 1948. Effect of coconut milk on the growth of explants from carrot root. *Sci.* **108**: 655–657.

CAPLIN, S. M., and F. C. STEWARD. 1949. A technique for the controlled growth of excised plant tissue in liquid media under aseptic conditions. *Nature* **163**: 920–924.

CARPENTER, E. 1942. Differentiation of chick embryo thyroids in tissue culture. *J. exp. Zool.* **89**: 407–431.

CARREL, A. 1911. Die Kultur der Gewebe ausserhalb des Organismus. *Berliner klin. Wochenschr.* **48**: 1364–1367.

CARREL, A. 1912a. On the permanent life of tissues outside of the organism. *J. exp. Med.* **15**: 516–528.

CARREL, A. 1912b. Pure culture of cells. *J. exp. Med.* **16**: 165–168.

CARREL, A. 1913a. Concerning visceral organisms. *J. exp. Med.* **18**: 155–161.

CARREL, A. 1913b. Artificial activation of the growth in vitro of connective tissue. *J. exp. Med.* **17**: 14–19.

CARREL, A. 1913c. Neue Untersuchungen über das selbstandige Leben der Gewebe und Organe. *Berliner klin. Wochenschr.* **5**: 1097.

CARREL, A. 1923. A method for the physiological study of tissues in vitro. *J. exp. Med.* **38**: 407–418.

CARREL, A. 1924. Tissue culture and cell physiology. *Physiol. Rev.* **4**: 1–20.

CARREL, A. 1934. Monocytes as an indicator of certain states of blood serum. *Sci.* **80**: 565–566.

CARREL, A., and L. E. BAKER. 1926. The chemical nature of substances required for cell multiplication. *J. exp. Med.* **44**: 503–521.

CARREL, A., and M. T. BURROWS. 1910. Le culture de tissus adultes en dehors de l'organisme. *C. r. Soc. Biol.* (Paris) **69**: 293–294.

CHILD, C. M. 1941. *Patterns and problems of development.* Chicago: University of Chicago Press.

CHOPRA, R. N. 1958. In vitro culture of ovaries of *Althaea rosea* Cav. In *Modern developments in plant physiology* (P. MAHESHWARI, ed.). *Proc. Delhi Univ. Seminar.* Pp. 81–89.

CLARK-KENNEDY, A. E. 1929. *Stephen Hales, D.D., F.R.S.: An eighteenth century biography.* London: Cambridge University Press.

CORIELL, L. L. 1962. Detection and elimination of contaminating organisms. In *Analytic cell culture,* Syverton Memorial Symposium. *Nat. Cancer Inst. Monogr.* **7**: 33–53.

COSTERO, I., and C. M. POMERAT. 1951. Cultivation of neurons from the adult human cerebral and cerebellar cortex. *Am. J. Anat.* **89**: 405–468.

CUNNINGHAM, B., and P. L. KIRK. 1942. Measure of "growth" in tissue culture. *J. cell. comp. Physiol.* **20**: 343–358.

D'AMATO, F. 1952. Polyploidy in the differentiation and function of tissues and cells in plants. *Caryologia* **4**: 311–358.

DANES, BETTY, and P. J. LEINFELDER. 1951. Cytological and respiratory effects of cyanide on tissue cultures. *J. cell. comp. Physiol.* **37**: 427–446.

DAS, N. K., K. PATAU, and F. SKOOG. 1956. Initiation of mitosis and cell division by kinetin and indoleacetic acid in excised tobacco pith tissue. *Physiologia Plantarum* **9**: 640–651.

DAVIDSON, F. F. 1950. The effects of auxins on the growth of marine algae. *Am. J. Bot.* **37**: 502–510.

DAWSON, R. F. 1938. A method for the culture of excised plant parts. *Am. J. Bot.* **25**: 522–524.

DAWSON, R. F. 1942. Nicotine synthesis in excised tobacco roots. *Am. J. Bot.* **29**: 813–815.

DAY, M. F., and T. D. C. GRACE. 1959. Culture of insect tissues. *Ann. Rev. Entomol.* **4**: 17–38

deBRUYN, WILLEMINA A. 1955. Het kweken van leucaemische cellen en van carcinomen in Kolven. In 5 Jaarboek v. Kankeronderzoek en Kankerbestrijding in Nederland. Pp. 137–142.

DERMEN, H. 1950. Pattern reversal in variegated plants. *J. Hered.* **41**: 324–328.

deROPP, R. S. 1947. The response of normal plant tissues and of crown-gall tumor tissues to synthetic growth hormones. *Am. J. Bot.* **34**: 53–62.

deROPP, R. S. 1948. The interaction of normal and crown-gall tumor tissue in in vitro grafts. *Am. J. Bot.* **35**: 372–377.

deROPP, R. S. 1955. The growth and behavior in vitro of isolated plant cells. *Proc. Roy. Soc. London B.* **144**: 86–93.

deTOROK, D., and P. R. WHITE. 1959. Cytological instability in tumors of *Picea glauca. Sci.* **131**: 730–732.

Difco manual of dehydrated culture media and reagents. 1959. 10th ed. Detroit: Difco.

DOLJANSKI, L., and R. S. HOFFMAN. 1943. The growth activating effect of extract of adult tissue on fibroblast colonies in vitro. III. The cultivation for prolonged periods. *Growth* **7**: 67–72.

DUHAMEL DU MONCEAU, H. L. 1758. *La physique des arbres, où il est traité de l'anatomie des plantes et de l'économie végétale, pour servir d'introduction au traité complet des bois et des forêts; avec une dissertation sur l'utilité des méthodes de botanique.* 2 vols. Paris: Guérin et Delatour.

DUJARDIN, F. 1835. Recherches sur les organismes inférieurs. *Ann. Sci. Naturelle, Zool.* **4**: 343–376.

DULBECCO, R., and M. VOGT. 1954. Plaque formation and isolation of pure lines with poliomyelitis viruses. *J. exp. Med.* **99:** 167–182.

DURE, L. S., and W. A. JENSEN. 1957. The influence of gibberellic acid and indole-acetic acid on cotton embryos cultured in vitro. *Bot. Gaz.* **118:** 254–261.

EAGLE, H. 1955a. The specific amino-acid requirements of a human carcinoma cell (Strain HeLa) in tissue culture. *J. exp. Med.* **102:** 37–48.

EAGLE, H. 1955b. Nutrition needs of mammalian cells in tissue culture. *Sci.* **122:** 501–504.

EARLE, W. R. 1943a. Production of malignancy in vitro. I. Method of cleaning glassware. *J. Nat. Cancer Inst.* **4:** 131–134.

EARLE, W. R. 1943b. Production of malignancy in vitro. IV. The mouse fibroblast cultures and changes seen in the living cells. *J. Nat. Cancer Inst.* **4:** 165–212.

EARLE, W. R. *et al.* 1954. The growth of pure strain-L cells in fluid-suspension cultures. *J. Nat. Cancer Inst.* **14:** 1159–1171.

EBELING, A. H. 1921. Measurement of the growth of tissues in vitro. *J. exp. Med.* **34:** 231–243.

EBELING, A. H. 1924. Action des acides aminés sur la croissance des fibroblastes. *C. r. Soc. Biol.* (Paris) **90:** 31–33.

EHRMANN, R. L., and G. O. GEY. 1953. The use of cell colonies on glass for evaluating nutrition and growth in roller tube cultures. *J. Nat. Cancer Inst.* **13:** 1099–1122.

ENDERS, J. F. 1952. Propagation of viruses and rickettsiae in tissue cultures. Chapter 6 in *Viral and rickettsial infections of man* (2d ed.) (T. M. RIVERS, ed.). Philadelphia: J. B. Lippincott Co.

ENDERS, J. F. 1954. Tissue culture in the study of immunity: Retrospection and anticipation. *J. Immunol.* **73:** 62–66.

ENDERS, J. F., T. H. WELLER, and F. C. ROBBINS. 1949. Cultivation of the Lansing strain of poliomyelitis virus in cultures of various human embryonic tissues. *Sci.* **109:** 85–87.

EVANS, VIRGINIA J., J. C. BRYANT, MARY C. FIORAMONTI, W. T. McQUILKIN, KATHERINE K. SANFORD, and W. R. EARLE. 1956a. Studies of nutrient media for tissue cells in vitro. I. A protein-free chemically defined medium for cultivation of Strain L cells. *Cancer Res.* **16:** 77–86.

EVANS, VIRGINIA J., J. C. BRYANT, W. T. McQUILKIN, MARY C. FIORAMONTI, KATHERINE K. SANFORD, B. B. WESTFALL, and W. R. EARLE. 1956b. Studies of nutrient media for tissue cells in vitro. II. An improved protein-free chemically defined medium for long-term cultivation of strain L-929 cells. *Cancer Res.* **16:** 87–94.

EVANS, VIRGINIA J., J. C. BRYANT, W. T. McQUILKIN, MARY C. FIORAMONTI, KATHERINE K. SANFORD, B. B. WESTFALL, and W. R. EARLE. 1957. Studies on nutrient media for tissue cells in vitro. III. Whole egg extract ultrafiltrate for long-term cultivation of Strain L cells. *Cancer Res.* **17:** 317–324.

EVANS, VIRGINIA J., and W. R. EARLE. 1947. The use of perforated cellophane for the growth of cells in tissue culture. *J. Nat. Cancer Inst.* **8:** 103–119.

EVANS, VIRGINIA J., W. R. EARLE, KATHERINE K. SANFORD, J. E. SHANNON, and H. K. WALTZ. 1951. The preparation and handling of replicate tissue cultures for quantitative studies. *J. Nat. Cancer Inst.* **11:** 907–927.

FAWCETT, C. W., and B. L. VALLEE. 1952. Studies on the separation of cell types in serosanguinous fluids, blood, and vaginal fluids by flotation on bovine plasma albumin. *J. lab. clin. Med.* **39:** 354–364.

FELL, HONOR B. 1928a. The development in vitro of the isolated otocyst of the embryonic fowl. *Arch. exp. Zellforsch* **7:** 69–81.

FELL, HONOR B. 1928b. Experiments on the differentiation in vitro of cartilage and bone. Part I. *Arch. exp. Zellforsch* **7:** 390–412.

FELL, HONOR B. 1931. Osteogenesis in vitro. *Arch. exp. Zellforsch* **11:** 245–252.

FELL, HONOR B. 1932. Chondrogenesis in cultures of endosteum. *Proc. Roy. Soc. London B.* **112:** 417–427.

FELL, HONOR B. 1953. Recent advances in organ cultures. *Sci. Progress* **162**: 212–231.

FELL, HONOR B., and E. MELLANBY. 1952. The effect of hypervitaminosis A on embryonic limb-bones cultivated in vitro. *J. Physiol.* **116**: 320–349.

FELL, HONOR B., and E. MELLANBY. 1953. Metaplasia produced in cultures of chick ectoderm by high vitamin A. *J. Physiol.* **119**: 470–488.

FELL, HONOR B., and R. ROBISON. 1929. The growth, development and phosphatase activity of embryonic avian femora and limb-buds cultivated in vitro. *Biochem. J.* **23**: 767–784.

FELL, HONOR B., and R. ROBISON. 1930. The development and phosphatase activity in vivo and in vitro of the mandibular skeletal tissue of the embryonic fowl. *Biochem. J.* **24**: 1905–1921.

FELL, HONOR B., and R. ROBISON. 1934. The development of the calcifying mechanism in avian cartilage and osteoid tissue. *Biochem. J.* **28**: 2243–2253.

FELLER, A. E., J. F. ENDERS, and T. H. WELLER. 1940. The prolonged coexistence of vaccinia virus in high titre and living cells in roller tube cultures of chick embryonic tissues. *J. exp. Med.* **72**: 367–380.

FIEDLER, H. 1936. Entwicklungs- und reizphysiologische Untersuchungen an Kulturen isolierter Wurzelspitzen. *Ztschr. Bot.* **30**: 385–436.

FIFE, J. M., and V. L. FRAMPTON. 1936. The pH gradient extending from the phloem into the parenchyma of the sugar beet and its relation to the feeding behavior of *Eutettix tenellus*. *J. agr. Res.* **53**: 581–593.

FIROR, W. M., and G. O. GEY. 1945. Observations on the conversion of normal into malignant cells. *Ann. Surg.* **121**: 700–703.

FISCHER, A. 1922. Cultures of organized tissues. *J. exp. Med.* **36**: 393–397.

FISCHER, A. 1925. Sur la transformation *in vitro* des gros leucocytes mononucleaires en fibroblastes. *C. r. Soc. Biol.* (Paris) **92**: 109–112.

FISCHER, A. 1926. The growth of tissue cells from warm blooded animals at lower temperatures. *Arch. exp. Zellforsch.* **2**: 203–305.

FISCHER, A. 1941. Die Bedeutung der Aminosaüren für die Gewebezellen *in vitro*. *Acta physiol. Scandinav.* **2**: 145–188.

FISCHER, A., T. ÅSTRUP, G. EHRENSVARD, and V. OEHLENSCHLAGER. 1948. Growth of animal tissue cells in artificial media. *Proc. Soc. exp. Biol. Med.* **67**: 40–46.

FORD, C. E., P. A. JACOBS, and L. C. LAJTHA. 1958. Human somatic chromosomes. *Nature* **181**: 1565–1568.

FORD, C. E., and R. H. MOLE. 1958. Chromosomes and carcinogenesis: Observations on radiation-induced leukemias. *Proc. 2d. U.N. Internat. Conf. Peaceful Uses Atomic Energy* **22**: 126–133.

FRASER, A. S., and B. F. SHORT. 1958. Studies of sheep mosaic for fleece type. I. Patterns and origin of mosaicism. *Austral. J. biol. Sci.* **11**: 200–208.

FRÉDÉRIC, J. 1951. La transformation histiocytaire des cellules hépatiques cultivées "in vitro" et son déterminisme. *Rev. Hématal.* **6**: 423–447.

FREW, J. G. H. 1928. Technique for the cultivation of insect tissue. *Brit. J. exp. Biol.* **6**: 1–11.

GAILLARD, P. J. 1948. Growth, differentiation and function of explants of some endocrine glands. *Symp., Soc. exp. Biol.* **2**: 139–145.

GAILLARD, P. J. 1953. Growth and differentiation of explanted tissues. *Internat. Rev. Cytol.* **2**: 331–401.

GAILLARD, P. J. 1955. Parathyroid gland and bone in vitro. *Exp. Cell Res., Suppl.* **3**: 154–169.

GAILLARD, P. J. 1957. Greffes à l'homme de tissus cultivés "in vitro." *Coll. Internat. du C.N.R.S.* **78**: 157–165.

GAUTHERET, R. J. 1934. Culture du tissu cambial. *C. r. Acad. Sci.* (Paris) **198**: 2195–2196.

GAUTHERET, R. J. 1935. *Recherches sur la culture des tissus végétaux: Essais de culture de quelques tissus méristématiques*. Paris: Librairie E. le François.

GAUTHERET, R. J. 1938. Sur le repiquage des cultures de tissu cambial de *Salix capraea*. *C. r. Acad. Sci.* (Paris) **206**: 125–127.

GAUTHERET, R. J. 1939. Sur la possibilité de réaliser la culture indéfinie des tissus de tubercules de carotte. *C. r. Acad. Sci.* (Paris) **208**: 118–120.

GAUTHERET, R. J. 1942a. Hétéro-auxines et cultures de tissus végétaux. *Bull. Soc. Chim. Biol.* **24**: 13–47.

GAUTHERET, R. J. 1942b. *Manuel technique de culture des tissus végétaux*. Preface by A. CARREL. Paris: Masson et Cie.

GAUTHERET, R. J. 1948a. Sur la culture indéfinie des tissus de *Salix capraea*. *C. r. Soc. Biol.* (Paris) **142**: 807–808.

GAUTHERET, R. J. 1948b. La culture des tissus végétaux. *Endeavor* **7**: (April, 1948).

GAUTHERET, R. J. 1950. Remarques sur les besoins nutrifis des cultures de tissus de *Salix capraea*. *C. r. Soc. Biol.* (Paris) **144**: 173–174.

GAUTHERET, R. J. 1959. *La Culture des Tissus Végétaux: Techniques et réalisations.* Paris: Masson et Cie.

GAW ZAN-YIN, LIU NIEN TSUI, and ZIA TIEN UN. 1959. Tissue culture methods for cultivation of virus grasserie. *Acta Virologica* **3**: (Suppl. 55–60).

GEY, G. O. 1933. An improved technic for massive tissue culture. *Am. J. Cancer* **17**: 752–756.

GEY, G. O., and M. C. GEY. 1936. The maintenance of human normal cells and tumor cells in continuous culture. I. Preliminary report: Cultivation of mesoblastic tumors and normal tissue and notes on methods of cultivation. *Am. J. Cancer* **27**: 45–76.

GEY, G. O., G. E. SEEGAR, and L. M. HELLMAN. 1938. The production of a gonadotrophic substance (prolan) by placental cells in tissue culture. *Sci.* **88**: 306–307.

GILCHRIST, F. G. 1928. The effect of a horizontal temperature gradient on the development of the egg of the Urodele, *Triturus torosus*. *Physiol. Zool.* **1**: 231–268.

GIOELLI, F. 1938. Morfologia, istologia, fisiologia e fisiopathologia di meristemi secondari *in vitro*. *Atti Accad. Sci. Ferrara* **16**: 1–87.

GOEBEL, K. 1908. Organographie der Pflanzen. Fischer. Jena, 1898–1901.

GRACE, T. D. C. 1958a. Effects of various substances on growth of silkworm tissues in vitro. *Austral. J. biol. Sci.* **2**: 407–417.

GRACE, T. D. C. 1958b. The prolonged growth and survival of ovarian tissue of the Prometheus moth (*Callosamia promethea*) in vitro. *J. gen. Physiol.* **41**: 1027–1034.

GRACE, T. D. C. 1962. The establishment of four strains of cells from insect tissues grown in vitro. *Nature* **195**: 788–789.

GRAFF, S., and K. S. McCARTY. 1957. Sustained cell culture. *Exp. Cell Res.* **13**: 348–357.

GREW, NEHEMIAH. 1682. *The anatomy of plants, with an idea of a philosophical history of plants, and several other lectures, read before the Royal Society.* London: W. Rawlins.

GROBSTEIN, C. 1955. Tissue interactions in the morphogenesis of mouse embryonic rudiments in vitro. In *13th growth symposium* (DOROTHEA RUDNICK, ed.). Princeton, N.J.: Princeton University Press.

GROBSTEIN, C. 1956. Trans-filter induction of tubules in mouse metanephrogenic mesenchyme. *Exp. Cell Res.* **10**: 424–440.

HABERLANDT, G. 1902. Kuturversuche mit isolierten Pflanzenzellen. *Sitzungsber. Akad. der Wiss. Wien, Math.-Naturwiss. Kl.* **111**: 69–92.

HANKS, J. H. 1947. Low temperature in leprosy studies: A study of the bacilli in tissue culture of lepromata in serum media. *Internat. J. Leprosy* **15**: 21–30.

HANKS, J. H. 1948. The longevity of chick tissue cultures without renewal of medium. *J. cell. comp. Physiol.* **31**: 235–260.

HANKS, J. H., and R. E. WALLACE. 1958. Determination of cell viability. *Proc. Soc. Exp. Biol. Med.* **98**: 188–192.

HANKS, J. H., and R. E. WALLACE. 1949. Relation of oxygen and temperature in the preservation of tissues by refrigeration. *Proc. Soc. Exp. Biol. Med.* **71:** 196–20.

HARRIS, M. 1943. The compatibility of rat and mouse cells in mixed tissue cultures. *Anat. Rec.* **87:** 107–117.

HARRIS, M. 1952. The use of dialyzed media for studies in cell nutrition. *J. cell. comp. Physiol.* **40:** 279–302.

HARRIS, M. 1954. The role of bicarbonate for outgrowth of chick heart fibroblasts in vitro. *J. exp. Zool.* **125:** 85–98.

HARRIS, M. 1959. Growth measurements on monolayer cultures with an electronic cell counter. *Cancer Res.* **19:** 1020–1024.

HARRISON, R. G. 1904. Experimentelle Untersuchungen über die Entwicklung der Sinnesorgane der Seitenlinie bei den Amphibien. *Arch. mikr. Anat.* **63:** 35–149.

HARRISON, R. G. 1907. Observations on the living developing nerve fiber. *Proc. Soc. exp. Biol. Med.* **4:** 140–143.

HARRISON, R. G. 1908. Embryonic transplantation and development of the nervous system. *Anat. Rec.* **2:** 385–410.

HARRISON, R. G. 1910. The outgrowth of the nerve fiber as a mode of protoplasmic movement. *J. exp. Zool.* **9:** 787–848.

HARRISON, R. G. 1912. The cultivation of tissues in extraneous media as a method of morphogenetic study. *Anat. Rec.* **6:** 181–193.

HARRISON, R. G. 1928. On the status and significance of tissue culture. *Arch. exp. Zellforsch.* **6:** 4–27.

HAUSCHKA, T. S., J. T. MITCHELL, and I. J. NIEDERPRUEUR. 1959. A reliable frozen tissue bank: Viability and stability of 82 neoplastic and normal cell types after prolonged storage at −78° C. *Cancer Res.* **19:** 643–653.

HEALY, G. M., DOROTHY C. FISHER, and R. C. PARKER. 1955. Nutrition of animal cells in tissue culture; synthetic medium No. 858. *Proc. Soc. exp. Biol. Med.* **89:** 71–77.

HELLER, R. 1949. Sur l'emploi de papier filtre sans cendres comme support pour les cultures de tissus végétaux. *C. r. Soc. Biol.* (Paris) **143:** 335–337.

HELLER, R. 1953. Recherches sur la nutrition minérale des tissus végétaux cultivés in vitro. *Ann. Sci. Naturelle, Bot., Biol. Végét.* **14:** 1–223.

HELLER, R., and R. J., GAUTHERET. 1947. Sur l'emploi d'un ruban de verre comme support pour les cultures de tissus végétaux. *C. r. Soc. Biol.* (Paris) **141:** 662–665.

HILDEBRANDT, A. C., and A. J. RIKER. 1953. Influence of concentrations of sugars and polysaccharides on callus tissue growth in vitro. *Am. J. Bot.* **40:** 66–76.

HILDEBRANDT, A. C., A. J. RIKER, and B. M. DUGGAR. 1946. The influence of composition of the medium on growth in vitro of excised tobacco and sunflower tissue cultures. *Am. J. Bot.* **33:** 591–597.

HOAGLAND, D. R., and W. C. SNYDER. 1933. Nutrition of strawberry plant under controlled conditions. *Proc. Am. Soc. Hort. Sci.* **30:** 288–294.

HOFFMAN, R. S., J. DINGWALL, and W. ANDRUS. 1951. Growth effects on chick fibroblast cultures of fractions of adult and embryonic tissue extracts following differential centrifugation. *Sci.* **113:** 268–269.

HOOKE, R. 1667. *Micrographia: Or some physiological descriptions of minute bodies made by magnifying glasses with observations and inquiries thereupon.* London: John Martyn and James Allestry (John Martyn—Printer to the Royal Society). (Pritzel No. 4198).

HOTSON, H. H. 1953. The growth of rust in tissue culture. *Phytopathology* **43:** 360–363.

HOTSON, H. H., and V. M. CUTLER. 1951. The isolation and culture of *Gymnosporangium Juniperi-virgineanae* Schw. upon artificial media. *Proc. Nat. Acad. Sci.* (Wash.) **37:** 400–403.

HSU, T. C. 1959. Numerical variation of chromosomes in higher animals. In *16th growth symposium: Developmental cytology* (DOROTHEA RUDNICK, ed.). New York: The Ronald Press Co. Pp. 47–62.

Hsu, T. C., and P. S. Moorhead. 1957. Mammalian chromosomes in vitro. VII. Heteroploidy in human cell strains. *J. Nat. Cancer Inst.* **18:** 463–473.

Hsu, T. C., and C. M. Pomerat. 1953a. Mammalian chromosomes in vitro. II. A method for spreading the chromosomes of cells in tissue culture. *J. Hered.* **44:** 23–29.

Hsu, T. C., and C. M. Pomerat. 1953b. Mammalian chromosomes in vitro. III. On somatic aneuploidy. *J. Morphology* **93:** 301–319.

Hughes, A. 1952. Some effects of abnormal tonicity on dividing cells in chick tissue cultures. *Quart. J. micr. Sci.* **93:** 207–219.

Huxley, J. S. 1926. Modification of development by means of temperature gradients. *Anat. Rec.* **34:** 126–127.

Jacquiot, C. 1947. Effet inhibiteur des tannins sur le développement des cultures *in vitro* du cambium de certains arbres fruitiers. *C. r. Acad. Sci.* (Paris) **225:** 434–436.

Jolly, J. 1903. Sur la durée de la vie et de la multiplication des cellules animales en dehors de l'organisme. *C. r. Soc. Biol.* (Paris) **55:** 1266–1268.

Jones, L. E., A. C. Hildebrandt, A. J. Riker, and J. H. Wu. 1960. Growth of somatic tobacco cells in microculture. *Am. J. Bot.* **47:** 468–475.

Knop, W. 1865. Quantitative Untersuchungen über den Ernährungsprozess der Pflanzen. *Landw. Versuchs-Stat.* **7:** 93–107.

Knop, W. 1884. Bereitung einer concentrierten Nährstofflösung für Pflanzen. *Landw. Versuchs-Stat.* **30:** 292–294.

Knudson, L. 1925. Physiological study of the symbiotic germination of orchid seeds. *Bot. Gaz.* **29:** 345–379.

Kotte, W. 1922a. Wurzelmeristem in Gewebekultur. *Ber. Deut. bot. Ges.* **40:** 269–272.

Kotte, W. 1922b. Kulturversuche mit isolierten Wurzelspitzen. *Beitr. Allg. Bot.* **2:** 413–434.

Kuchler, R. J., and D. J. Merchant. 1956. Propagation of strain-L (Earle) cells in agitated fluid suspension cultures. *Proc. Soc. Exp. Biol. Med.* **92:** 803–806.

Kulescha, A., and R. J. Gautheret. 1948. Sur l'élaboration de substances de croissance par 3 types de cultures de tissus de Scorsonère: Cultures normales, cultures de Crown-Gall et cultures accoutumées à l'hétéro-auxine. *C. r. Acad. Sci.* (Paris) **227:** 292–294.

LaRue, C. R. 1953. Studies on growth and regeneration in gametophytes and sporophytes of gymnosperms: Abnormal and pathological plant growth. *Brookhaven Sym. Biol.* **6:** 187–208.

Lasfargues, E. Y. 1957a. Cultivation and behavior in vitro of the normal mammary epithelium of the adult mouse. II. Observations on the secretory activity. *Exp. Cell Res.* **13:** 553–562.

Lasfargues, E. Y. 1957b. Cultivation and behavior in vitro of the normal mammary epithelium of the adult mouse. *Anat. Rec.* **127:** 117–126.

Leighton, J. 1951. A sponge matrix method for tissue culture: Formation of organized aggregates of cells in vitro. *J. Nat. Cancer Inst.* **12:** 545–562.

Leighton, J. 1954. The growth patterns of some transplantable animal tumors in sponge matrix tissue cultures. *J. Nat. Cancer Inst.* **15:** 275–282.

Levi-Montalcini, Rita, H. Meyer, and V. Hamburger. 1954. In vitro experiments on the effects of mouse sarcoma 180 and 37 on the spinal and sympathetic ganglia of the chick embryo. *Cancer Res.* **14:** 49–57.

Lewis, Margaret R. 1916. Sea water as a medium for tissue cultures. *Anat. Rec.* **10:** 287–299.

Lewis, Margaret R. 1928. A simple method of drawing blood from the heart of a fowl. *Arch. exp. Zellforsch.* **7:** 82–86.

Lewis, Margaret R., and W. H. Lewis. 1911a. The cultivation of tissues from chick embryos in solutions of NaCl, $CaCl_2$, KCl and $NaHCO_3$. *Anat. Rec.* **5:** 277–293.

Lewis, Margaret R., and W. H. Lewis. 1911b. The growth of embryonic chicken tissues in artificial media, agar and bouillon. *Bull. Johns Hopkins Hosp.* **22**: 126–127.

LEWIS, MARGARET R., and W. H. LEWIS. 1911c. The cultivation of tissues in salt solution. *J. Am. Med. Assoc.* **56**: 1795–1796.

LEWIS, MARGARET R., and W. H. LEWIS. 1912a. The cultivation of sympathetic nerves from the intestine of chicken embryos in saline solutions. *Anat. Rec.* **6**: 7–32.

LEWIS, MARGARET R., and W. H. LEWIS. 1912b. The cultivation of chicken tissues in media of known chemical constitution. *Anat. Rec.* **6**: 207–211.

LEWIS, MARGARET R., and W. H. LEWIS. 1926. Transformation of mononuclear blood-cells into macrophages, epithelioid cells, and giant cells in hanging-drop blood-cultures from lower vertebrates. *Carnegie Inst. Wash., Publ. 363, Contrib. Embryol.* **18**: 95–120.

LEWIS, W. H. 1929. The effect of various solutions and salts on the pulsation rate of isolated hearts from young chick embryos. *Carnegie Inst. Wash., Publ. 115 Contrib. Embryol.* **20**: 173–192.

LEWIS, W. H. 1935. Rat malignant cells in roller tube cultures and some results. *Carnegie Inst. Wash., Publ. 459, Contrib. Embryol.* **25**: 161–172.

LEWIS, W. H., and ELSIE S. WRIGHT. 1935. On the early development of the mouse egg. *Carnegie Inst. Wash., Publ. 459, Contrib. Embryol.* **148**: 113–144.

LI, C. R., and T. M. RIVERS. 1930. Cultivation of vaccine virus. *J. exp. Med.* **52**: 465–470.

LIMASSET, P., and R. J. GAUTHERET. 1950. Sur le caractère tumoral des tissus de tabac ayant subi le phénomène d'accoutumance aux hétéro-auxines. *C. r. Acad. Sci.* (Paris) **230**: 2043–2045.

LIPMANN, F. 1932. Versuche zur methodik der Messung der Zuwachses *in vitro* wachsender Gewebe durch Messung des Umsatzanstiegs. *Biochem. Ztschr.* **244**: 177–186.

LIPMANN, F. 1933. Stoffwechselversuche an Gewebekulturen, insbesondere über die Rolle der Glykolyse in Stoffwechsel embryonaler Zellen. *Biochem. Ztschr.* **261**: 157–164.

LIPMANN, F., and A. FISCHER. 1932. Proliferationsgrösse von Gewebezellen *in vitro* and Stoffumsatz. *Biochem. Ztschr.* **244**: 187–189.

LIU NIEN TSUI, T. E. SCHICK, and ZAN-YIN GAW. 1958. (Cultivation of silkworm tissue.) (In Chinese.) *Scientia* **7**: 219.

LJUNGGREN, C. A. 1897–98. Von der Fähigkeit des Hautepithels, ausserhalb des Organismus sein Leben zu behalten, mit Beruchsichtigung der Transplantation. *Deutsch. Ztschr. f. Chir.* **47**: 608–615.

LOCKE, F. S. 1895. Artificial fluids as uninjurious as possible to animal tissues. *Boston med. surg. J.* **134**: 173. Reprinted in *J. Boston Sci. Med.* **1**, No. 1:2–3.

LOEB, L. 1902. On the growth of epithelium in agar and blood-serum in the living body. *J. med. Res.* **8**: 109–115.

LOO, S. W. 1945. Cultivation of excised stem-tips of asparagus in vitro. *Am. J. Bot.* **32**: 13–17.

LÖWENSTADT, H. 1925. Einige neue Hilfsmittel zur Angebung von Gewebekulturen. *Arch. exp. Zellforsch* **1**: 251–256.

LWOFF, A., R. DULBECCO, MARGUERITE VOGT, and MARGUERITE LWOFF. 1955. Kinetics of the release of poliomyelitis virus from single cells. *Virol.* **1**: 128–139.

MCLAREN, A., and J. D. BIGGERS. 1958. Successful development and birth of mice cultivated in vitro as early embryos. *Nature* **182**: 877–878.

MCLIMANS, W. F., E. V. DAVIS, F. L. GLOVER, and G. W. RAKE. 1957a. The submerged culture of mammalian cells: The spinner culture. *J. Immunol.* **79**: 428–433.

MCLIMANS, W. F., F. E. GIARDINELLO, E. V. DAVIS, C. J. KUCERA, and G. W. RAKE. 1957b. Submerged culture of mammalian cells: The five liter fermentor. *J. Bact.* **74**: 768–774.

MAHESHWARI, NIRMALA. 1958. In vitro culture of excised ovules of *Papaver somniferum. Sci.* **127**: 342.

MAHESHWARI, NIRMALA, and M. LAL. 1961. In vitro culture of ovaries of *Iberis amara* L. *Phytomorphology* 11: 17–23.

MAITLAND, H. B., and M. C. MAITLAND. 1928. Cultivation of vaccinia virus without tissue culture. *Lancet* 2: 596–597.

MALPIGHI, M. 1675. Anatome plantarum. *Regiae Societati Londini ad Scientiam Naturalem Promovendem Institutae Dicta.* Johannis Martyn impensis (London).

MARCHAL, J. G., and A. MAZURIER. 1944. Culture *in vitro* de cellules végétales isolées. *Bull. Soc. Bot. Fr.* 91: 76–77.

MARTINOVITCH, P. N. 1953. A modification of the watch glass technique for the cultivation of endocrine glands of infantile rats. *Exp. Cell Res.* 4: 490–493.

MARTINOVITCH, P. N. 1955. Infantile rat adrenal transplanted into the anterior eye chamber of adrenalectomized hosts after cultivation in vitro. *J. exp. Zool.* 129: 99–128.

MAXIMOW, A. 1925. Tissue cultures of young mammalian embryos. *Carnegie Inst. Wash., Publ. 361, Contrib. Embryol.* 16: 47–113.

MEDVEDEVA, NATALIE B. 1960. On the cultivation of insect tissues in vitro. (Russian, English summary). *Rev. d'Entomol. U.S.S.R.* 39: 77–85.

MEIER, R. 1931. Zur Methodik der Stoffwechseluntersuchungen an Gewebekulturen. II. Gewichtsbestimmung an einzelnen Gewebekulture: Gewichtszunahme und Flächenzunahme. Vorläufige Mitteilung. *Biochem. Ztschr.* 231: 253–259.

MELCHERS, G., and L. BERGMANN. 1957. Kritische Versuche zur sogenannten Chemotherapie der Virus-Krankheiten. IV. *Internat. Pflanzenschutzkongresses Hamburg.*

MELCHERS, G., and L. BERGMANN. 1959. Infektionsversuche an submers kultivierten Geweben mit Tabakmosaikvirus. *Zeitschr. f. Naturforsch.* 14: 73–76.

MELCHERS, G., and V. ENGELMANN. 1955. Die Kultur von Pflanzengewebe in flüssigen Medium mit Dauerbeluftung. *Naturwiss.* 20: 564–565.

MELNICK, J. L., CATHERINE RAPPAPORT, D. D. BANKER, and P. N. BHATT. 1955. Stabilized suspensions of monkey kidney cells suitable for intercontinental shipment. *Proc. Soc. Exp. Biol. Med.* 88: 676–678.

METZGER, J. F., M. H. FUSILLO, I. CORNMAN, and D. M. KUHNS. 1954. Antibiotics in tissue culture. *Exp. Cell Res.* 6: 337–344.

MOLLIARD, M. 1921. Sur le développement des plantules fragmentées. *C. r. Soc. Biol.* (Paris) 84: 770–772.

MOORHEAD, P. S., and P. C. NOWELL. *Chromosome cytology of cultured cells.* (*Methods of medical research,* Vol. IX.) Chicago: Year Book Publishers, Inc. In press.

MOORHEAD, P. S., P. C. NOWELL, W. J. MELLMAN, D. M. BATTIPS, and D. A. HUNGERFORD. 1960. Chromosome preparations of leukocytes cultured from human peripheral blood. *Exp. Cell Res.* 20: 613–616.

MOREL, G. 1944. Le développement du mildiou sur les tissus de vigne cultivés *in vitro. C. r. Acad. Sci.* (Paris) 218: 50–52.

MOREL, G. 1946. Action de l'acide pantothénique sur la croissance des tissus d'Aubépine cultivés *in vitro. C. r. Acad. Sci.* (Paris) 223: 166–168.

MOREL, G. 1947. Transformations des cultures de tissus de vigne produits par l'hétéro-auxine. *C. r. Soc. Biol.* (Paris) 141: 280–282.

MOREL, G. 1948. Recherches sur la culture associée de parasites obligatoires et de tissus végétaux. *Ann. Epiphyties* 14: 123–234.

MORGAN, J. F., L. F. GUERIN, and HELEN J. MORTON. 1956. The effect of low temperature and storage on the viability and mouse strain specificity of ascitic tumor cells. *Cancer Res.* 16: 907–911.

MORGAN, J. F., HELEN J. MORTON, and R. C. PARKER. 1950. Nutrition of animal cells in tissue culture. I. Initial studies on a synthetic medium. *Proc. Soc. Exp. Biol. Med.* 73: 1–8.

MORTON, HELEN J., A. E. PASIEKA, and J. F. MORGAN. 1956. The nutrition of animal tissues cultivated in vitro. III. Use of a depletion technique for determining specific nutritional requirements. *J. biophys. biochem. Cytol.* 2: 589–596.

MOSCONA, A. 1952. Cell suspensions from organ rudiments of chick embryos. *Exp. Cell Res.* 3: 535–539.

Moscona, A. 1956. Development of heterotypic combinations of dissociated embryonic chick cells. *Proc. Soc. Exp. Biol. Med.* **92:** 410–416.

Moscona, A. 1957. The development in vitro of chimeric aggregates of dissociated embryonic chick and mouse cells. *Proc. Nat. Acad. Sci.* (Wash.) **43:** 184–194.

Muir, W. H., A. C. Hildebrandt, and A. J. Riker. 1954. Plant tissue cultures produced from single isolated cells. *Sci.* **119:** 877–878.

Muir, W. H., A. C. Hildebrandt, and A. J. Riker. 1958. The preparation, isolation and growth in culture of single cells from higher plants. *Am. J. Bot.* **45:** 589–597.

Murneek, A. E. 1935. Physiological role of asparagine and related substances in nitrogen metabolism of plants. *Plant Physiol.* **10:** 447–464.

Murray, Margaret R., and Gertrude Kopech. 1953. *A bibliography of the research in tissue culture: 1884–1950.* 2 vols. New York: Academic Press, Inc.

Murray, Margaret R., and A. P. Stout. 1942. Characteristics of human Schwann cells in vitro. *Anat. Rec.* **84:** 275–285.

Murray, Margaret R., and A. P. Stout. 1947a. Adult human sympathetic ganglion cells cultivated in vitro. *Am. J. Anat.* **80:** 225–250.

Murray, Margaret R., and A. P. Stout. 1947b. Distinctive characteristics of the sympathicoblastoma cultivated in vitro: A method for prompt diagnosis. *Am. J. Pathol.* **23:** 429–435.

Murray, Margaret R., and A. P. Stout. 1954. The classification and diagnosis of human tumors by tissue culture methods. *Tex. Rep. Biol. Med.* **12:** 898–915.

Naylor, E. E. 1931. The morphology of regeneration of *Bryophyllum calycinum*. *Am. J. Bot.* **19:** 32–40.

Nickell, L. G. 1951. Embryo culture of weeping crabapple. *Proc. Am. Soc. Hort. Sci.* **57:** 401–405.

Nickell, L. G. 1956. The continuous submerged cultivation of plant tissue as single cells. *Proc. Nat. Acad. Sci.* (Wash.) **42:** 848–850.

Nickell, L. G., and W. Tulecke. 1960. Submerged growth of cells of higher plants. *J. Biochem. Microbiol. Technol. Eng.* **2:** 287–297.

Nitsch, J. P. 1949. Culture of fruits in vitro. *Sci.* **110:** 499.

Nitsch, J. P. 1951. Growth and development in vitro of excised ovaries. *Am. J. Bot.* **38:** 566–577.

Nobécourt, P. 1937. Cultures en série de tissus végétaux sur milieu artificiel. *C. r. Acad. Sci.* (Paris) **205:** 521–523.

Nobécourt, P. 1939. Sur la perennité et l'augmentation de volume des cultures de tissus végétaux. *C. r. Soc. Biol.* (Paris) **130:** 1270.

Nobécourt, P. 1940. Synthèse de la vitamine B₁ dans des cultures de tissus végétaux. *C. r. Soc. Biol.* (Paris) **133:** 530–532.

Novick, A., and L. Szilard. 1950. Description of the chemostat. *Sci.* **112:** 715–716.

Osgood, E. E., and J. H. Brooke. 1955. Continuous tissue culture of leucocytes from human leukemic bloods by application of "gradient" principles. *Blood* **10:** 1010–1022.

Overbeek, J. van. 1939. Evidence for auxin production in isolated roots growing in vitro. *Bot. Gaz.* **101:** 450–456.

Overbeek, J. van. 1942. Cultivation in vitro of small *Datura* embryos. *Am. J. Bot.* **29:** 472–477.

Overbeek, J. van, M. E. Conklin, and A. F. Blakeslee. 1941. Factors in coconut milk essential for growth and development of very young *Datura* embryos. *Sci.* **94:** 350–351.

Owens, Olga von H., M. K. Gey, and G. O. Gey. 1954. Growth of cells in agitated fluid medium. *Ann. N.Y. Acad. Sci.* **58:** 1039–1055.

Paál, A. 1914. Über phototropische Reitzleiteungen. *Ber. Deut. bot. Ges.* **32:** 499–502.

Painter, J. T., C. M. Pomerat, and D. Ezell. 1949. The effect of substances known to influence the activity of the nervous system on fiber outgrowths from living embryonic chick spinal cords. *Tex. Rep. Biol. Med.* **7:** 417–455.

PARKER, R. C. 1932. The races that constitute the group of common fibroblasts. I. The effect of blood plasma. *J. exp. Med.* **55**: 713–734.

PARKER, R. C. 1936. The cultivation of tissues for prolonged periods in single flasks. *J. exp. Med.* **64**: 121–130.

PARKER, R. C. 1961. *Methods of tissue culture.* 3d ed. New York: Paul B. Hoeber, Inc.

PARTANEN, C. R., I. M. SUSSEX, and T. A. STEEVES. 1955. Nuclear behavior in relation to abnormal growth in fern prothalli. *Am. J. Bot.* **42**: 245–256.

PAUL, J. 1960. *Cell and tissue culture.* 2d ed. Baltimore: The Williams & Wilkins Co.

PLANTEFOL, L. 1938. Sur les échanges respiratoires des tissus végétaux en culture. *C. r. Acad. Sci.* (Paris) **207**: 1121–1123.

PLANTEFOL, L., and R. J. GAUTHERET. 1939. Le glucose et la respiration des cultures de tissus végétaux. *C. r. Acad. Sci* (Paris) **208**: 927–929.

POMERAT, C. M. (ed.). 1951. Tissue culture methods. Section IV in *Methods of medical research*, Vol. 4. Chicago: Year Book Publishers, Inc.

POMERAT, C. M. 1959 Rhythmic contraction of Schwann cells *Sci.* **130**: 1759–1760.

POMERAT, C. M., and E. L. SEVERINGHAUS (eds.). 1954. Tissue culture technique in pharmacology. *Ann. N.Y. Acad. Sci.* **58**: 971–1326.

PORTER, K. R. 1947. The culture of tissue cells in clots formed from purified bovine fibrinogen and thrombin. *Proc. Soc. exp. Biol. Med.* **65**: 309–314.

PRICE, W. C. 1940. Generalized defense reactions in plants. *Am. Nat.* **74**: 117–128.

PRIESTLEY, J. H. 1928. The meristematic tissue of the plant. *Biol. Rev.* **3**: 1–20.

PUCK, T. T. 1958. Growth and genetics of somatic mammalian cells in vitro. *J. cell. comp. Physiol.* **52**: 287–311.

PUCK, T. T., and H. W. FISHER. 1956. Genetics of somatic mammalian cells. I. Demonstration of the existence of mutants with different growth requirements in a human cancer cell strain (HeLa). *J. exp. Med.* **104**: 427–433.

PUCK, T. T., and P. I. MARCUS. 1955. A rapid method for viable cell titration and clone production with HeLa cells in tissue culture: The use of X-irradiated cells to supply conditioning factors. *Proc. Nat. Acad. Sci.* (Wash.) **41**: 432–437.

PUCK, T. T., P. I. MARCUS, and S. J. CIECIURA. 1956. Clonal growth of mammalian cells in vitro: Growth characteristics of colonies from single HeLa cells with and without a "feeder" layer. *J. exp. Med.* **103**: 273–283.

RANGA SWAMY, N. S. 1961. Experimental studies on female reproductive structures of *Citrus microcarpa* Bunge. *Phytomorphology* **11**: 109–127.

RECHINGER, C. 1893. Untersuchungen über die Grenzen der Teilbarkeit im Pflanzenreich. *Abh. zool.-bot. Ges.* (Wien) **43**: 310–334.

REINERT, J., and P. R. WHITE. 1956. The cultivation in vitro of tumor tissues and normal tissues of *Picea glauca*. *Physiologia Plantarum* **9**: 177–189.

RINGER, S. 1886. Further experiments regarding the influence of lime, potassium and other salts on muscular tissue. *J. Physiol.* **7**: 291–308.

RIVERS, T. M., E. HAAGEN, and R. S. MUCKENFUSS. 1929. Development in tissue cultures of the intracellular changes characteristic of vaccinal and herpetic infections. *J. exp. Med.* **50**: 665–672.

ROBBINS, W. J. 1922a. Cultivation of excised root tips and stem tips under sterile conditions. *Bot. Gaz.* **73**: 376–390.

ROBBINS, W. J. 1922b. Effect of autolyzed yeast and peptone on growth of excised corn root tips in the dark. *Bot. Gaz.* **74**: 59–79.

ROBBINS, W. J., and MARY A. BARTLEY. 1937. Vitamin B₁ and the growth of excised tomato roots. *Sci.* **85**: 246–247.

ROBBINS, W. J., and W. E. MANEVAL. 1923. Further experiments on growth of excised root tips under sterile conditions. *Bot. Gaz.* **76**: 274–287.

ROBBINS, W. J., and W. E. MANEVAL. 1924. Effect of light on growth of excised root tips under sterile conditions. *Bot. Gaz.* **78**: 424–432.

ROBBINS, W. J., and MARY B. SCHMIDT. 1938a. Growth of excised roots of the tomato. *Bot. Gaz.* **99**: 671–728.

ROBBINS, W. J., and MARY B. SCHMIDT. 1938b. Growth of excised tomato roots in a synthetic solution. *Bull. Torrey Bot. Club* **66**: 193–200.

ROBBINS, W. J., and MARY B. SCHMIDT. 1939a. Further experiments on excised tomato roots. *Am. J. Bot.* **26**: 149–159.

ROBBINS, W. J., and MARY B. SCHMIDT. 1939b. Vitamin B₆, a growth substance for excised tomato roots. *Proc. Nat. Acad. Sci.* (Wash.) **25**: 1–3.

ROBBINS, W. J., VIRGINIA B. WHITE, J. E. McCLARY, and MARY A. BARTLEY. 1936. The importance of ash elements in the cultivation of excised root tips. *Proc. Nat. Acad. Sci.* (Wash.) **22**: 636–639.

ROBERTSON, G. G. 1945. Homoplastic ovarian transplantability in the house mouse. *Proc. Soc. exp. Biol. Med.* **59**: 30–31.

ROSE, G. G., C. M. POMERAT, T. O. SHINDLER, and J. B. TRUNNELL. 1958. A cellophane-strip technique for culturing tissue in multipurpose culture chambers. *J. biophys. and biochem. Cytol.* **4**: 761–764.

ROSENE, H. F. 1941. Comparison of rates of water intake in contiguous regions of intact and isolated roots. *Plant Physiol.* **16**: 19–38.

ROSENE, H. F., and E. J. LUND. 1937. Effect of an applied electric current on the external longitudinal polarity potentials of Douglas fir. *Am. J. Bot.* **24**: 390–399.

ROUS, P., and F. S. JONES. 1916. A method for obtaining suspensions of living cells from the fixed tissues, and for plating out of individual cells. *J. exp. Med.* **23**: 549–555.

ROUX, W. 1885. Beiträge zur Entwicklungsmechanik des Embryo. *Ztschr. Biol.* **21**: 411–526.

SACHAR, R. C., and B. BALDEV. 1958. In vitro growth of ovaries of *Linaria moroccana* Hook. *Current Sci.* **27**: 104–105.

SACHAR, R. C., and KUSUM KANTA. 1958. Influence of growth substances on artificially cultured ovaries of *Tropaeolum majus* L. *Phytomorphology* **8**: 202–218.

SALK, J. F. 1953. Studies in human subjects on active immunization against poliomyelitis: preliminary report of experiments in progress. *J. Am. Med. Assoc.* **151**: 1081–1098.

SANFORD, KATHERINE K., W. R. EARLE, V. J. EVANS, H. K. WALTZ, and J. E. SHANNON. 1951. The measurement of proliferation in tissue cultures by enumeration of cell nuclei. *J. Nat. Cancer Inst.* **11**: 773–795.

SANFORD, KATHERINE K., W. R. EARLE, and GWENDOLYN D. LIKELY. 1948. The growth in vitro of single isolated tissue cells. *J. Nat. Cancer Inst.* **9**: 229–246.

SANFORD, KATHARINE K., GWENDOLYN D. LIKELY, and W. R. EARLE. 1954. The development of variations in transplantability and morphology within a clone of mouse fiibroblasts transformed to sarcoma-producing cells in vitro. *J. Nat. Cancer Inst.* **15**: 215–230.

SCHABERG, A. 1955. Regeneration of the adrenal cortex in vitro. *Anat. Rec.* **122**: 205–214.

SCHABERG, A., and C. A. deGROOT. 1958. The influence of the anterior hypophysis on the morphology and function of the adrenal cortex in vitro. *Exp. Cell Res.* **15**: 475–483.

SCHERER, W. F., and A. C. HOOGASIAN. 1954. Preservation at subzero temperatures of mouse fibroblasts (strain L) and human epithelial cells (strain HeLa). *Proc. Soc. exp. Biol. Med.* **87**: 480–487.

SCHERER, W. F., et al. 1955. *An introduction to cell and tissue culture.* Minneapolis: Burgess Publishing Co.

SCHLEIDEN, M. J. 1838. Beiträge zur Phytogenesis. *Arch. Anat., Physiol. u. Wiss. Med.* (J. Müller) **1838**: 137–176.

SCHOPFER, W. H., and W. RYTZ, JR. 1937. La ouate comme source de facteur de croissance de microörganisme. *Arch. Mikrobiol.* **8**: 244–248.

SCHWANN, T. 1839. *Mikroskopische Untersuchungen über die Übereinstimmung in der Struktur und dem Wachstume der Tiere und Pflanzen.* Leipzig: W. Engelmann, Nr. 176, Ostwalds Klassiker der exakten Wissenschaften, 1910.

SHAFFER, B. M. 1956. The culture of organs from the embryonic chick on cellulose-acetate fabric. *Exp. Cell Res.* **11:** 244–248.

SHARP, L. W. 1926. *An introduction to cytology.* 2d ed. New York: McGraw-Hill Book Co., Inc.

SHAW, D. T., L. C. KINGSLAND, and A. M. BRUES. 1940. A roller bottle tissue culture system. *Sci.* **91:** 148–149.

SIMMS, H. S., and M. SANDERS. 1942. Use of serum ultrafiltrate in tissue cultures for studying deposition of fat and for propagation of viruses. *Arch. path.* **33:** 619–635.

SKOOG, F. 1951. Chemical control of growth and organ formation in plant tissues. *Année biol.* **26:** 545–562.

SKOOG, F., and C. TSUI. 1948. Chemical control of growth and bud formation in tobacco stem segments and callus cultured in vitro. *Am. J. Bot.* **35:** 782–787.

SOLT, MARIE L., R. F. DAWSON, and D. R. CHRISTMAN. 1960. Biosynthesis of ana-basine and of nicotine by excised root cultures of *Nicotiana glauca. Plant Physiol.* **35:** 887–894.

SPEMANN, H. 1936. *Experimentelle Beiträge zu einer Theorie der Entwicklung.* Berlin: J. Springer.

STANLEY, W. M. 1938. Aucuba mosaic virus protein isolated from diseased, excised tomato roots grown in vitro. *J. Biol. Chem.* **126:** 125–131.

STEEVES, T. A., and I. M. SUSSEX. 1952. In vitro cultures of a fern callus. *Nature* **170:** 672–673.

STEVENS, L. C. 1957. A modification of Robertson's technique of homiotropic ovarian transplantation in mice. *Transplantation Bulletin* **4:** 106–107.

STEVENS, L. C. 1960. Embryonic potency of embryoid bodies derived from a trans-plantable testicular teratoma. *Developmental Biology* **2:** 285–297.

STEVENS, L. C., E. S. RUSSELL, and J. L. SOUTHARD. 1957. Evidence on inheritance of muscular dystrophy in an inbred strain of mice using ovarian transplantation. *Proc. Soc. Exp. Biol. Med.* **95:** 161–164.

STEWARD, F. C., and S. M. CAPLIN. 1951. A tissue culture from potato tuber: The synergistic action of 2,4-D and of coconut milk. *Sci.* **113:** 518–520.

STEWARD, F. C., and S. M. CAPLIN. 1954. The growth of carrot tissue explants and its relation to the growth factors present in coconut milk. I(A): The development of the quantitative method and the factors affecting the growth of carrot tissue explants. *Ann. Biol.* **30:** 385–394.

STEWARD, F. C., MARION O. MAPES, and JOAN SMITH. 1958a. Growth and organized development of cultured cells. I. Growth and division of freely suspended cells. *Am. J. Bot.* **45:** 693–703.

STEWARD, F. C., MARION O. MAPES, and JOAN SMITH. 1958b. Growth and organized development of cultured cells. II. Organization in cultures grown from freely suspended cells. *Am. J. Bot.* **45:** 705–708.

STEWARD, F. C., and J. C. MARTIN. 1937. The distribution and physiology of *Valonia* at the Dry Tortugas with special reference to the problem of salt accumulation in plants. *Carnegie Inst. Wash., Publ. 475,* pp. 87–170.

STEWARD, F. C., and E. M. SCHANTZ. 1954. The growth of carrot tissue explants and its relation to the growth factors in coconut milk. II. The growth-promoting prop-erties of coconut milk for plant tissue cultures. *Ann. Biol.* **30:** 399–415.

STEWARD, F. C., and E. M. SCHANTZ. 1955. The chemical induction of growth in plant tissue cultures: The chemistry and mode of action of plant growth sub-stances. *Proc. Sym. Wye College* 165–186.

STONE, H. B., J. C. OWINGS, and G. O. GEY. 1934a. Transplantation of living grafts of thyroid and parathyroid glands. *Ann. Surg.* **1934:** 262–277.

STONE, H. B., J. C. OWINGS, and G. O. GEY. 1934b. Living grafts of endocrine glands. *Am. J. Surg.* **24:** 386–392.

STRANGEWAYS, T. S. P., and HONOR B. FELL. 1926. Experimental studies on the differentiation of embryo tissues growing in vivo and in vitro. Part I. *Proc. Roy. Soc. London B.* **99:** 340–366; Part II. *Proc. Roy. Soc. London B.* **100:** 273–283.

STRAUS, J. 1954. Maize endosperm tissue grown in vitro. II. Morphology and cytology. *Am. J. Bot.* **41**: 833–839.

STRAUS, J., and C. D. LaRue. 1954. Maize endosperm tissue grown in vitro. I. Culture requirements. *Am. J. Bot.* **41**: 687–694.

STREET, H. E. 1950. The role of high-energy phosphate bonds in biosynthesis. *Sci. Progress* **38**: 43–66.

STULBERG, C. S., H. D. SOULE, and L. BERMAN. 1958. Preservation of human epithelial-like and fibroblast-like cell strains at low temperatures. *Proc. Soc. Exp. Biol. Med.* **98**: 428–431.

SUSSEX, I. M., and T. A. STEEVES. 1953. Growth of excised fern leaves in sterile conditions. *Nature* **172**: 624–627.

SWIM, H. E., and R. F. PARKER. 1955. Preservation of cell cultures at 4° C. *Proc. Soc. Exp. Biol. Med.* **89**: 549–553.

SWIM, H. E., R. F. HAFF, and R. F. PARKER. 1958. Some practical aspects of storing mammalian cells in the dry-ice chest. *Cancer Res.* **18**: 711–717.

TANAOKI, T., A. C. HILDEBRANDT, and A. J. RIKER. 1960. Use of pectinase in preparation of mitochondria from tobacco-tissue cultures. *Sci.* **132**: 1766–1767.

THEOPHRASTUS OF ERESSOS. Ca. 320 B.C. *Enquiry into plants.* Translated by A. HORT, 1916. New York: G. P. Putnam's Sons, Inc., Loeb Classical Library.

TORREY, J. G. 1957. Cell division in isolated single plant cells in vitro. *Proc. Nat. Acad. Sci.* (Wash.) **43**: 887–891.

TORREY, J. G. 1959. Experimental modification of development in the root. (In *17th growth symposium: Cell, organism, and milieu.* DOROTHEA RUDNICK, ed.) New York: The Ronald Press Co., pp. 189–222.

TORREY, J. G., J. REINERT, and NANCY MERKEL. 1962. Mitosis in suspension cultures of higher plant cells in a synthetic medium. *Am. J. Bot.* **49**: 420–425.

TORREY, J. G., and Y. SHIGEMURA. 1957. Growth and controlled morphogenesis in pea root callus tissue grown in liquid media. *Am. J. Bot.* **44**: 334–344.

TRAGER, W. 1935. Cultivation of the virus of grasserie in silkworm tissue cultures. *J. exp. Med.* **61**: 501–513.

TRELEASE, S., and H. M. TRELEASE. 1933. Physiologically balanced culture solutions with stable hydrogen-ion concentration. *Sci.* **78**: 438–439.

TROWELL, O. A. 1959. The culture of mature organs in a synthetic medium. *Exp. Cell Res.* **16**: 118–147.

TSCHERMAK-WOESS, E. 1956. Karyologische Pflanzenanatomie. *Protoplasma* **46**: 798–834.

TUKEY, H. B. 1933. Artificial culture of sweet cherry embryos. *J. Hered.* **24**: 7–12.

TUKEY, H. B. 1934. Artificial culture methods for isolated embryos of deciduous fruits. *Am. Soc. Hort. Sci.* **32**: 313–322.

TULECKE, W. R. 1953. A tissue derived from the pollen of *Ginkgo biloba.* *Sci.* **117**: 599–600.

TULECKE, W. R. 1957. The pollen of *Ginkgo biloba:* In vitro culture and tissue formation. *Am. J. Bot.* **44**: 602–608.

TYRODE, M. V. 1910. The mode of action of some purgative salts. *Arch. internat. Pharmacodyn.* **20**: 205–223.

UNDERWOOD, W. B. 1941. *A textbook of sterilization.* Erie, Pa.: American Sterilizer Co.

USPENSKI, E. E., and W. J. USPENSKAIA. 1925. Reinkultur und ungeschlechtliche Fortpflanzung der *Volvox minor* und *Volvox globator* in einer synthetischen Nährlösung. *Ztschr. Bot.* **17**: 273–308.

VAGO, C., and S. CHASTUNG. 1958. Obtention de lignées cellulaires en culture de tissus d'invertébrés. *Experientia* **14**: 110–111.

VASIL, I. K. 1957. Effect of Kinetin and gibberellic acid on excised anthers of *Allium cepa. Phytomorphology* **7**: 138–149.

VICKERY, H. B., G. W. PUCHER, and H. E. CLARK. 1936. Glutamine metabolism of the beet. *Plant Physiol.* **11**: 413–420.

VICKERY, H. B., G. W. PUCHER, A. J. WAKEMAN, and C. L. LEAVENWORTH. 1937.

Chemical investigations of the tobacco plant. VI. Chemical changes that occur in leaves during culture in light and darkness. *Conn. Agr. Exp. Sta. Bull.* **399**: 757–832.

VIRCHOW, R. 1858. *Die Cellularpathologie in ihrer Begründung auf physiologische und pathologische Gewebelehre.* Berlin: A. Hirschwald.

VÖCHTING, H. 1878, 1884. *Über Organbildung im Pflanzenreich.* I. Theil. 1878. II. Theil. 1884. Bonn: Max Cohen.

VÖCHTING, H. 1892. *Über Transplantation am Pflanzenkörper: Untersuchungen zur Physiologie und Pathologie.* Tübingen: H. Laupp.

VÖCHTING, H. 1894. Über die durch Pfropfen herbeigeführte Symbiose des *Helianthus tuberosus* und *Helianthus annuus. Sitzngsber. K. Preuss. Akad. Wiss.* (Berlin) **1894**: 705–721.

VÖCHTING, H. 1918. *Untersuchungen zur experimentelle Anatomie und Pathologie des Pflanzenkörpers.* Tübingen: H. Laupp.

VOGELAAR, J. P. M., and ELEANOR ERLICHMAN. 1933. A feeding solution for cultures of human fibroblasts. *Am. J. Cancer* **18**: 28–38.

VOGELAAR, J. P. M., and ELEANOR ERLICHMAN. 1939. Contributions to tissue culture technic. *Am. J. Cancer* **35**: 510–520.

VOGT, W. 1932. Einige Ergebnisse aus Versuchen mit halbseitiger Temperaturhemmung am Amphibienkeim. *Rev. Suisse Zool.* **39**: 309–324.

WALKER, B. E. 1958. Polyploidy and differentiation in the transitional epithelium of mouse urinary bladder. *Chromosoma* **9**: 105–118.

WALLACE, R. E., and J. H. HANKS. 1958. Agar substrates for study of microepidemiology and physiology of cells in vitro. *Sci.* **128**: 658–659.

WARBURG, O. 1923. Versuche an überlebenden Karzinomgewebe. *Biochem. Ztschr.* **142**: 317–350.

WARBURG, O., and F. KUBOWITZ. 1927. Stoffwechsel wachsender Zellen (Fibroblasten, Herz, Chorion). *Biochem. Ztschr.* **189**: 242–248.

WAYMOUTH, CHARITY. 1956a. A rapid quantitative hematocrit method for measuring increase in cell population of strain L (Earle) cells cultivated in serum-free nutrient solution. *J. Nat. Cancer Inst.* **17**: 305–311.

WAYMOUTH, CHARITY. 1956b. A serum-free nutrient solution sustaining rapid and continuous proliferation of strain L (Earle) mouse cells. *J. Nat. Cancer Inst.* **17**: 315–325.

WAYMOUTH, CHARITY. 1959. Rapid proliferation of sublines of NCTC Clone 929 (strain L) mouse cells in a simple chemically defined medium (MB 752/1). *J. Nat. Cancer Inst.* **22**: 1003–1017.

WEINSTEIN, L. H., L. G. NICKELL, H. J. LAURENCOT, and W. R. TULECKE. 1959. Biochemical and physiological studies of plant tissue cultures and the plant parts from which they are derived. I. Agave toumeyana Trel. *Contrib. Boyce Thompson Inst.* **20**: 239–250.

WEISS, L. P., and D. W. FAWCETT. 1953. Cytochemical observations on chicken monocytes, macrophages and giant cells in tissue culture. *J. Histochem. Cytochem.* **1**: 47–58.

WEISS, P. 1929. Erzwingung elementarer Strukturverschiedenheiten am *in vitro* wachsenden Gewebe: Die Wirkung mechanischer Spannung auf Richtung und Intensität des Gewebewachstums und ihre Analyse. *Arch. Entw. mech. Org.* **116**: 438–554.

WENT, F. W. 1928. Wuchstoff und Wachstum. *Rec. trav. bot. Néerl.* **25**: 1–116.

WEST, F. R., and E. S. MIKA. 1957. Synthesis of atropine by isolated roots and root callus of belladonna. *Bot. Gaz.* **119**: 50–54.

WETMORE, R. H., and S. SOROKIN. 1955. On the differentiation of xylem. *J. Arnold Arboretum* **36**: 305–317.

WHITE, P. R. 1931. Plant tissue cultures: The history and present status of the problem. *Arch. exp. Zellforsch.* **10**: 501–518.

WHITE, P. R. 1932a. Plant tissue cultures: A preliminary report of results obtained in the culturing of certain plant meristems. *Arch. exp. Zellforsch.* **12**: 602–620.

White, P. R. 1932b. Influence of some environmental conditions on the growth of excised root tips of wheat seedlings in liquid media. *Plant Physiol.* **7**: 613–628.

White, P. R. 1933a. Plant tissue cultures: Results of preliminary experiments on the culturing of isolated stem-tips of *Stellaria media. Protoplasma* **19**: 97–116.

White, P. R. 1933b. Concentrations of inorganic ions as related to growth of excised root-tips of wheat seedlings. *Plant Physiol.* **8**: 489–508.

White, P. R. 1934a. Potentially unlimited growth of excised tomato root tips in a liquid medium. *Plant Physiol.* **9**: 585–600.

White, P. R. 1934b. Multiplication of the viruses of tobacco and aucuba mosaic in growing excised tomato roots. *Phytopathology* **24**: 1003–1011.

White, P. R. 1937a. Separation from yeast of materials essential for growth of excised tomato roots. *Plant Physiol.* **12**: 777–791.

White, P. R. 1937b. Amino acids in the nutrition of excised tomato roots. *Plant Physiol.* **12**: 793–802.

White, P. R. 1937c. Vitamin B_1 in the nutrition of excised tomato roots. *Plant Physiol.* **12**: 803–811.

White, P. R. 1937d. Comparison of nutrient salt solutions for the cultivation of excised tomato roots. *Growth* **1**: 182–188.

White, P. R. 1937e. Survival of isolated tomato roots at suboptimal and supraoptimal temperatures. *Plant Physiol.* **12**: 771–776.

White, P. R. 1938a. Accessory salts in the nutrition of excised tomato roots. *Plant Physiol.* **13**: 391–398.

White, P. R. 1938b. "Root-pressure": An unappreciated force in sap movement. *Am. J. Bot.* **25**: 223–227.

White, P. R. 1939a. Potentially unlimited growth of excised plant callus in an artificial nutrient. *Am. J. Bot.* **26**: 59–64.

White, P. R. 1939b. Controlled differentiation in a plant tissue culture. *Bull. Torrey Bot. Club* **86**: 507–513.

White, P. R. 1939c. Glycine in the nutrition of excised tomato roots. *Plant Physiol.* **14**: 527–538.

White, P. R. 1940a. Does "C. P. grade" sucrose contain impurities significant for the nutrition of excised tomato roots? *Plant Physiol.* **15**: 349–354.

White, P. R. 1940b. Sucrose vs. dextrose as carbohydrate source for excised tomato roots. *Plant Physiol.* **15**: 355–358.

White, P. R. 1942. "Vegetable Dynamicks" and plant tissue cultures. *Plant Physiol.* **17**: 153–164.

White, P. R. 1943a. *A handbook of plant tissue culture.* Tempe, Ariz.: The Jaques Cattell Press, Inc.

White, P. R. 1943b. Nutrient deficiency studies and an improved inorganic nutrient for cultivation of excised tomato roots. *Growth* **7**: 53–65.

White, P. R. 1945. Respiratory behavior of bacteria-free crown-gall tissues. *Cancer Res.* **5**: 302–311.

White, P. R. 1946. Cultivation of animal tissues in vitro in nutrients of precisely known constitution. *Growth* **10**: 231–289.

White, P. R. 1949. Prolonged survival of excised animal tissues in vitro in nutrients of known constitution. *J. cell. comp. Physiol.* **34**: 221–242.

White, P. R. 1953. A comparison of certain procedures for the maintenance of plant tissue cultures. *Am. J. Bot.* **40**: 517–524.

White, P. R. 1954. *The cultivation of animal and plant cells.* New York: The Ronald Press Co.

White, P. R. 1955. An approach to chemically defined nutrients for strain L mouse cells. *J. Nat. Cancer Inst.* **16**: 769–787.

White, P. R. (ed.). 1957. Proceedings of the Decennial Review Conference on Tissue Culture (1956). *J. Nat. Cancer Inst.* **19**: 467–843.

White, P. R. 1959. Contribution apportée à la connaissance du cancer par la technique de la culture des tissus. *Lejeunia* **23**: 5–138.

WHITE, P. R., and A. C. BRAUN. 1942. A cancerous neoplasm of plants: Autonomous bacteria-free crown-gall tissue. *Cancer Res.* 2: 597–617.

WHITE, P. R., and E. Y. LASFARGUES. 1949. Some effects of dilution on the nutritive value of dialyzed plasma and embryo juice. *Proc. Soc. Exp. Biol. Med.* 71: 479–484.

WHITE, P. R., and W. F. MILLINGTON. 1954a. The distribution and possible importance of a woody tumor on trees of the white spruce, *Picea glauca*. *Cancer Res.* 14: 128–134.

WHITE, P. R., and W. F. Millington. 1954b. The structure and development of a woody tumor affecting *Picea glauca*. *Am. J. Bot.* 41: 353–361.

WHITTEN, W. K. 1956. Culture of tubal mouse ova. *Nature* 177: 96.

WHITTEN, W. K. 1957. The effect of progesterone on the development of mouse eggs in vitro. *J. Endocrinol.* 16: 80–85.

WILDE, C. E. 1959. Differentiation in response to the biochemical environment. In *17th growth symposium: Cell, organism, and milieu* (DOROTHEA RUDNICK, ed.). New York: The Ronald Press Co. Pp. 3–43.

WILSON, HILDEGARD, ELIZABETH B. JACKSON, and A. M. BRUES. 1942. The metabolism of tissue cultures. I. Preliminary studies on chick embryo. *J. gen. Physiol.* 25: 689–703.

WINKLER, H. 1935. Chimären und Burdonen. *Der Biologe* 4: 279–290.

WOLF, K., M. C. QUIMBY, E. A. PYLE, and R. P. DEXTER. 1960. Preparation of monolayer cell cultures from tissues of some lower vertebrates. *Sci.* 132: 1890–1891.

WOLFF, EMILIENNE. 1955. Les besoins spécifique en acides aminés de la syrinx de l'embryon de poulet cultivée *in vitro* sur un milieu entièrement synthétique. *C. r. Acad. Sci.* (Paris) 240: 1016–1017.

WOLFF, EMILIENNE. 1957a. Nouvelles recherches sur la culture organotypique de la syrinx d'oiseau: Culture sur différents milieux naturels et amélioration de ces milieux par des acides aminés. *Arch. Anat. Microsc. Morphol. Exp.* 46: 2–38.

WOLFF, EMILIENNE. 1957b. Analyse des besoins nutritifs d'un organe embryonnaire, la syrinx d'oiseau, cultivée en milieu synthétique. *Arch. Anat. Microsc. Morph. Exp.* 46: 407–468.

WOLFF, ET. 1954. Potentialités et affinités des tissus reveléées par la culture in vitro d'organes en associations hétérogènes et xénoplastiques. *Bull. Soc. Zool. France* 79: 357–368.

WOLFF, ET. 1957. Les propriétés générales des organes embryonnaires en culture in vitro. *Acta anat.* 30: 952–969.

WOLFF, ET., KATY HAFEN, MADELEINE KIENY, and EMILIENNE WOLFF. 1953. Essais de cultures *in vitro* d'organes embryonnaires en milieux synthétiques. *J. Embryol. Exp. Morph.* 1: 55–84.

WOLFF, ET., and J. P. WENIGER. 1954. Recherches préliminaires sur les chimères d'organes embryonnaires d'oiseaux et de mammifères en culture *in vitro*. *J. Embryol. Exp. Morph.* 2: 161–171.

WOODWORTH, J. 1699. Some thoughts and experiments concerning vegetation. *Philos. Trans. Roy. Soc.* (London) 21: 193–227.

WYATT, S. S. 1956. Culture in vitro of tissue of the silkworm, *Bombyx mori* L. *J. gen. Physiol.* 39: 841–852.

ZIEGLER, D. W., *et al.* 1958. The propagation of mammalian cells in a 20-liter stainless steel fermentor. *Appl. Microbiol.* 6: 305–310.

INDEX